Olive Shoots Around Your Table

"Visser documents *Olive Shoots Around Your Table* with many case histories he has personally experienced, citing both successes and failures, and covering a broad range of typical modern problems such as substance abuse, divorce, abuse, poverty, shame and loneliness. He also calls on his own family nurturing experiences, and points out how prayer, scriptural advice, but mostly love and forgiveness, have produced successful results."

Jack Evans
Review in the Belleville Intelligencer

"For years I have struggled with a past I couldn't outrun, and a sense of shame and guilt that crippled me. This book helped me understand not only where I have been wounded and how I've passed that wounding on to my child, but also how to get healing. The strategies, wisdom and understanding offered in this book have been incredibly helpful in my life. I recommend it highly!"

Single mother

"For anyone struggling with family problems, *Olive Shoots Around Your Table* brings hope when nothing else works. Pastor John Visser provides the foundation for families to build on, the structure to reside in, and the faith to make it work. *Olive Shoots Around Your Table* should be read by all parents encountering the daily challenges of child rearing, and by all family therapists who want to give hope to families who cannot move forward. John Visser provides the vision that is so often missing when people struggle with family dynamics."

Alan Mathany, B.A., M.S.W.
Director of Operations,
Frontenac Community Mental Health Services

"The courts are back-logged with litigation ranging from child abuse to divorce. In this complex society, *Olive Shoots Around Your Table* offers a menu for life that will provide practical answers – unattainable in the courts – for those seeking to establish functional families. I recommend it highly!"

D. Kent Kirkland
Judge, Ontario Court of Justice

Olive Shoots
Around Your Table

JOHN VISSER

Essence
PUBLISHING

Belleville, Ontario, Canada

Olive Shoots Around Your Table

Breaking the Cycle of Family Dysfunction

Copyright © 1996, 2005 John Visser

First printing, August 1996
Second printing, November 1996
Third printing, September 1998
Revised edition, December 2005

ISBN: 1-896400-14-0

Cover Design: Juliet deWal

Essence Publishing is a Christian Book Publisher dedicated to furthering the work of Christ through the written word. For more information, contact: 20 Hanna Court, Belleville, ON, Canada K8P 5J2.
Phone: 1-800-238-6376. Fax: (613) 962-3055.
E-mail: publishing@essencegroup.com
Internet: www.essencegroup.com

Printed in Canada
by

Essence
PUBLISHING

To
My wife, Michelle,
all our children
and
grandchildren.

Other Books by John Visser:

Handling Stress

Setting the Captives Free

To Have and to Hold:
Biblical Reflections on Marriage, Sex & Courtship

Blessings & Curses:
The Key to Lasting Change

Table of Contents

LIST OF FIGURES

Acknowledgements

I thank my God every time I remember you.
Philippians 1:3

I t's been almost 10 years since *Olive Shoots Around Your Table* was first published. I have been extremely gratified by the warm reception it has received. Many people have testified how the book has not only helped them identify patterns of dysfunction in their own lives and family, but has also helped them break free from these patterns by God's grace. For that I give God all the glory! Only eternity will fully reveal the fruit this has borne!

As well, the book has received a warm reception in the Netherlands after having been translated and published in the Dutch language by Navigator Boeken, the Dutch branch of the Navigators. My heartfelt thanks to Rob Barzilay and Thea Heidemeijer for making this possible!

Since demand for the book continues to be strong, we've decided to publish this updated edition with a new cover design to match my latest book, *Blessings & Curses: The Key to Lasting Change.*

I want to express my deepest appreciation to Alida Tuinman, Diana Bouma, Joanne Arbuckle, Judy Brown and the staff at *Essence Publishing*, for providing invaluable assistance in preparing this book for publication; to Fred Riemersma, who did many of the illustrations; and to Juliet deWal, who did the cover design. I couldn't have done it without you! Thanks so much for a job well done!

I am also very grateful to Dr. Terry Burrows for his help in reviewing the manuscript and providing excellent insights, as well as graciously consenting to write the *Foreword*. Thank you so much for your encouragement and support! We truly have a similar vision.

The same goes for my friend and colleague, Jeff Boerger, who all along has shown a keen interest in this project and who gave hours of his valuable time reading the manuscript and giving suggestions. Thanks so much Jeff!

I also want to thank the Maranatha Church community for its help and encouragement. You were the laboratory in which many of these truths were put to the test. Many of you have graciously allowed your stories to be used and, through our church council, have given me the time to complete this book on schedule. May God reward each of you for your faithfulness!

Many authors and publishers have graciously allowed us to use their copyrighted material. For this also, we are very grateful. We have attempted to locate the owners of all copyrighted selections used in this book, but where we have failed in this, we beg your indulgence.

Finally, I want to thank my wife, Michelle, and our four children — David, Michael, Deborah and Jonathan — all of whom have contributed immeasurably to my life and ministry. Thank you for giving me the time and space to write this book and have it published. Your lives are a living demonstration that having a functional family in a dysfunctional world is not only a possibility, it can be a reality. I love you all!

Foreword

How beautiful on the mountains are the
feet of those who bring good news.
Isaiah 52:7

I welcome the publication of this book. It is a valuable contribution to the growing and increasingly important field of Christian Psychotherapy. It is a Christian book about dysfunctional Christian families – something that is "supposed" to be a contradiction in terms, but is in fact common.

It is also a book about family dysfunction in general, which makes it applicable to everyone, whether Christian or not. Its author, John Visser, is a capable and gifted man. He pastors an alive and innovative congregation in Belleville, Ontario – the Maranatha Christian Reformed Church. Both he and his congregation have a vital and practical commitment to the healing ministry of our Lord Jesus Christ.

I first met John in May of 1996 when Maranatha Church hosted the Annual Meeting of the Christian Medical Foundation. I was fascinated to learn that the congregation, under his leadership, is interested in the psychological and spiritual aspects of people's personal problems in living. They are committed to a ministry of healing, including ministering as a therapeutic community to people suffering from Multiple Personality Disorder (also known as Dissociative Identity Disorder) as a result of severe childhood sexual abuse. These are difficult patients to help and there is a limit to the ability of the secular mental health system to treat them – and more and more are coming forward every day. That a church congregation in a small city in eastern Ontario is taking on such a burden and learning to help therapeutically in ways that the secular mental health system cannot is an exciting community development – with implications for mental health care for our entire country.

The Health Care Crisis

I have been burdened for many years by the recognition that the needs for emotional, mental and spiritual care of the citizens of our nation have been increasing dramatically and have long since overtaken the capacity of the medical and mental health systems to deal with them effectively. Also, we have reached the ceiling of the ability of purely secular paradigms and methods of psychotherapy and psychiatry to effect healing of our patients' many problems in any definitive way. The implications of these two factors point to a potentially explosive ministry challenge for the Body of Christ as we approach the end of the century.

As medicare continues to contract in the face of our struggling economy and more and more people who need help are simply unable to access the mental health system – whether for minor problems in living or for full blown major psychoses – they will turn increasingly to private and community resources. Understandably, they will turn to people to whom they do not have to pay therapy fees and who have always been saying, *"Come to me, all you who are weary and burdened, and I will give you rest"* (Matt. 11:28). That is to say, they will turn increasingly for help, a trickle at first and then drove after drove, to the Church of Jesus Christ.

Are we ready for such an onslaught, which will be simultaneously our greatest challenge and our greatest opportunity for bringing the lost to our Lord that the Church has ever seen? Do we have the understanding, the training and the experience to scale up our resources to be able to meet this scary but wonderful unfolding development? Not yet. But men of God like John Visser and his congregation have started part of the pioneering process of showing the way. This book is an important sharing of his experience for all Christians who wish to enlarge their understanding and become better prepared to play their part in the bringing in and healing of the lost.

As John points out in this book, the cradle of mental health, or the destructive fiery forge of mental illness, is the family. As the family goes, so goes the nation – and both are becoming increasingly dysfunctional, as we observe with mounting distress day by day. His book is therefore not just theory. It is born out of experience and of learning by doing. As he describes himself, he is "one who spends the bulk of his time working with Christians through their problems."

The book addresses a wide variety of interested Christian audiences – from fellow pastors, counsellors and sufferers from dysfunctional families to parents wishing to avoid creating one. In fact, any thoughtful person striving to understand how people and life can get as messed up as they so often do, will be educated by this book. The integration of a fully Christian perspective with many useful ideas drawn from other psychological sources, based on years of practical pastoral experience in the field, gives it a unique character and strength. John himself sums this up best when he says, "The pain has to be faced and worked through, in the strength of the Lord."

Parts One and Two are rich in description and example discussing the nature of family dysfunctions and what the major dynamics and issues are in understanding them. I personally found the sections on understanding the religiously dysfunctional family and the importance of recognizing personal idolatries, and the facing and grieving of losses as integral parts of the psychotherapeutic process particularly helpful. Part Three gives a masterful overview of the Eriksonian schema of child development and experienced practical advice to parents on handling the often tricky and difficult dilemmas of child rearing and discipline – from infancy, childhood and adolescence to young adulthood.

Chapter 25 of the book deals with the importance and dynamics of forgiveness in the process of therapy and recovery from the traumas and woundings of family dysfunction. Together with the last chapter, it is a strong and unifying conclusion to a strong book.

Taking Risks

As I reflected upon this book and the innovative therapeutic relevance of the ministry at Maranatha Church that is put into daily practice, I was struck at how important it is for us to take risks in life if anything new and valuable is ever going to be brought to fruition. And how difficult it is and how much inertia and opposition it so often engenders to take those risks.

Developing healing ministries in the church certainly entails a risk. There is ample opportunity for the rigidly "religious" or the territorially "professional" to say that John Visser is straying out of his proper boundaries into where he doesn't "belong." But as a physician psychotherapist, I believe that as a pastor, John and his congregation are exactly where they do belong. I hope soon to see more and more churches standing shoulder to shoulder with them.

John and I are from different professional backgrounds, but I know we are in complete agreement on the importance and need for a widely applied professional Christian psychotherapy.

I am grateful to have the privilege of standing with him for the healing ministry of our Lord Jesus Christ in the real world.

The cry of the emotionally wounded and the spiritually lost now deafens us. The traditional medical and mental health systems are overwhelmed and all but visibly failing. I know – I work on the inside.

In 1984, I started an organization to protect and improve the ability of family doctors in Canada to be able to offer psychotherapy to their patients. But we know that we GP psychotherapists, and all the others – the psychiatrists, psychologists and social workers put together – can only help a tiny percentage of the millions who are in need. The only people who have the true solution to all the problems, who have the people and the physical resources to meet them, and who have the Great Commission to deliver it, are the Church of Jesus Christ. Soon all eyes will turn to us. We need to get ready.

As John Visser says, "The church community needs to be a safe place where people can come with their wounds and hurts and be loved back to life. God is in the business of taking broken and wounded people and putting them back together again. He wants to present us before all the nations as His workmanship so everyone can marvel at His wisdom and love. Only then will we be a light to the nations and a fitting channel of God's marvellous grace."

I commend this fine book to your reading and instruction.

Terry Burrows, B.Sc., M.D.
Founder
General Practice Psychotherapy Association
Toronto, Ontario
July 1996

Introduction

*He tends His flock like a shepherd: He gathers the
lambs in His arms and carries them close to His
heart; He gently leads those that have young.*
Isaiah 40:11

It was, as I remember, a Wednesday morning – sermon-making day. As is wont to happen when one craves solitude, the phone rang. A man I didn't know was on the other end. My name had jumped out at him from the phone book, he said, and would I please come to see him? Since he obviously didn't sound too "with it" and I had plenty of other work to do, I wasn't too keen on getting involved. After all, crisis counselling is not my speciality. Besides, I was trying to put a sermon together.

On further reflection, though, it occurred to me that I should maybe practice what I preach. (I hate it when that happens!) For quite some time, I had been encouraging our church people to seriously invest themselves in the lives of people God placed around them. How did I know this was not some providential ordering that needed an obedient response? Besides, my sermon wasn't getting anywhere anyway! So I went.

That's how I met Bob. Bob proved to be an interesting man. In his late thirties or early forties, he had a long history of psychiatric disorders. Variously diagnosed as schizophrenic and manic-depressive, he would, by times, develop real illusions of grandeur. He would see himself first as a nurse, then as a doctor and eventually as God Almighty. Needless to say, that got him into all kinds of trouble!

Bob had actually been born into a reasonably well-to-do family. His father, as I recall, had been a railroad man. After his parents died, Bob had inherited the family property, which he immediately squandered in wild and reckless living. At one point, he took to driving around in a Cadillac, though he didn't even have a driver's licence! By the time I met him, the alcohol, the drugs and the gambling had left him virtually destitute. His wives — he had been married twice — had left him and so had all his friends. He was one lonely man.

Yet, for all his grandiosity, there was something very endearing about Bob. For the next several years, I and others with me, poured our lives and love into Bob's life. Like a parched desert, he drank it up and then began to bloom. He gave his life to Christ. He quit his drinking and his drugs. He got his finances under some measure of control. Slowly but surely his life began changing before our very eyes.

By times we despaired whether he would ever make it, particularly when his old friends started coming out of the woodwork. Now that Bob was getting on his feet again and even had a little money, they wanted to be his friends again. For a while it seemed that Bob was going to choose them over his new friends in Christ. But eventually, grace prevailed and Bob made the choice to break with the past once and for all.

Then, suddenly, Bob died. To this day, I have no idea what caused his death. Maybe his body was just worn out from all the years of abuse. Maybe he was just tired of living and wanted to be with the Lord. Maybe the Lord just took him to spare him any further pain and suffering. I really don't know.

I do know this though: During the years I knew Bob and worked with him, I learned more about the complexity of the human personality and the long-term consequences of the choices we make than I had in all my previous interactions with "normal" people. What I learned from Bob was that many of the destructive patterns that were so clearly evident in his life, exist in all of our lives, only to a lesser degree. We hide them better and our coping mechanisms are perhaps more refined, but many of our dysfunctions are not so different. They are just harder to spot.

For example, Bob was incredibly shame-based. He could not bear to look at his real fears and insecurities. Much of his grandiosity was an attempt to build himself up. The fact that this came at considerable cost to himself, his wives and his one son, was quite incidental to the real fear that drove him – that somehow he was deficient and would therefore be rejected. Only gradually, and even then only to a limited degree, was God's grace able to penetrate that deep root of fear in his life.

What that did for me is set the stage for much of my subsequent counselling ministry. My passion has always been to see men and women set free to become all they are destined to be in Christ. If the Gospel is true, it should work not only for the average "normal" person, but it should also work for the "Bobs" of this world. It should be able to transform their lives and break the cycle of generational sin. And indeed it does, provided we are willing to take seriously both the complexity of the human condition and the endless resources that we have in Christ.

In the pages that follow, I share some of the insights I have gained from a variety of sources for the purpose of helping individuals and families break free from the destructive patterns of the past and start a new life in Christ.

I want to make it clear at the outset that I do not write from the standpoint of a professional counsellor. I am not a professional counsellor in the traditional sense of the word. I am a pastor who does a great deal of counselling out of the conviction that God desires to see the Body of Christ grow up to maturity. Much of my counselling, therefore, is more closely akin to discipling than it is to purely clinical work.

The advantage of this is that the principles presented in the pages that follow can readily be adapted and applied in any congregational setting. Indeed, that is my passion – to see churches take more and more seriously the healing ministry of Jesus Christ, and for them to be places where the broken and the wounded can find the abundant life that Jesus has so readily promised them.

As our society increasingly experiences the bitter fruit of family dysfunction in its many forms, and soaring health costs push existing health care programs to the brink, the Church will once again need to be on the forefront in pointing the way to wholeness through faith in Christ.

The stories in this book are gleaned from a variety of sources. Many of them I have personally witnessed first hand. In some instances, names and identifying details have been changed to protect the parties involved. I am deeply grateful for the many who have allowed their stories to be used. We learn best by example and it is my hope and prayer that the Lord will use what is presented in the following pages to help the Christian community, in cooperation with the appropriate mental health agencies, to discover and develop the resources that are needed to stem the tide of dysfunction that is mushrooming in our society and to build families and individuals that are truly healthy. I believe the well-being of society and the future of the Church depends on it.

John Visser
Belleville, Ontario

PART ONE:

Understanding Family Dysfunction

1 | Family: Whose Idea is it Anyway?

*Your children will be like olive
shoots around your table.*
Psalm 128:3

It is no secret that the traditional model of the family is under serious attack today. According to noted psychologist and author Dr. James Dobson, this current attack on the family first became evident in the early '70s with the publication of a book called *The Death of the Family*, by the British psychotherapist, David Cooper. In his book, Dr. Cooper argued for the need to abolish the traditional family unit and to substitute new forms of human relationships.[1]

In 1971, the now-defunct *Look* magazine published an interview with that famed American guru of wisdom, Shirley MacLaine. Here is what Shirley had to say about the family:

"I don't think it's desirable to conform to having one mate, and for those two people to raise children. But everyone believes that's the ideal. They go around frustrated most of their lives because they can't find one mate. But who said that's the natural basic personality of man? To whom does monogamy make sense?... To a muskrat maybe... why should they then adhere to this state of monogamy?

"In a democratic family, individuals understand their natural tendencies, bring them out in the open, discuss them, and very likely follow them. And these tendencies are definitely not monogamous." [2]

She is arguing, as is David Cooper, for the dissolution of the family and the restructuring of the family unit.

Now, it is easy to write off Shirley MacLaine's ideas as being on the fringe of society, and there may be some truth to that. But history shows an interesting pattern. Very often, new ideas which first begin on the fringes of society are eventually, with some modification, adopted by the mainstream of society.

Roll the clock forward some twenty years to 1992. In the Fall of 1992, *Time* magazine published a special edition entitled, *Beyond the Year 2000: What to Expect in the New Millennium.* It contains 93 pages of dreary predictions and analyses of the future. It spends a lot of time on the family, marriage and parenthood. One section bore this thought-provoking title: *The Nuclear Family Goes Boom!* Here are some of *Time's* predictions as to what will happen to the family in the year 2000 and beyond:

> *The family as we have known it will soon die. It is nothing more than an interesting anomaly — a mere blip in human history. We thought of it as "normal," but we were wrong. The very term "nuclear family" will give off a musty smell in the days ahead.*
>
> *Replacing it will be multiple marriages, or what will be known as "serial monogamy." Divorce will be so common as to be considered normal. Some marriage contracts will have "sunset clauses" to automatically terminate at a given age. Couples reaching their 50th anniversaries will be as rare as today's piano or cello virtuosos — gifted masters of their craft.*
>
> *An even more radical approach may evolve. It is reasonable to ask whether there will be a family at all. Given the propensity for divorce, the growing number of adults who choose to remain single, the declining popularity of*

having children and the evaporation of the time families
spend together, another way may eventually evolve. It may
be quicker and more efficient to dispense with family-based
reproduction. Society could then produce its future genera-
tions in institutions that might resemble state-sponsored
baby hatcheries....[3]

That is the wisdom of the editors of *Time* magazine and their vision for the future!

Fortunately, the track record of people who have made predictions concerning the future of the human race is dismal indeed. The same year that *Time* published its predictions on the family, two Canadians, Reginald Bibby and Don Posterski conducted the largest ever survey among Canadian teenagers. They found that our youth haven't yet discovered *Time* magazine's dreary predictions concerning marriage; 85% of the young people surveyed said they planned to get married someday and 84% of them still expected to have a family! [4] Fully 75% of children in the country still live in a traditional household with a father and a mother, though not necessarily their original father or mother.

Nevertheless, ideas have consequences. And ideas that once were on the fringe of society are finding their way into the seats of power. The so-called "hippies" and other fringe groups of the '60s and '70s are now very often the men and women who occupy seats of power in our society. Many of them, to a very large degree, have rejected biblical thoughts and values. If you listen carefully to what they are saying, they have an entirely different social agenda for all of life, including the family, than what most of our culture has taken for granted for thousands of years. Let me give some examples.

Audrey McLaughlin, former leader of the federal New Democratic Party in Canada, went on record during the 1993 federal election to say this concerning the family: "I've always said the family is whatever you choose it to be." [5] Do you catch the implications? This is a rather obvious attempt to mollify the gay rights activists who so desperately want to see the definition of family changed to include them.

And then, on May 8, 1994, at George Washington University in Washington, D.C., U.S. former First Lady Hillary Clinton received an honourary doctorate and then delivered the Mother's Day commencement address. Her speech that afternoon dealt with the institution of the family and how she thinks it has changed. Here is what she said:

> "If it ever did, [the traditional family] *no longer does consist of two parents, two children, a dog, a house with a white picket fence and a station-wagon in the driveway. Instead of families looking like the Cleavers on "Leave it to Beaver," we have families that include test-tube babies and surrogate moms. Instead of Sunday night family dinners, we now have cross-country telephone conference calls. Instead of aunts and uncles and grandmas and grandpas, we have nannies and daycare centers."* [6]

She went on then to recommend what she called an "extended family" to fill the void as traditional families dwindle. She urged the graduates to look out for their friends, neighbours and fellow citizens as they would members of their own families, and concluded by saying, "When the traditional bonds of family are too often frayed, we all need to appreciate that in a very real sense we have become an extended family." [7]

Please note carefully that *what* Mrs. Clinton says is not bad in and of itself. What *is* bad is what she *doesn't* say. Nowhere in her whole address on the subject of family and how it has changed does she express any regret for the forces in society, or in government, that contribute to the undermining of the family.

That, of course, is a large part of the problem. Increasingly, legislative decisions that are being made are not geared to defending and nurturing the traditional family. Instead, they are geared towards supporting alternate life-styles, thus weakening the family.

Here is a case in point. Under the latest federal budget handed down in early March 1996, in Canada, a household with a single-income earner making $60,000 annually pays $4,841 or 36.2% more income tax than a dual-income family where each person is making $30,000. That is a big tax advantage for dual-income earners. That, in turn, undermines the stability of families where the wife might want to stay home to look after the children.[8] Other reports indicate that the tax difference is even greater if they are not married and have at least one child.[9] With tax laws like that, it is not hard to understand why an accounting group, in 1992, issued a satirical pamphlet entitled, *Ten Taxing Reasons Not to Marry!*

Christians need to be alert to these trends. More and more the laws of the land are being changed so that the rights and privileges, which have historically been extended to the traditional family, are now being extended to a wide variety of other "families." That is particularly evident today in the on-going battle to give family recognition to gay couples living together.

One of the most eagerly awaited Supreme Court of Canada decisions in early 1995 was the Egan and Nesbit decision. James Egan and Jack Nesbit are a gay couple that have been together for forty-seven years. They were seeking spousal benefits and had taken their case all the way to the Supreme Court of Canada. Their argument was that they are every bit as much a couple as heterosexual couples and should therefore be allowed the same spousal benefits. According to the former Executive Director of the Evangelical Fellowship of Canada, Brian Stiller, the Federal government mounted a largely ineffectual presentation trying to defend the present law, which makes them ineligible to receive spousal benefits.

When the Supreme Court finally rendered its decision on May 25, 1995, both sides in the gay rights debate claimed victory. In a 5-4 vote, the court decided that gay couples are not eligible for spousal benefits since the heterosexual relationship is unique in its ability to procreate children. At the same time, the court also ruled in a 9-0 vote that the Canadian Charter of Rights and Freedoms bars discrimination on the basis of sexual orientation, *even though this is not specifically mentioned in the text!* [10]

Another piece of legislation that reflects this on-going shift is Bill C-41, which was passed in June 1995 by the Canadian Government amid howls of protest. Bill C-41 was an anti-hate bill, which included an anti-discrimination clause against a wide variety of people, including homosexuals. It included the term "sexual orientation" as one of a series of crimes for which particularly harsh penalties may be applied.

Even more recently, in a case involving two lesbian ex-partners, Madam Justice Gloria Epstein of the Ontario Court's General Division ruled that the province's Family Law Act, which limits the understanding of marriage to a man and a woman in a committed relationship, was at odds with the Charter of Rights. Accordingly, she chose to redefine marriage as "between two persons." [11] In a similar vein, Ontario Court Judge James Nevins has ruled that lesbian couples can legally adopt children. [12] And so the battle goes on. With only the occasional reprieve, court decision after court decision seeks to stretch the definition of family until it includes just about every possible combination of persons. [13]

WHAT IS AT STAKE

Now, if you are like me, the tendency is to get bored with all of this. The temptation is to say, "Why bother to make a fuss? It's a free country. If other people want to live that way, that's their business. Let them. Just let me live my life my way."

I believe that kind of thinking is extremely short-sighted for both ourselves and our country. What is at stake here is nothing less than the question: What is family? Are there biblical norms that dictate what the model of the family should be? Does it matter to society as a whole how we define family?

I firmly believe that it does. How well a person turns out or how productive he or she is to society has a great deal to do with the stability of the family in which he or she was raised. It is within the family that our personalities are shaped, particularly in the first four or so years of our life. That being the case, our society has a long-term interest in upholding the family as the basic unit of a society and as the norm for living. Yet when we take the rights and privileges that are traditionally reserved for the family unit and share these with other forms of relationships, we undermine the security and well-being of the nation. We are setting in motion a cycle of unrighteousness that has already begun to bear bad fruit and one day may well destroy our culture.

The thing to understand is that family is not how you choose to define it or how you constitute it. It is something that God has instituted and it should be structured according to His Word. When we listen and adhere to these biblical norms as a society, then we will reap a harvest of righteousness. The blessings we will experience as a society will be in direct proportion to our obedience to God's Word.

That is what the psalmist means in Psalm 128 when he says:

Blessed is every one who fears the Lord, who walks in His ways! You shall eat the fruit of the labour of your hands; you shall be happy, and it shall be well with you. Your wife will be like a fruitful vine within your house; your children will be like olive shoots around your table. Lo, thus shall the man be blessed who fears the Lord. The Lord bless you from Zion! May you see the prosperity of Jerusalem all the days of your life! May you see your children's children! Peace be upon Israel! (RSV).

The picture here is one of well-being, isn't it? Here is a man who is happy in his relationship with his wife. His table is surrounded by children who are full of promise, like young olive shoots. Stability and security are the order of the day and his whole community prospers because of the contribution his family is making.

How does he get this way? Well, it is because he walks in the fear of the Lord. Verse 1 says, *Blessed is every one who fears the Lord, who walks in His ways!* As he seeks to build his life around God's principles for marriage and family, he is enabled to create a safe and secure place in which children can be born, raised and launched into life. With the blessing of God, they can become productive and useful citizens both in society at large and in the Kingdom of God.

Please don't misunderstand me. I know that even the church community is not immune to the forces that come against the family. Every church has its share of broken and dysfunctional families. I am not saying that unless your family has it all together, your children have no chance of growing up normal. Not at all! The grace of God is amazing. If we truly seek Him, He will do some wonderful things for us and our children. What I am saying, though, is that the family is important in shaping who we are. Since who we are is what later shapes society, we ought, as Christians, to do all we can to try to preserve and support the traditional family in a way that gives glory to God.

With that in mind, let us take a closer look at the family as God has intended it.

THE IDEAL FAMILY

Please refer to *Figure 1.1.* This diagram represents the *'ideal' family.*[14] For our purposes, we have pictured a father, a mother and a child. As we will see later, any number of children could be added.

There are several things to note in this arrangement. First of all, *the parents are face to face.* That is significant because it symbolizes that spiritually, emotionally and intellectually they are in tune with each other. Note, too, that on one side, *their hands are joined,* symbolizing that physically they are in touch with each other. They have a meaningful love relationship.

Figure 1.1
The 'Ideal' Family

On the same side, *their feet are facing each other* because their movement in life is constantly towards one another and towards a greater degree of intimacy. *Their other feet face outward* because, in the course of being more and more intimate with each other, they are also jointly engaged in moving out into the world doing the task to which God has called them. That calling is governed by the Scriptures, which *they are jointly holding* with their other hands. Each of them, through the Scriptures, is connected with God, through faith in Jesus. Each of them is submitted to God's authority, and each thus draws his or her life from the Lord. That is what enables them to give to each other rather than just leaning on each other and depleting each other's resources. This Scripture is a lamp to their feet; it is the guide that governs their lives. So even when sometimes their relationship goes through rocky times, they are still joined in union with the Lord who gives them the resources and the means to re-connect and re-establish their relationship.

Now into this perfect marriage is born *a child*. Note what happens when this child comes into the family. The union between husband and wife does not have to be broken to make way for the child. Whether the child is there or whether the child is not there, they still have a relationship with each other. The child is not the glue that keeps them in contact with one another.

Notice, too, that the child *can spin around freely* in the circle, indicating that she is *free to have communication* with both the mother and the father. She is free to exercise and to develop each of these relationships quite independently. Notice, too, that she is *a person in her own right*. She is not a possession. She is not controlled or owned by either of the parents. She is *a trust given by God* to the parents to train up in the way that she ought to go. As she comes of age, she can be launched into life grounded in Scripture and, with Scripture as her guide, she can grow in her relationship with Jesus. Rooted and grounded in God's love, she can become her own person, choosing freely to come and go with regards to her family. She won't be controlled or manipulated to preserve the family structure.

Because there is unity between the father and the mother, there is *room in the family* for more children. Each of the children is able to have that special relationship with father and mother. There is plenty of love to go around. What the one gets does not diminish the supply of the other one. This is the family as God designed it.

Unfortunately, none of our families is perfect. In the chapters that follow, we will take a look at why that is and how, with God's help, we can break out of the cycle of family dysfunction.

NOTES

1. James C. Dobson, *Focus on the Family Newsletter*, August 1994, p. 1.

2. John Kronenberger, "Is the Family Obsolete?" *Look*, 26 January 1971, p. 35.

3. Claudia Wallis, "The Nuclear Family Goes Boom!" *TIME*, Fall 1992, pp. 42-44.

4. R. Bibby and D. Posterski, *Teen Trends: A Nation in Motion*, 1992. (as quoted by Dr. James Dobson in *Focus on the Family Newsletter*, August 1994, p. 3.)

5. *Vancouver Sun*, 1 September 1993.

6. Hillary Rodham Clinton, commencement address at George Washington University, 8 May 1994. (as quoted by Dr. James Dobson in *Focus on the Family Newsletter*, August 1994, p. 1)

7. *Ibid.*

8. "Discrimination Against the Single-Income Family Continues," *Reality*, March/April 1996, p. 5.

9. Analysis by Dr. Chris Gerrard, *The Taxpayer*, Winter 1992.

10. "Both Sides Claim Victory in Gay Rights Ruling," *Faith Today*, July/August 1995, p. 45.

11. Frank Stirk, "Family Issues Alert/Pastor's Briefing," *Focus on the Family (Canada)*, 20 February 1996.

12. Daniel Girard, "Lesbian Couples Can Adopt," *Toronto Star*, 11 May 1995, p. A1, A26.

13. Since I first wrote these words, the gay rights movement has made significant additional gains to the point that Bill C-38, extending civil marriage rights to same-sex couples, is before Parliament as of April, 2005.

14. I am indebted to Sam DaSilva of Renewal Christian Counselling, St. Catharines, Ontario for this model.

Growing Up is Hard to Do

2

Our steps are made
firm by the Lord.
Psalm 37:23

One Sunday morning after I had spoken in one of our services about the importance of the biblical family, a young, single mom came to me and said somewhat defensively, "You know, traditional families have just as many problems and raise just as many problem children as do other kinds of 'families.'" Having just come out of a bad marriage and struggling to raise her children alone, she was understandably looking for some confirmation that she had made the right choice in walking away from an abusive husband.

Her comments, though, set me to thinking. Why can gay couples not raise children just as effectively as heterosexual parents? What is wrong with a single parent valiantly struggling to bring up her child or children in the best way she knows how? What is there about the biblical model of the family, even with all its flaws, that makes it so essential to the well-being of society?

The answer, I decided, lies in what it means to grow up. Let's take a closer look at that in this chapter.

THE PROCESS OF GROWING UP

Growing up is an incredibly complicated experience. For most of us, it happens so naturally that we don't even stop to think about it, until something starts to go wrong. Then, we begin to understand how complex this process really is.

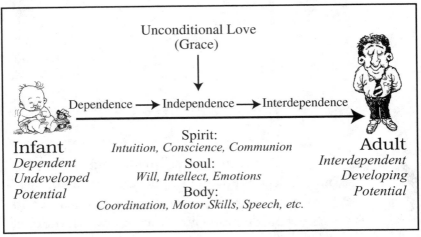

Figure 2.1
The Development of Personality

Please refer to *Figure 2.1* above. What is the difference between a child and an adult? The primary difference between them is a matter of development. The child has undeveloped potential; the adult has potential that, hopefully, has come to some measure of maturity. The challenge of raising children is to take an infant – helpless, dependent, yet full of potential – and provide a nurturing and protective environment so that, by God's grace, the child's potential can come to full expression.

If we consider parents as a bow, the child as an arrow and God as the archer, then God's aim is to use parents to launch their children into the world so that they can increasingly become the individuals God has intended them to be.

This maturity and development needs to take place at each level of the child's existence: *spirit, soul* and *body*. Each of these faculties needs to be developed properly if the child is to grow into a healthy adult. Let's look at each of these in more detail.

Spirit

The *spirit* is a part of our being that includes things like *conscience, intuition* and *communion*. The best known of these is probably the conscience.

Our *conscience* is that little voice on the inside that tells us right from wrong. Sometimes it is our mind speaking to us, but more often it is just a sense deep down in our being telling us what to do. It is the rudder by which we live our lives. The Bible says that if we ignore our conscience, we will shipwreck our faith (1 Tim. 1:19). That does not mean that our conscience is always right or dependable. Our conscience is a function of our knowledge and it has been known to be wrong. For example, I knew a young woman once whose conscience was so distorted that when she went on a date, she felt duty-bound to express her appreciation to the guy by going to bed with him. If for some reason she didn't, she felt guilty! Obviously, our conscience can be way out of whack. Nevertheless, it is the yardstick that God has given us to help us make correct moral choices. It just needs to be informed by truth.

Intuition is our capacity for creativity and inspiration. It is that brilliant burst of wisdom or insight that comes to us at the oddest of times. It is not a rational process. It comes intuitively. Without consciously working at it, ideas and inspiration often come spontaneously. They provide us with excitement, joy and exhilaration because they are often so unexpected. A lot of people think of them as *"hunches,"* but they are really a function of the human spirit.

Communion is the ability to have fellowship with both God and other people. Perhaps you have noticed that sometimes when you meet a person for the first time, you instantly connect. You really understand each other and pretty soon there is a bond between you that is beyond language. That is communion. The reverse of that is also true. You may know a person well, perhaps even come out of the same background and family. Humanly speaking, you should understand each other well and get along with each other. But something gets in the way. You don't "click." It's nothing you can put your finger on perhaps, but you just do not connect. That's a function of communion, or rather, the lack of it.

Soul

Many people confuse *soul* and *spirit* and think that both refer to the part of us that continues on after death. We talk of a person's "soul" or "spirit" as having gone to heaven, for example, and often use the terms interchangeably. There is probably no harm in that. Technically speaking, though, the term *soul* is better used to refer to that part of us that gives us consciousness, or an awareness of life around us. The Greek word for *soul* is *psuche* from which we get such English words as *psychology* and *psyche,* etc.

Used in this way, the soul consists of at least three components: the *will*, the *intellect* and the *emotions.*

Our *will* is what helps us make decisions. It helps us to decide whether or not we are going to follow a certain course of action. If you have ever been with people who don't know how to make decisions, you know how maddening that can be.

For some people, making decisions can be very difficult. I have friends who in their growing up years were not encouraged to make wise or responsible decisions. When they did step out and make a decision, it was often wrong and harmful and they or others got hurt. As a result, they drew their wagons around their little camp, so to speak, and made up their minds to not move unless circumstances compelled them. As a result, they have become indecisive. They are riddled with fear and insecurities. They let their friends, circumstances or culture become the driving force in their lives. This, of course, often drags them into places or things where they really don't want to go.

The *intellect* is the mind given by God to help us understand, process and interpret reality.

Emotions are our feelings or our affections. They can be rather complicated in that they have a life of their own. They have been given to us so that we can appropriately respond to situations. When danger threatens, adrenaline kicks into gear, our heartbeat increases, and strong emotions help us respond to that danger. When we are overcome by sorrow and our hearts are broken, emotions help us to vent our tears and our pain so that healing can take place. Our emotions are designed to enable us to rejoice when the situation warrants rejoicing and mourn and weep when the situation warrants mourning and weeping. They are such an important part of our lives that we are going to devote Chapter 13 to them.

Body

Our *bodies* are the vehicles by which we interact with the physical world. If our spirit enables us to connect with the spiritual world, and our soul, or personality, enables us to connect with other people, then our bodies enable us to connect with the physical creation. Bodily functions include such things as the five senses – sight, smell, hearing, taste and touch – the ability to speak, the ability to move from place to place, and so on. Truly, we are fearfully and wonderfully made!

• • • • • • • •

Now, a healthy baby has all of these capacities at birth. These capacities, however, are in embryo or seed form. They are also distorted by sin. The challenge for Christian parents, then, is to help their children grow up and develop their potential in a way that honours and glorifies God.

Practically speaking, it means we need to help them develop a *conscience* that is tender towards God and yielded to His Word; an *intuition* that has the capacity to hear from God and serve as a channel of His creative energy; a sense of *communion* that can have true fellowship both with God and other people; *minds* that can understand and embrace truth from God's point of view; *emotions* that are appropriate to the occasion; a *will* that is yielded in all things to God's will and *bodies* that can truly be instruments of righteousness in God's hands.

This is our goal as parents. How well we succeed in that becomes the measure of our success as parents. To fail here is to fail in the most important task of our lives.

THE IMPORTANCE OF LOVE

The question is, how do we do that? Well, it all starts with a thing called "love." Love means that our interests are being looked after. On the one hand, we are protected from harm and danger, and on the other hand, the basic needs of our lives are being met. That love needs to come, first of all, from God and secondarily, from our parents or other significant adults in our lives.

Where that love is present, all other factors being equal, our children are free to grow up and become what God has intended them to be. Where that love is not present, hurts and wounds will likely develop that will hinder their spiritual, emotional or even physical development.

Let's look at this issue more closely now in the context of the *Hierarchy of Human Needs*.

Psychologists have for many years understood that all of us have certain basic human needs that need to be fulfilled if we are to develop and mature properly. Different schools of psychology have developed different models. The most common one is Maslow's model (see *Figure 2.2*).[1]

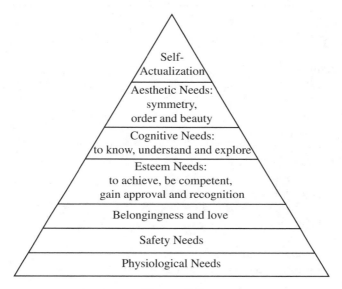

Figure 2.2
Maslow's Hierarchy of Human Needs

The one I personally find most useful is a modified version of Maslow's model that Dr. Charles Whitfield uses in his excellent book, *Healing the Child Within* (see *Figure 2.3*).[2]

Let's take a look at some of these:

Survival

The most fundamental needs of a child are food, safety and security. If we stop feeding our children, they are not going to be with us for very long. Likewise, if we don't protect them or provide safe places for them, they can be seriously hurt or even killed. To a very large degree, we take these things for granted. The fact remains, where these conditions are not present and these needs not met, the child cannot survive. It is as simple as that.

Attention and Mirroring

When you see a mother or a father with a new baby, you sometimes wonder which one is the child. Isn't that true? You

1. Survival
2. Safety
3. Touching, skin contact
4. Attention
5. Mirroring and echoing
6. Guidance
7. Listening
8. Being real
9. Participating
10. Acceptance
     Others are aware of, take seriously and admire the Real You
     Freedom to be the Real You
     Tolerance of your feelings
     Validation
     Respect
     Belonging and love
11. Opportunity to grieve losses and to grow
12. Support
13. Loyalty and trust
14. Accomplishment
     Mastery, Power, Control
     Creativity
     Having a sense of completion
     Making a contribution
15. Altering one's state of consciousness, transcending the ordinary
16. Sexuality
17. Enjoyment or fun
18. Freedom
19. Nurturing
20. Unconditional love (including connection with God)

Source: Whitfield. Used by permission.

Figure 2.3
Modified Hierarchy of Human Needs

know, "Kootchy-kootchy-koo, baby smile," and all that! You'd think there was never a baby as cute and intelligent as this one. Why do parents lose their dignity like that? They do it because something very important is taking place. The child is being validated as a person in his own right. By paying attention to him and mirroring his actions, you are letting him know that he has the right to exist as a separate person. You are telling him that the world is a safe place where people will take note of his needs and wants and are glad to have him around.

Acceptance

To be accepted is to be taken seriously, to be allowed to be who you really are. It's to be loved and appreciated, to be made to feel that you really belong.

All of us have been in situations where we feel we have not been accepted. Most of the time, we shrug it off and find a place where we do belong. For most of us, that is at home with our family. Imagine then the pain of a child who feels that even at home he or she is not wanted. The pain of that can be unbearable.

Later on when we look at the dysfunctional family, we will see that many such families have what is called the "lost" child. These are children who have made up their mind to not disturb the equilibrium of their families. They have made up their minds that they are not going to cause mom and dad any trouble. As a result, they die on the inside. Nobody knows who they really are. Chances are, they don't even know themselves.

Most of us have also been in situations where we did not feel free to be who we really are. People couldn't handle it. They rejected us. And so we learned to put on masks and pretend to be somebody we are not. At least that way we won't be rejected and filled with pain.

Opportunity to Grieve Losses and to Grow

Nobody goes through life without some measure of pain. Pain is tolerable, even useful, if we can work it through and learn from it. Opportunity to grieve our losses is a critical element of growing up.

Unfortunately, some people are never given that opportunity. They either do not take the time to grieve properly or else are not given that opportunity by the people around them. In either case, the results can be devastating.

A good friend of mine had a doll when she was little, which served as her security blanket. Her cousin, in a fit of jealous rage, mutilated it by tearing off its limbs. The little girl who owned it was furious and inconsolable. Though her parents tried to ease her pain by having it fixed, she refused to have anything further to do with it because it no longer lived up to her idea of perfection. By not working through her grief, she buried the pain deep inside.

I had something similar happen in my own life, though it didn't affect me as deeply. When I was a child, I had a train of which I was quite proud. One of my older brothers, bless him, wanted to take it apart to see how it worked. And yes, he promised he would put it back together again. Well, you can guess what happened. The last time I saw that train, it was lying in pieces on the floor and I never did get it back on track.

In the cosmic scope of things, I know that was no major loss, but I felt it and the resentment associated with that stayed with me much longer than I care to remember.

Accomplishment

This involves several different elements: mastery, creativity, having a sense of completion and making a contribution.

Few things are more frightening for anyone than being at the mercy of forces we can neither understand nor control. That is especially so for a child to whom the whole world seems so big. Witness how much smaller childhood places are when you visit them as an adult!

Part of growing up, therefore, is learning that we have some measure of control over life. It means having a realistic awareness of our strengths and weaknesses. It means having the creativity to come up with new and novel solutions to problems we experience. It also means we need to experience the satisfaction of knowing we have seen a project through to the end, as well as the joy of knowing that what we have done matters to other people.

Many of us perhaps take this process for granted. As children, we start a project. We run into some frustration. We want to give up on it. Mom or Dad or some teacher refuse to let us give up. They put our nose to the grindstone. They help us through our difficulties and, lo and behold, the thing is done, and we have the satisfaction of knowing we have climbed another mountain.

Every child needs to know something of that satisfaction. Children who don't are likely to grow up suffering from serious self-esteem problems which will in turn lead them into possible patterns of anti-social behaviour.

• • • • • • • •

All of these components, (together with the rest of the list in *Figure 2.3*), represent a *Hierarchy of Human Needs.* That is to say, from top to bottom, they represent the most fundamental needs of our lives. The degree to which we are deprived of these, is the degree to which our lives are likely to be influenced negatively. Deprive a child of food, he dies physically. Deprive a child of touch, attention and love, he dies emotionally. Deprive a child of a sense of accomplishment, he dies socially.

What we need to understand is that the normal way in which God pours these provisions into the lives of children is through their parents. As parents walk in fellowship with the Lord, love their children unconditionally and provide for them appropriately, life springs forth inside their children and they grow up with a minimum of fuss and bother. As I said earlier, most of the time this happens so naturally that we aren't even aware of the process. But what a joy it is to see our children developing and unfolding!

WHEN LOVE FAILS

Unfortunately, we live in a fallen world. None of us either gives or receives love perfectly. Most of the time we can learn to cope and make do. Every so often, though, the pain roots itself deeply into our souls and robs us of self-confidence and sometimes even the will to keep living. When that happens, we shut down. Spiritually, emotionally, sometimes even physically, we stop growing. Psychologists call these "fixations" – areas of our personality where growth has been arrested. We know them more commonly as "hang-ups" – areas where our growth has been stifled or "hung up."

An example may clarify what I mean. Let's suppose that you have a child who is just learning to walk. Now, you know what parents are like when their baby begins to walk, especially when it is the first one. You'd think there was no other baby in the world that could match the genius of this one! When he takes his first step, you cheer him on. When he falls and hurts himself, you pick him up, kiss him better and set him back on his feet. And sure enough, all other things being equal, by the time the child is a year-and-a-half old or so, he's walking. And what an accomplishment that is!

Now let's suppose that instead of being a loving and affirming parent, you are a sadistic parent. Every time little Jimmy gets up on his feet to start walking, you push him over. And you keep doing it. Each time he hurts himself a little more. What's going to happen to that child? Well, he's going to quit trying to walk, isn't he? The pain is too great. It hurts too much. It's much safer not to take any chances.

What happens when Jimmy no longer tries to walk? He doesn't develop walking skills. His muscles atrophy. He develops no sense of balance. He develops other ways of getting around. Maybe he learns to drag himself from place to place, and so on. Pretty soon what you have is a 19 or 20-year-old who has never walked.

Now picture someone coming along and saying, "Come on, you lazy-bones! These legs are made for walking. Get up and get at it!" What happens? He can't do it, can he? Why not? Because his early wounding has caused him to grow up distorted. He hasn't developed the skills necessary for walking and if he now tries it, the physical pain and the emotional humiliation are simply too much. He just can't do it! Chances are, he'll just give up. It's like commanding a person who is hospitalized with a broken leg to get up and walk. He cannot do it. The more you pressure him, the more despairing he becomes. His leg needs healing before he can stand on it, let alone walk with it.

We understand this physically, of course, and few, if any, of us would be so sadistic as to demand someone to walk when he obviously cannot. We have a much harder time, however, understanding this same principle emotionally and spiritually. For example, when someone is discouraged or depressed, we'll often say to them, "Just pull yourself together. Quit moping and make something of yourself." Or, to someone who cannot hold down a job, we might say, "If you would only get off your lazy behind and make some effort, you could easily achieve what I have achieved."

All of that may be true, but none of it is very helpful. People who are wounded emotionally or spiritually are every bit as much handicapped as people who are wounded physically. Before they can get up and walk, they need to be healed. Without that healing, they are likely to repeat the same self-defeating behaviour over and over again.

THE IMPORTANCE OF A FATHER AND A MOTHER

I believe that is why it is so important to defend the biblical family. God, in His wisdom, has decided that a committed relationship of fidelity and trust between a man and a woman is needed to create a safe and secure environment for children to grow up in a healthy way. People increasingly ask questions like, "Why is it so important for kids to have both a mom and a dad? Why can't a gay couple raise kids? Why can't we redefine the family any old way we want to? Why should we be concerned about the increasing number of single-parent families in the nation?"

The answer is this: From a biblical point of view, both mothers and fathers are of critical importance in the development of a child's personality. Each of them brings his or her own particular strengths to bear on the development of their children.

Mothers tend to be the nurturers. They are, in the words of Dr. Daniel Trobisch, "like a circle." [3] They enfold and protect. Fathers, on the other hand, tend to challenge and encourage. So, if the mother is the circle, then the father is the one who draws the children out of that circle into the broader world, encouraging them to take a stand and be their own persons.

The easiest way to understand this difference between masculinity and femininity is to look at your own family. What happens when Junior goes out the door to school? What are mom's last words very often? "Be careful!" Isn't that true? Her tendency is to embrace the child and say, "Do you have your lunch? Don't be late for the bus. Don't forget your jacket," and so on. What do fathers do? "Get out there and go get them, Grover!" And if you forget your jacket and catch a cold? Well, that's your own problem and you'll just have to learn for next time.

I realize, of course, these are generalizations. Some mothers lean more to the masculine side and some men more to the feminine. Yet the fact remains, kids need both! They need a place where they can be nurtured and made to feel safe. They also need someone who will challenge them to go out into the world, take risks and make something of themselves. Then, when they get hurt, as sometimes they will, they need to be able to run home again and be kissed better, so they can be strong enough to try again. In this way, they can grow up with a healthy understanding of who they are and what they can contribute to the world.

A BITTER HARVEST

That is why these issues of family redefinition are so critical in our day and age. We are currently reaping a harvest of social disorder that has its roots in the breakdown of the nuclear family. Statistics indicate an almost frightening parallel between non-marital births and violent crimes (See *Figure 2.4*).[4]

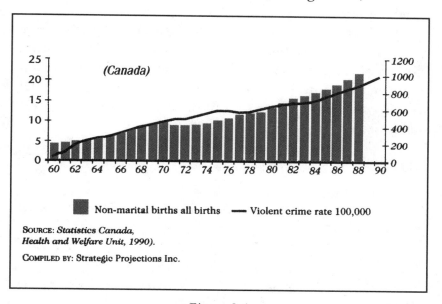

(Canada)

Non-marital births all births   ■— Violent crime rate 100,000

SOURCE: *Statistics Canada,*
Health and Welfare Unit, 1990).

COMPILED BY: Strategic Projections Inc.

Figure 2.4
Non-Marital Births as a Percentage of Total Live Births (Left Scale), and Violent Crimes per 100,000 Persons (Right Scale), 1960 to 1990

It appears we are raising a generation of dysfunctional kids who are reproducing many of their own dysfunctions in the next generation. One of the women in our church who teaches in a nearby public school tells that in a recent general level class of 30 students, only two kids were still living in their original nuclear family! All the rest were from broken homes or blended families.

Please don't misunderstand me. I don't want to make it sound as if single-parent, blended or broken families are doomed for failure. They are not. God's grace extends to all those who walk in faith. David said many years ago, *Though my father and mother forsake me, the Lord will receive me* (Ps. 27:10).

I have tremendous admiration for those who have had to shoulder the load of caring for their children single-handedly. Many do a marvellous job! The rest of us need to do all we can to help and encourage them.

At the same time, we need to understand that "as goes the home, so goes the nation." As citizens of our nation, as well as citizens of the Kingdom of God, we have a vested interest in doing all we can to build strong, healthy families. If we don't, we will continue to reap a harvest of brokenness that no social policy or agenda will ever be able to heal.

NOTES

1. Laura Lefton and Lester Valvante, "Maslow's Pyramid of Needs," *Mastering Psychology*, 4th ed. (Needham Heights, MA: Simon & Schuster, Inc., 1991) p. 375.

2. Charles I. Whitfield, *Healing the Child Within* (Deerfield Beach, FL: Health Communications, Inc., 1987) p. 18.

3. Leanne Payne, *Restoring the Christian Soul Through Healing Prayer* (Wheaton, IL: Crossway Books, 1991) pp. 36-37.

4. William D. Gairdner, *The War Against the Family* (Toronto: Stoddart, 1993) p. 192.

3 | Turning the Hearts of Fathers

*He will turn the hearts of the
fathers to their children.*
Malachi 4:6

I t is an indisputable fact that every human being on earth
has at least two things in common: Everyone is born of
a mother and everyone is begotten of a father. Having a
father and a mother is, therefore, significant because
each of them has a different impact on the life of that growing and developing child.

As we saw in the last chapter, a mother tends to nurture.
She has imparted her own life to the child, and so she seeks
to protect and enclose. A father's job, on the other hand, is to
draw the child out of that circle of nurture and to give it purpose and direction. That is why it is so important for our
society to commit itself to building strong and functional
homes. Foundations that are laid early in life make a tremendous impact in later years, both for good and evil.

Just to see again how important that is, let's take a look
at the job description the angel Gabriel gives in Luke 1:16-
17 to Zechariah concerning his soon-to-be-born son, John
the Baptist:

Many of the people of Israel will he bring back to the Lord their God. And he will go on before the Lord, in the spirit and power of Elijah, to turn the hearts of the fathers to their children and the disobedient to the wisdom of the righteous... (Luke 1:16-17).

John the Baptist was the forerunner of Jesus. Just as a king who is going to visit a particular region in his empire will send heralds before him, John the Baptist was the voice of one crying in the wilderness, *"Prepare the way for the Lord..."* (Isa. 40:3). John the Baptist's task was to restore the people to their God, and it is interesting to note in that context, that an important component of doing that was to *turn the hearts of the fathers to their children and the disobedient to the wisdom of the righteous.*

This verse is a paraphrase of the last couple of verses of the Old Testament book of Malachi:

See, I will send you the prophet Elijah before that great and dreadful day of the Lord comes. He will turn the hearts of the fathers to their children, and the hearts of the children to their fathers; or else I will come and strike the land with a curse (Mal. 4:5-6).

What is Malachi saying? He is saying, in effect, that "as goes the home, so goes the nation." Unless the issues between parents and children are resolved in a proper way, judgment comes upon the nation and the nation will not receive the blessings of God's Kingdom.

For that reason, whenever God moves historically in a nation to bring healing and restoration, He begins by raising up an Elijah-type ministry. The purpose of that ministry is to restore the hearts of children to their fathers and the hearts of fathers to their children. In this way, the impending judgment caused by family alienation is averted.

To understand this more clearly, let's review briefly how important family life is to personal and social well-being.

Home is where we are shaped to a very large degree, both by the parents we have and the circumstances we experience. Unfortunately, we live in a sinful world and even the best of parents are not perfect and neither are their children.

In the course of growing up, therefore, there are times when instead of being unfolded in the way that we should be, we experience trauma, pain and injury. When that happens at the hands of parents, it can build an incredible sense of anger and resentment towards the parents. Apart from God's grace, this can mark a child for the rest of his or her life, unless God is there to turn the hearts of the fathers to their children and the hearts of children to their fathers. Sometimes, of course, that wounding is more imaginary than real. In either case, unless God's grace intervenes, the damage done can be incalculable.

Let me give some examples.

Parental Favourites

Some parents favour one child over the other. I have never yet found any parent who would admit to that. All parents I have met usually go out of their way to say they treat all of their children equally. Perhaps they do. But I tell you, I have met a great many kids who swear that, at least in their perception, their parents did not treat them equally, but favoured one sibling over others. Some parents like boys better than girls. Some parents like one temperament better than another. Some parents favour children that have been named after their side of the family. Sometimes grandparents have that problem. Sometimes it is only a perception on the part of a child, but sometimes it is based on reality.

Listen to this letter written by an 8-year-old girl to her camp counsellor:

Can you help me? My father carries a picture around of my younger brother who is 4, and he looks just like Daddy. He also carries a picture of my older sister who is 15 and very pretty. My daddy doesn't carry my picture around at all. I gave him a picture of me. I cut it and made sure it would fit in his wallet, but he put it in his drawer. Is there any way I can get my Daddy to carry my picture? [1]

Can you imagine the pain in the heart of a child like that?

A mother in our church shared with me once that when she and her family visit her parents her own father favours one of their children. He makes a big show out of giving a gift to this particular child whom he especially likes, while completely ignoring the rest of their children. Understandably and properly, this makes the mother furious!

I know a man who tells a similar story. He remembers visiting his grandmother. She was one of those people who favoured kids that were named after her side of the family. He has vivid memories of her giving cookies to his cousins in his very presence, and then by-passing his plea for a cookie for himself. Can you imagine the damage that does to a young boy? Is it any wonder he grew up with a great deal of hate which caused incredible damage to his marriage and his children for years to come?

That is not to say all such incidents are rooted in reality. Sometimes they are merely perceived that way. Leanne Payne, in her book *Restoring the Christian Soul Through Healing Prayer,* tells the story of a woman who all her life had this nagging sense of guilt that would not leave her. As she got counselling and prayer, the Holy Spirit reminded her of an incident that had happened when she was born. As her father rushed her mother to the hospital for the delivery, he forgot to turn off the kitchen stove. As a result, the pot that was on the stove caught fire and the whole house burned down. All through her growing up years she had heard the connection between the burning house and her birth. Whenever the family talked about her birth, somebody was sure to say, "Oh, the house burned down when you were born." The result was that deep down inside her soul she felt she was the cause of the house burning down! [2]

Adults look at that and say, "That is stupid and ridiculous." And indeed it may be. But children don't view it that way. They often feel they are responsible even if that is not the intent. Parents, therefore, need to be careful in what they communicate to their children. And they need to be careful not to favour one child over another.

Parental Agendas

Some parents try to force their kids to be something other than what God has designed them to be. We all know that scenario: Father or mother never had an opportunity to go to school and so their kid is going to have the university education they never had, even if he or she is not cut out to be a scholar. Or Dad always wanted to become a professional hockey or ball player, but he never got the chance. Now his kid is going to become the fulfillment of his dreams, whether or not he has the interest or the ability to excel in sports.

Most parents, of course, would never say this overtly. But listen carefully to their conversations and observe the values they project onto their children, and you will see how much pressure some parents exert on their children to make them something other than what they have been designed to be. Children, of course, want to please their parents and gain their approval and so will often give in to that kind of pressure and expectation.

I, for one, am very grateful that in my parental home each of us, from very early on, was encouraged and given the freedom to be what we wanted to be. There is an interesting background to that as I discovered recently. When my mother was little, she really liked going to school. Her dream was to be a physician. In those days, not many girls became doctors and not many went to school beyond the sixth grade. And so, when she was 12, my grandfather took her out of school to help her mother at home, even though my mother always maintained there wasn't much work to be done at home. My mother resented that as she was growing up and remembers making a vow that should she ever have children, she would never do that to them. Consequently, most of us kids had the freedom to pursue our own goals and ideas. I say most, because, ironically enough, my oldest sister tells me that my mother put a lot of pressure on her to continue her education, when in fact she had little interest and only moderate ability to do so! That shows you the power of vows, both for good and ill. Another irony is that my youngest brother has gone on to become the physician my mother never became, not because of any family pressure but out of his own free choice. Mind you, I have always been glad my mother didn't go on to higher education, or else she would likely not have met my father, who was a farmer. Then where would I be?

Parental Abuse

Some parents abuse their children. Abuse can vary all the way from benign neglect of basic emotional, physical and spiritual needs to cruel teasing and severe emotional, physical and sexual abuse. We all know well enough how prevalent this is getting to be in our day and age.

Just recently in the news, I heard the very sad story of a father in his 40s and a mother in her 30s who were both sent to jail for the sexual abuse of their two girls. One was 10 and the other was 12. The mother would set the father up with these girls, one at a time, if you can imagine the perversity of all that. Yet these things are happening with increasing frequency. The more a society breaks down and people give in to the dark urges of their own souls, the more abuse there is.

Most of us have probably never experienced that degree of abuse. Many of us, though, can clearly remember incidents when we felt we were treated unjustly, or were blamed for things which were not our fault. Some of us, perhaps, can remember incidents of significant emotional, physical or even sexual abuse that have scarred us to the core of our being.

One of the men in our church called me one Sunday after I had spoken on the topic of abuse. He related how in his home, a good Christian home in many ways, his father, when angry, would take him by the neck and force him hard against the wall until he fainted. When he came to, he would usually find himself lying on the floor. That is abuse and it happens even in "good" Christian homes. It has been my observation that anger is the *one* emotion that has most commonly been acceptable in religiously dysfunctional families.

Now, I don't want to give the impression that every little injury we receive will scar us for life, nor do I want to leave the impression that if we are not careful, we are going to scar our children for life. Kids are amazingly resilient and have an amazing ability to recover, and as long as we walk in repentance and forgiveness and allow things to come out into the open so they can be worked through properly, God's grace will carry us through.

I remember one such incident very vividly from my own youth. A person I was very close to and really looked up to, really hurt me at one point. I was interrupting him at an inappropriate time, but instead of just telling me to wait until he was ready, he point blank told me to go to hell! I was crushed. Not only was that not the kind of language we used at our house, but to be told that by someone I respected and admired was devastating! Fortunately, my mother found out about it, stood up for me and straightened the situation out. I shudder to think what would have happened had she not been able to do that. It could have easily become a root of bitterness in me, because that is often what happens when these issues don't get resolved. They go deeper and deeper into the very core of our hearts. And if that happens when our personalities are still being shaped, the damage can be very severe indeed. We stop functioning in a normal way and our personalities get wounded and distorted.

CLOSING YOUR HEART

The response to such hurts in our lives is very similar to that of any pain or injury we experience. What is a body's natural reaction to pain? What happens when you burn your hand on the stove? Your reflexes kick in and you pull back. That is a safety device. We do that, not only physically, but also emotionally. If expressing my opinion is not safe in my household, then I am not going to express my opinion any longer. If being my own person in this household is not safe, then I am not going to be my own person anymore. I will build walls around my heart. The more serious the injury and the earlier in life it happens, the bigger the wall will be that I build around my heart. This is especially true in relation with the significant care-givers of our lives – our father, mother or guardian. We will close off our hearts against father and mother and this starts a cycle that may well lead to disaster.

What happens when you close off your heart against your mother and your father? You put yourself under a curse, because the Bible says, *Honour your father and mother... that it may go well with you and that you may enjoy long life on the earth. It is,* says Paul, *the first commandment with a promise* (Eph. 6:2-3).

In other words, if you do *not* honour your parents, then you are setting in motion a series of judgments that can affect you for the rest of your life. For as you cut yourself off from your mother or father, you also cut yourself off from their advice and influence in your life. That is significant, because even the worst of parents have a lot of wisdom they can speak into the lives of their children to help them make good and wise decisions.

Cut off from the wisdom of your parents, you now need to make decisions on the basis of your own limited thoughts and experience. That makes you susceptible to being led around by every pied piper that comes along. Without a history of experience to draw from, how can you decide whether or not the pied piper is going to lead you astray?

This is one of the reasons why Satan, through his social engineers and political and economic power brokers, has for years and years now been trying to break up the nuclear family. If he can take children out of their families and make them wards of the state, as has been done in some societies, then he can shape their minds and allegiances far more readily. That's what Hitler did with his Hitler Youth prior to and during World War II. They became pawns in his hands, unable, because of their youth and limited experience, to understand the true significance of where Hitler was leading them and their nation.

CONTINUING THE CYCLE

So, here is how the cycle continues: Cut off from the wisdom of a previous generation, the child is forced to find his own way in life based on his own limited experience and insight. As a result, he will tend to seek short-term gratification as opposed to long-term gain, and he won't have the discipline he needs to carry his tasks to completion. This is critical because completed tasks are an essential part of knowing who you are. When there is nobody to hold your nose to the grindstone, you have no way of finding out the range and scope of your ability.

As a result, people get down on themselves. They feel like they're not much good at anything and hate themselves because they've never had any help controlling their volatile emotions. That, in turn, makes them susceptible to peer pressure. They now begin to run around with friends who are just like them and who try to make them feel good. Because their consciences are often seared, the result is violence and trouble that multiplies in proportion to the brokenness of the individual's heart. You get all manner of people who lack the ability to form intimate and lasting relationships. Generation after generation now breeds a whole stream of broken and wounded people.

Brian Noel Raymond

Let me give you an example. The name Brian Noel Raymond probably won't mean much to you. You may remember, though, the news story that made him famous, or I should say, infamous.

Brian Noel Raymond was the driver of the jeep used in the drive-by shooting in March 1994 in Ottawa that left Nicholas Battersby dead and the city in shock. Battersby was a 27-year-old immigrant from England working as an engineer at Bell Northern Research. He was walking along the streets of Ottawa when suddenly a jeep came driving by, a random shot was fired and Nicholas Battersby was left dead on the ground. Brian Raymond was the driver of that jeep. Here is Brian Noel Raymond's background:

> *He grew up in the projects of Ottawa, raised by a single mother. His three siblings have different dads. Brian's dad was an alcoholic who left two years after Brian's birth.*
>
> *From infancy, Brian was difficult. He was active and hard to control with a short attention span at school. A psychologist notes this may have been an early indicator of his "attention hyperactivity disorder," an impulsive control problem that tends to make a person socially obnoxious.*
>
> *"People like Brian simply don't see the consequences of their actions," says Phillip Firestone, a University of Ottawa psychologist. A kindergarten teacher was prophetic: "Poor attitude, short attention span, creates behavioural problems in the classroom, not capable of controlling behaviour."*
>
> *Brian scored 80 on an IQ test, placing him in the bottom 10 per cent of kids his age. Poor academic skills dogged him in school. Drugs and crime soon entered the equation. By 14, he was using marijuana, hash and alcohol and then cocaine by 1994. Brian himself blames drugs, lack of a male role model and bad choices in friends for his problems.*
>
> *He started running with a tough crowd that lived*

without adult supervision. After binges, he stayed out all night rather than upset his mother. His youth court criminal record dates back to 1991, including assault, property crimes and escaping lawful custody.

In 1992, at the William E. Hay Centre for young offenders, he began counselling for anger management and drug and alcohol abuse but didn't attend regularly and finally quit. A final report said that his current level of drug use, his association with a negative group and support of anti-social values place him at a high risk of re-offending.[3]

That was seven weeks before Nicholas Battersby was shot down during his Sunday night stroll.

Statistics indicate that 80% of violent crimes in North American society are conducted by young men in their mid-twenties to their mid-thirties. They are raised in a low-income environment and in largely fatherless homes. This category of individuals has increased more than four-fold in our society in the last thirty years – from less than 5% of all live births in 1960 to more than 20% of live births as recently as 1990.[4] Is it any wonder that we are setting the stage for social disorder that is beyond our imagination?

A man in our church mentioned to me recently how he and his wife had just experienced the shock of their life. A gang of 40 to 50 youths had congregated in a parking lot across from their business and then went on a smashing rampage. The two businesses on either side of his business both suffered broken windows. Thank God that at least his windows were spared. And that's not some major metropolitan centre; that's only small-town Ontario! In big cities, of course, it's even worse. Swarming crowds of young people are increasingly creating social problems that police are hard-pressed to handle.

STABILIZING THE FAMILY

Some people say we should legislate more severe punishments to straighten them out. And that might help some. But, the fact remains, all the legislation in the world isn't going to change hearts that are wounded or damaged for lack of love. We can lock them up longer, impose stiffer sentences and call for a new social order, but none of these in and of themselves will curb crime that flows out of a wounded life. The only thing that will make a long-term difference is for society to recognize the importance of the nuclear family and do all it can to support it as the most significant social unit we have. And I, for one, cannot understand why the powers that be in our nation cannot see that. Instead of formulating policies that encourage and support the family, they seem hell-bent on bringing about its demise through their social engineering.[5]

Even Statistics Canada has been recruited into this little scheme. For years, the traditional family has been defined by Statistics Canada as *two or more people living together related by birth, marriage or adoption*. It has now decided to *exclude* from the term "traditional" any family where:

1. the wife earns an income;
2. either parent had been previously divorced;
3. children have been adopted;
4. they live in an apartment or duplex.

Isn't that interesting? The U.S. Bureau of Vital Statistics has just redefined the family in a similar way. On this basis it can now be stated that the traditional family in North America only comprises 30% of all families, while the actual figure is 77%. Even James Dobson doesn't qualify as a family under this new definition because one of his kids is adopted. I love what Link Byfield, editor of *Alberta Report* (August 15, 1994), had to say about this: *"Why not... exclude any family that doesn't live behind a white picket fence? That would surely have reduced the numbers to 1%!"* [6]

What do we do about all these attempts to break down the nuclear family and the social chaos that results? Obviously, we need to do all we can to preserve and strengthen the role of the traditional family in society. We need to teach our children the importance of healthy family relationships. We need to support and encourage legislation that helps rather than hinders healthy family life. We also need to support organizations like Dobson's *Focus on the Family*, John and Paula Sandford's *Elijah House* and many others like them that are committed to preserving the biblical model of the family.

What happens if we don't? We will continue to see the disintegration of our society and culture. Increasingly, individuals and families will become "dysfunctional," that is to say, not functioning normally. Fathers and mothers won't love their children and children won't love their parents. Instead, anger and hatred will fill the land with violence and every unimaginable evil. In succeeding chapters, we will take a look at how that happens and how, with God's help, we can break out of that cycle.

NOTES

1. Winkie Pratney, "Hurt and Bitterness," *The Last Days Newsletter*, Vol. 7, No. 3, 1984, p. 14.

2. Leanne Payne, *Restoring the Christian Soul Through Healing Prayer* (Wheaton, IL: Crossway Books, 1991) p. 148.

3. Adapted from *Ottawa Citizen* articles written by Mike Blanchfield, Court Reporter.

4. William D. Gairdner, *The War Against the Family* (Toronto: Stoddart, 1993) p. 182.

5. Bill C-33, which added the words "sexual orientation" as a prohibited ground of discrimination in the Canadian Human Rights Act on May 9, 1996, is a good case in point. Though Justice Minister Allan Rock insisted this was merely a matter of prohibiting discrimination against homosexuals, and had nothing to do with redefining the family, the gays themselves see it differently. Said Svend Robinson, an openly gay Member of Parliament, the day after Bill C-33 was passed: "Justice Minister Allan Rock was 'wrong' to argue the legislation will not affect these issues. I am confident that the amendments to this legislation will in fact assist in the recognition of gay and lesbian families and gay and lesbian relationships."

Subsequent court rulings have already demonstrated this prediction to be accurate. (See "Liberal Tyranny Over Homosexual Legislation," *Reality*, May/June 1996, p.3).

6. "Statistics Canada Jumping Into Political Waters," *Reality*, September/October 1994, p. 19.

The Dysfunctional Family

I am poor and needy, and my heart
is wounded within me.
Psalm 109:22

It was late one Saturday night in the early years of my ministry. My wife and I were sitting on the living room floor, sorting through a supply of books that the nearest Christian book store had made available to our small-town congregation. Suddenly the phone rang. Sobbing hysterically, a woman friend of ours related the latest episode of abuse that she was suffering at the hands of her very cruel husband.

While I was sympathetically trying to calm her down, there was a terrific pounding on our back door. There stood our neighbour lady in her nightgown, tears streaming down her face, panic in her eyes. Could she please use our phone to call the police? Apparently, her husband had come home drunk that night and gone on a wrecking spree in their house and she feared for her life. I remember the next day seeing the kitchen window completely knocked out of its casement. In his drunken fury, the husband had heaved his remaining case of beer straight through the window!

Thus began our introduction to family dysfunction.

A dysfunctional family is a family that is not functioning the way it should. It is not a safe place for children to grow up and become what God has intended them to be. Instead, they get battered and bruised and learn to develop coping mechanisms that encourage the dysfunction to be passed on to the next generation. Because we live in a fallen world, all families are, of course, dysfunctional to some degree. None of us is perfect and none of us turns out perfectly adjusted kids! Nevertheless, some families are considerably more dysfunctional than others and the damage they cause has more lasting effects.

THE ALCOHOLIC FAMILY

With that in mind, let's take a look in this chapter at how dysfunctional families work, or, I should say, how they don't work! Because the alcoholic family is so clearly dysfunctional and has been studied extensively, we will begin with it. Later on, we will broaden our scope and take a look at other factors that also contribute to making families dysfunctional.

The Alcoholic Father

Figure 4.1 represents an alcoholic family. Notice two things about the *husband* as he stands there: *He is elevated* above the rest of his family and his position is wobbly and precarious. There is a reason for that. He is elevated because an alcoholic, like any addict in a family, is the person around whom the family rotates. Everybody has to adjust to his habit.

That is one of the characteristics of family systems. They hang together like a mobile and tend to balance each other out to retain equilibrium. If one person moves out in one direction then somebody else has to move out further in the opposite direction in order to maintain stability. You have perhaps noticed that in your own family.

For example, if you have a person in your family who is angry a lot and you want to keep your family together, then you have to compensate for that other person's anger. You walk around on eggshells, you watch carefully what you say, you keep the kids out of his hair, and so on. You compensate by being more careful and making sure you don't trigger his anger. If you don't do that, the family may well explode.

Figure 4.1
The Alcoholic Dysfunctional Family

That is how it is with every dysfunctional family, including the alcoholic family. The whole family rotates around the alcoholic and his addiction. They never know what kind of a mood he is going to be in when he wakes up. Will he be hung over from the night before? Is he going to be able to make it to work? Will the boss call up and ask where he is? An alcoholic needs help to stabilize his precarious position.

The Co-Dependent Wife

Enter his *wife*. An alcoholic cannot function without the support of family members who will help stabilize the family system. Notice two things about her position:

First, *her back faces her husband*. This is because it is virtually *impossible to have eye-to-eye and heart-to-heart contact* with the person who is addicted. An addict focuses his or her life on the addiction. Consequently, this couple is emotionally, psychologically and perhaps even physically far removed from each other. They have no eye-to-eye or heart-to-heart contact.

Second, *her husband is ambivalently dependent on her*. She is the *stabilizing influence* in his life. She makes excuses for him. When the boss calls up and asks why her husband is not at work, she says something like, "He is sick today. I'm sorry. He'll be in tomorrow." Or, when the kids wonder why their dad is not keeping his promises, she covers for father and says, "Well, you know, he's just not feeling very well today. Maybe tomorrow." She soon discovers that he's not very good at paying the bills and that she is going to have to keep the creditors off their back and make excuses for payments that have not been made. She will very likely go out and work, because his job performance will increasingly deteriorate as the alcoholism becomes more and more a part of his life.

So, there tends to be a lot of pressure on her. She cannot readily leave him because, psychologically, he is very manipulative. An alcoholic usually has a phenomenal capacity to make the spouse feel she is the cause of his problems. Once she buys into that, she feels responsible for making the family work.

Mother's Helper

Understandably, with all this pressure, this woman needs help to maintain her own sense of equilibrium. Enter the *first-born*. The first-born in the alcoholic family often becomes a substitute spouse. He or she tends to become an extension of the father and will try to compensate for the things the father is not. For our illustration, we'll make the oldest child a son.

Notice three things:

First, *mother and son are eye-to-eye and heart-to-heart*. The tendency in this relationship will be for the eldest son, or daughter if that is the case, to become the mother's confidant. Things she cannot share with her husband or her younger children, she will try to share with the eldest child. That can become a very heavy load for the first-born who is not designed to carry such adult responsibilities.

Second, *the son is holding his mother's hand*. He literally becomes an extension of her life. He helps her out. Maybe he helps run the household. Perhaps he does some of the cooking or looks after the younger children. In these, and other ways, he becomes emotionally, psychologically and even physically close to his mother.

Third, *the relationship between father and son is indirect*. Because there isn't much of a relationship between the father and the mother and an unwarranted closeness exists between mother and son, father and son have no relationship except indirectly through the mother. This creates tension between father and son. The father is jealous because he is excluded from this cozy relationship. He feels, not without justification, that his son is taking his place. At the same time, the son is angry because he feels his father is neglecting his mother and making life miserable for her as well as for himself. Life in this family is now starting to be hampered by some very significant tension. Enter the eldest daughter.

The Acting-Out Child

The eldest daughter in this family system, or the *second child*, is known as the *acting-out child*, or the rebellious teenager. She will go through life being labelled the black sheep of the family. She's the one who commonly gets into trouble. When she goes to school, she is the one who skips classes. She is the one who causes concern for the teacher. She fails to live up to her potential. She is the rebel who gets into trouble with the law and will commonly be the first child in the family who gets dragged into therapy.

The second child is acting out the pain in the family. She is trying to draw the attention of the world, in the only way she knows how, to the fact that she is having a difficult time and there is pain in the family. The thinking in the back of her mind, subconsciously most often, is that when she is troublesome and rebellious, somebody has to take note and start asking questions. And maybe, if someone starts asking questions, father and mother's problems can be resolved, the family can be stabilized and their problems can be fixed. That is why so often she is the most open in the family to therapy. The rest of the family may think she is the wild one and the one with the most problems. In actual fact, though, she is the one who is crying out for help because she has become the dumping ground for the whole family's pain. It is often nearly impossible for families to understand that the problems of the black sheep are most likely an expression of pain in the family system.

So, this family is getting to be pretty dysfunctional. Father is unstable and mother is weighed down with a heavy load. The eldest son is doing his best to support mom, but he is angry because he has far more responsibility than he ever bargained for. The rebel is getting into trouble with people all over the place. That stirs up the whole family nest. It is time for a little levity.

The Family Clown

Enter the second daughter, or *third child,* known as the *family mascot* or *clown.*

One of the aspects of dysfunctional families is that you are *forced into roles.* In a healthy family, you can choose your own role, depending on who you are and how you want to live. For example, if you want to stay home and be a source of support to mom and dad, you are free to do that. You are equally free at a given point to decide that you no longer want to do that, and make a life of your own. Sure, there may be tensions associated with such a decision, but in a normal family that is a natural part of growing up.

In a dysfunctional family, you don't have the liberty of making your own choices. Roles are foisted on you, whether or not that is what you want to be, because that is what is needed to keep the family system functioning. For example, the rebel serves to deflect attention from the parents' own dysfunction. As long as the child is the one who keeps throwing the whole family into turmoil all the time, the child can be blamed for all the trouble. Were the child to start behaving, the turmoil in the family would still continue, since it comes from the alcoholic parent. Only now, there is no one to blame for it. So the rebel is needed in order to shift blame from the real cause.

Nobody can live with tension all the time and so the next child tends to compensate for his sibling's rebellion by being the *clown*. The clown is the person who, when the conversation around the table gets a little too tense, has learned to throw in a joke to divert the attention from the seriousness at hand. She is the one who always does funny things and always makes people laugh. There are two reasons for that: It diverts the attention from the pain in the family, and it keeps her from having to deal with the serious pain in her own life. And wouldn't you know it, it also keeps the world at bay. For when the world sees all the fun in this family, the world says, "Aren't they a marvellous family?"

One of the serious complications of dysfunctional families is the constant need for cover-up. They do not want others to know, let alone see, that they are having serious family problems. They must at all costs present a harmonious facade to the world. Hence, the need for a clown.

Unfortunately, the clown is cast into a role. She has to be happy, whether or not she feels like it. As a result, she develops her own set of problems. She lives superficially because she hasn't learned to handle her emotions very well. When she is grumpy, she is told to cheer up. When she wants to cry, she is told to laugh. Emotionally, she lives in denial, unable to understand and handle her own emotions. Consequently, she deals with emotionally-charged issues by laughing everything off. Few, if any, people are ever allowed to get really close to her. She has difficulty establishing intimate relationships. The moment someone tries to get too close, the walls go up, even while her heart is crying out for true intimacy. Unless her husband is very giving and understanding, chances are good that her marriage will fail. She just doesn't have what it takes to form a really intimate relationship.

The Lost Child

There is one child remaining in this picture. He is known as the *lost child*. If the clown tries to solve the pain in the family by light-hearted levity, joking and ignoring the pain, the lost child absorbs all the pain and feels it most intensely. The lost child, perhaps before he is even born, discovers that the world is not a nice place to be. While still in his mother's womb, he has already heard and sensed the tension that exists in his family. He doesn't want to contribute to this and so he withdraws into his own little world. He is the one who always sits in his room and cranks up the stereo to try to drown out all the fighting going on in the family. He is also the child in the family who is most likely to commit suicide. When he does, everybody will shake their heads and say, "Isn't that a shame? I never knew he had a problem. He was such a nice, quiet child." He was quiet and he was nice at the cost of his own soul because he could not afford to be his own true self.

So much for the alcoholic family. As we will see later, apart from God's grace, each of these children is going to reproduce some aspect of their dysfunction in the next generation. Even when they make a conscious effort not to, many of their dysfunctional patterns will be repeated.

Alcoholism is, of course, but one condition that produces dysfunctional families. There are a number of others, as well. Let's take a look at these.

OTHER PARENTAL CONDITIONS PRODUCING FAMILY DYSFUNCTION

Chemical Dependence

Chemical dependence includes such things as drug addiction and any other form of chemical addiction. It may include "soft" drugs such as tobacco, marijuana, hash, etc. It may also include "hard" drugs such as heroine, cocaine, LSD, speed, etc. As with alcohol, family life will again revolve around the person with the addiction.

A cocaine addict was explaining to me some time ago the power of his addiction. He said, "The strangest thing about addiction is that you are willing to sacrifice anybody and everybody, including the ones whom you love, in order to get your fix." Needless to say, this causes chaos in the family and will force dysfunctional patterns to develop very quickly. Already, his children were beginning to exhibit the classic roles of the dysfunctional family.

I would also include less commonly recognized addictions such as being hooked on TV, eating too much food, spending too much money, pornography, or even being a workaholic who gets his sense of identity out of the work he does. All of these are people whose attention is focused on meeting their addictions. Everything and everybody else becomes secondary to having these needs met. If you are part of a family like that and you want to keep the family unit functioning, then you have to make the adjustments necessary to keep the system afloat. You have to deny yourself and your own needs for the sake of the addict. When you do that, chances are pretty good you are going to lose your own sense of identity.

Co-dependency

In recent years, co-dependency has come to be recognized as a phenomenally complex but very prevalent psychological illness that has a far-reaching impact on family life. Co-dependency is a disease in which one becomes so concerned about other people's well-being that one doesn't properly take care of one's own legitimate needs. For example, the wife of the alcoholic husband, in allowing herself to become the martyr who upholds the whole family, may be said to be co-dependent. Some of her own unresolved needs are being met by the role she plays. While she may complain about her husband's alcoholism and want him to change, part of her wouldn't know what to do if he did!

Co-dependency is a very complicated process. It very often begins with a minimizing of your own personal feelings and thoughts. You can't afford to worry about your own needs and feelings, because you are so busy looking after the needs of others. Furthermore, there is something about meeting other people's needs that in turn meets a deep need inside you. You need to be needed. This constant giving of yourself to others and assuming responsibility for things you are not responsible for leads to anger and resentment. If these are not resolved, they will eventually lead to a deadening numbness of your own feelings. You no longer know who you are. This, in turn, often leads to depression and compulsive behaviour. Depression and compulsive behaviour lead to deep feelings of shame, further depression and, eventually, chronic illnesses of many kinds.

In a family where either the father or the mother, or both, are co-dependent in the sense that they are living to please other people in order to meet their own unresolved needs, there isn't much love or energy left to be poured into their children. The children often have to meet the needs of the parents rather than vice-versa. This is called "parental inversion" and makes the children responsible for the parents rather than the other way around.

Chronic Mental and Physical Illness

We have all experienced times in our families when someone is not feeling well. Mother has a headache, father has an injury, or brother has the flu. In a healthy family, there is enough flexibility for others to take that person's load temporarily until the person in question is back on his or her feet and life can resume its normal course. God has built amazing healing provisions into His creation.

Sometimes, though, you get situations where the illness or the injury is long-term rather than short-term. Mother or father suffers from a long-term mental illness or gets crippled or injured for life. When that happens, the stage is set for producing dysfunctional offspring.

Take for example, a mother who is emotionally very unstable. She doesn't just yell at her kids occasionally, she goes completely bonkers.

One woman I know tells me that when she was growing up her mother suffered from violent, irrational attacks. She has vivid memories as a child of her mother hollering at the top of her lungs that she was going to kill herself that night. In addition to that, the woman would often be accused of doing things she knew she hadn't done. Is it any wonder that little girl grew up to be a woman with significant emotional problems in her own life? Only God's grace can deliver us from such a heritage as that!

Another woman I know has told me the story of how her mother had bouts of emotional instability. As a little girl, she remembers going to school scared. She remembers her mother shouting after her as she left for school that she had better be good at school or else her mother wouldn't be there when she got home. At the same time, her mother was putting coats over her younger sibling's pajamas as well as her own as if she were planning to leave immediately! Talk about scaring that little girl! What an awesome sense of responsibility to have placed on shoulders that young.

A family that has a debilitating mental or physical illness has to fight against tremendous odds if it is to remain healthy and functional. Please understand, I am not placing blame on parents who find themselves in this situation. No one chooses these kinds of problems. Nevertheless, they do happen, and when they do, they can have a devastating impact on the life of a child. Apart from God's grace, they may well be scarred for life. How badly injured they are depends, of course, on the severity and duration of the situation, as well as their own ability to cope with it.

Overly Rigid, Judgmental and Demanding Parents

All parents, of course, want their children to turn out well, and each has his or her own ideas of how that can best be accomplished. Some are too lenient – they allow their children to do whatever they want. Others are too rigid and demanding – they establish levels of performance that a normal child can seldom attain. Failure of any kind is not tolerated. Punishment is swift and often out of proportion to the supposed infraction. Tragically, people with a distorted concept of God and religion often fall into this category. For that reason, this group will be explored more fully in the next chapter.

Child Abuse

Some parents abuse their children. This abuse can be physical, emotional or spiritual and it can take the form of *neglect* or the more common *active abuse*.

By *neglect*, I mean the things parents fail to do for their children when it is in their power to do so. For example, not providing food, clothing or shelter for a child entrusted to your care is neglect. Not allowing them to express their emotions in appropriate ways, not providing a spiritually supportive environment or a safe and secure environment when it is in your power to do so, are all forms of neglect that can leave children emotionally damaged.

A father and a mother in the Mirimachi region of New Brunswick were sentenced in July 1995 to 16 year terms in a federal penitentiary. Their crime? For reasons neither they nor anyone else has been able to explain, they systematically starved their 3-year-old son to death. Perhaps he was hard to handle, or maybe they were trying to discipline him. I don't know. I do know that neglect of this nature is a serious form of abuse.[1]

Recently, I heard in the news the tragic story of a 15-year-old girl in the city of Chicago who gave birth to a baby. Apparently, though she was living at home, her parents didn't even know she was pregnant! While her mother was sleeping in a nearby bedroom, she gave birth to the baby all alone in the bathroom. Obviously not thinking too clearly and anxious to hide the birth of her child from her parents, she took the newborn baby and threw her out the window into a snow bank and then went to school! Can you imagine that?

Well, it just so happened, by the providence of God, that a neighbour's car wouldn't start that morning. As she was debating what to do, she heard what sounded like a cat, she said. She followed the sound to its source, and lo and behold, found this blood-covered, new-born baby lying in the snow, suffering, as they found later, from a concussion and several other injuries. That is not merely neglect. That is active abuse.

Active abuse is pain that is foisted on a child by something that somebody does to them. It is not motivated by love but rather by the needs, wants and desires of the perpetrator. It can range all the way from physical to emotional to spiritual abuse.

Physical abuse hurts a child physically. Inappropriate and excessive physical punishment, injury to life or limb and inappropriate sexual touching are all readily understood examples of physical abuse. Not so readily understood examples of *sexual abuse* include more subtle things like coarse jesting, telling off-colour stories to children, ridiculing or shaming their sexuality or taking advantage of their sexual naiveté. All of these are a form of abuse because they all shame the child. It makes the child wonder, "What is wrong with me? Why is he doing this to me?" That is why physical and emotional abuse are inevitably tied together.

Emotional abuse is damage caused to a child's feelings or emotions. A common example of emotional abuse is shaming. Shaming is making fun of or ridiculing a person for what he is, as opposed to what he does. Shaming says, "You are an evil child, a no good, rotten bum. I wish I had never had you. You have caused me nothing but grief." Note how far removed this is from biblical correction and discipline. This is not a correction of a person's behaviour, which is what discipline is supposed to be. Rather it is a rejection of what they are.

Children who have been shamed go through life rejecting fundamental aspects of their being. They tend to think, "I am a mistake, I ought not to be here. I cause trouble everywhere I go." And sure enough, words like that often become prophetic as the angry child tries to make his or her way through life.

Another common example of emotional abuse is withholding or withdrawing love. You know the scenario: You're angry with your child, and because you are angry, you withdraw emotionally and sometimes even physically. You pretend he is not there. You give him the cold shoulder. You let him know that inappropriate behaviour means he can no longer count on your love. That, of course, puts a child in a terrible bind because it means it is never safe for him to be his own person. Later on, this is likely to lead to many boundary problems because he has come to associate being real and saying, "No!" with a withdrawing of love.

Closely tied into this is cruel teasing. There is an old proverb that says, "Sticks and stones may break my bones, but names will never hurt me." In most cases, this is a blatant lie! Many kids are deeply wounded by cruel teasing, sometimes even more than by physical abuse.

The story is told of a man on a trolley street-car in the city of New York who wanted to play a joke on his 3-year-old son. The two of them travelled together regularly on a double-decker trolley. One day as they boarded the trolley, the father sent his little son ahead of him down the aisle of the bottom deck. Then, while his little boy was unsuspectingly making his way down the aisle, the father quickly sneaked upstairs and stayed there for the duration of the trip. Imagine the little boy's horror when he came to the end of the aisle, turned around fully expecting to see his father, only to be greeted by a sea of strange faces! No father anywhere.

The father thought it was a great practical joke; little did he realize the lifetime of agony and counsel to which he would subject his son.

Post-Traumatic Stress Disorder

Post-traumatic Stress Disorder (PTSD) is a well-attested psychological disorder that results from undergoing either extended periods of stress or very traumatic experiences in one's life. Soldiers returning from battle, victims of serious abuse and survivors of accidents or natural disasters will often suffer from this disorder. It is defined by the following conditions:

A recognizable stressor

A stressor is anything that brings stress into our lives. It can range anywhere from a mild problem we experience to the catastrophic disasters that overtake people. Some examples are extended sexual, physical or emotional abuse, a concentration camp experience, a devastating natural disaster, multiple deaths in your family and so on. Tragedies like this can hit you like a ton of bricks and just crush the life right out of you.

A periodic reliving of the trauma

Truly traumatic experiences are not easily overcome. Even when they have consciously been put out of our minds, they often live on in the subconscious. From there they will often try to re-emerge in many different forms: nightmares, bad dreams or flashbacks that come out of nowhere are probably the most common. Often they are triggered by some experience that relates to the original trauma. Understandably, this causes great conflict and pain for the victim because the cycle of pain just never seems to end.

Let me give an example. One woman I know has undergone serious sexual abuse. Even today, many years later, she will repeatedly wake up in the middle of the night feeling violated all over again. That is reliving the trauma. It can be very, very scary to the point of driving people to alcohol or drugs or to seriously consider suicide. It is also one of the most common causes of panic attacks. It is not the only cause, of course, but certainly a common one.

Psychic numbing

What do you do when the pain becomes more than you can bear? You try to turn it off. This is known as psychic numbing. We all do this to some degree. When something unpleasant or painful happens, what do we do? We stop thinking about it. We put our mind on something else.

The problem with psychic numbing is that it not only kills the bad feelings, it also kills the good feelings. The result is that we become people without souls. The bad doesn't move us, but neither does the good. Consequently, we have a very difficult time forming intimate relationships. Nobody can get really close to us; we can't even get close to ourselves because a part of us has died. If you have ever had a relationship with such a person, you will know that it takes a great deal of energy because the responsibility for making the relationship work falls on your shoulders. For that reason, many such marriages and friendships end in failure.

Additional symptoms

A person who experiences *Post-traumatic Stress Disorder* generally will exhibit any or all of the following additional characteristics:

Hypervigilance or hyperactivity

If you never know who or what is going to hit you, then you live in a constant fear that you are going to be hit again at any time. A minor example: Some years ago, I was involved in a traffic accident in the town where we live. I was making a left turn on an advance green when a car from the opposite direction came through the intersection without waiting for the traffic to clear and I got hit. What stands out in my memory is the sound of the crunch. Ever notice that? When someone hits your car in a big way, what a noise it makes!

On the scale of traumatic experiences, it probably does not rate very high. But you know, for the longest time after that, when coming up to that intersection, my insides would churn and I would be extra careful to ensure that I wouldn't be hit again. That is hypervigilance or hyperactivity.

A young woman by the name of Tillie was seriously abused at the hands of a close relative over an extended period of time. After the rest of the family had gone to bed, he would come to visit her in her bedroom and abuse her in the most traumatic ways imaginable. For years after that, her nights were a nightmare. She would try to stay awake all night, just to make sure he wasn't coming for her. When she did finally fall asleep, the slightest noise would wake her up. When she was in a crowd of people, she'd have to keep track of people all the time, lest someone should suddenly come up behind her and grab her. When the memories became too much, she'd throw herself into a flurry of activity to try to dull the pain on the inside. Such was the legacy of her trauma. Only God's grace was able to eventually heal it all.

Avoiding activities associated with the pain

Traumatic memories are often triggered by events or activities which are similar to the original traumatic event. For example, in the story above, the very act of going to bed would trigger the nightmares of the abuse. Consequently, victims of Post Traumatic Stress Disorder will tend to avoid events, activities or places associated with the pain. If I have survived a traumatic car accident, I may choose never to ride in a car again and so on.

Survival guilt

People who have survived a natural disaster often feel oddly guilty for surviving. They feel that in surviving they have betrayed or abandoned the others who did not. This is especially true if they've had to do things in violation of their conscience in order to survive. Unprocessed, these emotions often lead to a subconscious death wish which is likely to surface in chronic depression.

Multiple Personality Disorder (MPD)

This disorder, better called *Dissociative Identity Disorder (DID)*,[2] is a condition whereby the mind splits into different parts and all the pain becomes compartmentalized. It happens commonly to victims of sexual abuse and is increasingly being recognized as one way in which the mind seeks to keep itself from being totally destroyed in the face of unspeakable pain. A person who suffers from this disorder will commonly create different personalities to handle different aspects of life.

Sometimes the personalities are acquainted with each other. Other times they are not. Some personalities may be Christian; others virulently anti-Christian. Integration is hard work and usually takes several years to accomplish, but it is a precious thing to behold.[3]

PASSING ON THE PATTERN

What we need to understand is this: In each of the situations described above, the child is not able to be the person God has made him or her to be. He is forced to become something other than what he really is. This causes him to develop a variety of coping mechanisms, as we will see later on, that distort his personality and set in motion a series of events that cause the dysfunction to be repeated from generation to generation. As a result, son number one in our alcoholic family model will probably marry somebody very much like his mother because he gets his role in life out of being that kind of support person. The clown will most likely go through life clowning her way out of trouble and having difficulty in personal relationships. The acting-out child will likely get herself into trouble at school and perhaps even with the law. She may have to live with the consequences of some very bad decisions she makes while living out of her pain. And the lost child, if he or she survives, will very likely go through life suffering from very low self-esteem, trying to minimize his or her presence and seeking to draw life out of other people because he or she has very little to contribute to life.

That is the dysfunctional pattern. It gets repeated from generation to generation. The good news is that, in Jesus Christ, God will break into that cycle. He will set us free so that we won't have to repeat the patterns of the past. We can be cleansed and redeemed by the blood of Jesus. We'll see more about that in later chapters.

NOTES

1. "Parents Jailed 16 Years For Starving Son," *Toronto Star*, 25 July 1995, p. A2.

2. The fourth edition of the *Diagnostic and Statistical Manual of Mental Disorders (DSM-IV)* of the American Psychiatric Association (1993), the official diagnostic manual of psychiatry in North America, has officially changed the name of MPD to "Dissociative Identity Disorder." The term "Multiple Personality Disorder" has been retained, in brackets, in *DSM-IV*, and may therefore still be used diagnostically.

3. For more information on this topic, please refer to James G. Friesen's book *Uncovering the Mystery of MPD* (San Bernardino, CA: Here's Life Publishers, Inc., 1991).

The Religiously Dysfunctional Family

5

These people honour me with their lips,
but their hearts are far from me.
Matthew 15:8

In the Fall of 1994, a young Turk by the name of Abdullah, a Muslim immigrant to France, was sentenced by a French court to life in prison while his father, mother and cousin were each sentenced to 20 years in prison. Their crime? They had ganged up on Abdullah's 15-year-old sister, Nazmiye, and brutally murdered her for religious reasons.

Apparently, in having moved from Turkey to the very secular nation of France, the young girl had become enamoured by the French way of life. In the course of so doing, she had rejected her family's traditional religious values. She had resisted the pre-arranged marriage which her parents were trying to foist upon her. She had disgraced and dishonoured their name by looking for a foster family, and to top it all off, she had started going out with a French boy. This really incensed her family. Thus, while the parents looked on and the cousin held her to the ground, her elder brother killed her by strangulation. They did it in the name of religion. Hence their prison sentences.[1]

When I hear a story like that, the question that comes to my mind is, "How in the world can people do something like this and then think they are doing it in the name of God?" Yet that is precisely what happens all over the world today — violence and great pain perpetrated in the name of religion.

Time magazine, in an article on terrorism, gave the following profile of a suicide bomber: A young Palestinian by the name of Radi strapped 6 kilograms of dynamite around his waist and tried to board an Israeli military bus. The driver saw that Radi wasn't wearing military fatigues, so he closed the door and pulled the bus ahead. The bomb went off and, predictably, many people were wounded, but the only person killed was Radi himself. His limbs were blown off and his head and torso remained to be photographed and imaged all around the world.

Radi was a very devout Muslim. He prayed the required five times a day. He was a loner whose only close friends were those who shared his religious convictions. You ask yourself the question, "What is it that motivates religious people like this to perform dastardly acts of cowardice, mayhem and murder all over the world?"[2]

VIEW OF GOD

The answer is, a distorted view of God. Many don't see God as the Bible reveals Him: the Creator and Redeemer of the world, who is a loving Father to those who believe in Christ. He longs for all men to be saved and come to the knowledge of the truth; He longs for His love, truth, justice and mercy to be demonstrated to all the nations of the world.

Instead, many people see Him as an angry ogre in heaven who runs the world with an arbitrary series of black and white rules; a God who favours those who keep the "rules" and who, without mercy, exercises violence and judgment against all those who deviate from them.

It is this distorted view of God that colours the extreme wing of many fanatic religious movements today. It is also this distorted view of God that colours almost everything that happens in a religiously dysfunctional family.

CHARACTERISTICS OF THE RELIGIOUSLY DYSFUNCTIONAL FAMILY

In this type of family, either the father, mother or both walk through life with a sadly distorted image of God. They tend not to understand the nature of grace. They tend to want to establish their own self-righteousness, either by their religious fervour or by their religious activity. And they reproduce in their own lives and in the life of their family, an image of God as they see Him.

For this reason, a religiously dysfunctional family tends to be, on average, coloured by many or all of the following characteristics and parental conditions associated with family dysfunction:

Extreme Rigidity

That is to say, the parents are not very flexible. Their rules are rules that are to be observed because they flow out of their understanding of who God is. And if God made these rules, and you live in the fear of God, then you had better stick to these rules or you are going to get into trouble. So, a religiously dysfunctional family tends to be one that operates by black and white rules, with not too many shades of grey in between.

Punitive or Punishment Oriented

Because a religiously dysfunctional family operates under rules of right and wrong, stepping outside of those rules means swift and severe punishment.

Judgmental

The parents are judgmental because in this kind of religious system, the parents have God all figured out. They know exactly what is right and wrong. They define that, of course, on the basis of what they themselves can manage to get away with! And because they have now figured out what is a right and a wrong way to live, they judge everybody else by their standards. So when people aren't living for God in the way they think is right, they look down their noses and judge them. They say judgmentally, "Those people aren't believers at all. If they were really believers they wouldn't do the kinds of things they're doing."

Non-loving

The religiously dysfunctional family is non-loving because the rules are black and white. When you operate under this kind of legalism, you don't have the strength, energy or capability to try to discern the complex motives that make people tick. Because you're externally oriented, and you are trying to make the family do all the right things on the outside, you have no comprehension of the struggle and the rages in people's inner lives. Love has no place in this legalistic family.

Perfectionistic

It is a system that is geared towards doing the best that you can – not because you love God and want to please Him, but because in this legal system your place is determined by your ability to keep the law. And because your place is determined by how good you are, you have got to be good in order to be accepted. That means that you are always striving to be accepted, you can't admit your own mistakes and you weary yourself and everybody around you by trying to be all the things you *think* a good religious person ought to be.

Sense of Inadequacy

The result of all of the above, of course, is a constant feeling of inadequacy. There is always more to be done. There is always a higher standard to meet. And so, in a religiously dysfunctional system, whether that is a church or a family, there is always that internal sense that says, "I am not good enough. I am never going to measure up, but I have to keep trying to prove to myself and everybody else that I am okay." These patterns are then passed on from one generation to another and bear the fruit of unrighteousness for generations to come, unless God's grace intervenes.

THE RELIGIOUSLY DYSFUNCTIONAL FAMILY

With that in mind, let's take a look at a model of the religiously dysfunctional family. (Please refer to *Figure 5.1*).

Figure 5.1
The Religiously Dysfunctional Family

The Father

Once again, there are several things we should note. *The husband is elevated.* This is because, like in the alcoholic family, life in the religiously dysfunctional family focuses on his addiction. His addiction, of course, is much more subtle than it was in Chapter 4 where the addiction was alcohol. This man's addiction is religion – and religious work. That is why he is holding a Bible. *He is a Bible-thumping man* who rules his family, and his life, by *his* interpretation of what the Bible says.

The collection plate he is holding stands for the fact that *he is a religious workaholic.* He is the kind of man who serves on every committee in the church, participates in every Christian organization he can find, and is often on the forefront of religious movements.

You ask what is wrong with being a Christian worker? Absolutely nothing, as long as it is done for the right motivation and out of love for God. This man *does not know or understand the love of God.* This man *sees God with the distorted viewpoint* of a dysfunctional person. He sees God as an angry God. He is insecure in his relationship with God because he feels that he needs to work in order to be "in the good" with God. He thinks that if he throws himself into Christian service, out of a sense of duty, then he will somehow make the bad feelings inside go away. In all likelihood, he will be seen in the church as a good man. In actual fact, however, he will be an angry, insecure man. He doesn't have the capacity to relate to other people in a meaningful way in everyday life.

The Co-Dependent Wife

This man is usually married, and his *wife* is drawn into the dysfunction with him. His wife becomes *an enabler.* She helps him carry out his dysfunctional religious tasks. If you look at her externally, she appears to be a woman who is wholeheartedly in support of her husband's religious work. After all, how could you argue with working for God?

When he is gone every night, busy saving all the rest of the world, never having time for her, part of her justifies that. She thinks, "As a good, dutiful, religious wife, I need to submit to that and accept that." But at the same time, she feels cheated because this man is using his religion to avoid intimacy with his wife. Notice that even though they are facing each other in the diagram, *they are not face-to-face.* Her emotional needs are not being met by him because she has to go through the Bible, and through the church, in order to ever meet the man.

She tends to be an angry woman. She will often suffer from bouts of depression because she really doesn't know how she is going to get out of this situation. So, even while *she is support-ing him with her left arm, with her right arm she is trying to pull him down to her own level.* She is crying out for intimacy. She is saying, "Won't you please come and be with me? Throw all the religious role-playing aside! Quit spouting off Scripture! Please tell me what is really in your heart. Be a real living person."

Mother's Helper

This mother is under a lot of strain. She is like Moses years ago praying for someone to help her out. Enter *daughter num-ber one.* The eldest daughter supports her mother, who in turn supports her father's religious dysfunction. This young lady will tend to be a *hyper-responsible individual* because she is her mother's helper.

She will also have a lot of unresolved fear and anger. That fear and anger may be directed towards her father because he is always gone and makes life miserable for the mother. It can also be directed at the mother for being a wimp and taking all the father's abuse. In either case, there is a good chance that when this daughter grows up she will have an identity prob-lem. As she grows up, she will go the opposite direction of what she sees modelled in her mother. She tends to judge her mother and father and vows to herself, "I am never going to be like that." This will start a cycle of dysfunction in her life.

The Acting-Out Child

Family systems balance out, as you will recall from Chapter 4. In this family, the *second child* is the first-born son – the *acting-out child*. This young man is angry with his father and acts out the anger in the family because he longs for a relationship with his father that is real. The son knows, if not intellectually, at least in his heart, that the job of his father is to affirm him in his manhood. The job of the father is to help him gain control over his own emotions. A father directs his son in life so he is able to bounce questions off him, learn his identity and go through life in the way God has designed.

Yet when the son tries to reach out to his father, his father is not there. This father does not have the capacity to be there for his son physically, emotionally or spiritually. This young man is angry, and he is usually the first to leave the family. The acting-out child is the kind of person who, most likely, will go through a significant period of rebellion. Ironically enough, when he bounces back from his rebellion, he is, undoubtedly, going to become almost identical to his father. Why? Because his father has modelled for him the religiously dysfunctional and controlling role.

The Nice Child

Enter the second son or *third child*. Again, because family systems tend to balance out, the second son in this family is the *nice child*. The reason he is the nice child is because his identity is shaped almost exclusively in reaction to his elder brother. Because he doesn't want to be like his elder brother and cause his family the same problems, he is the nice kid that just sort of goes along with the flow. He only has one problem. He has no identity. He is somebody different with everybody he meets because he has learned that this is how you keep everyone happy and avoid strife.

The Mediator

Now we need a *mediator*. This is the role of the second daughter *(fourth child)*. She feels her job is to keep this family together. By now the whole family is in each other's hair. That causes a lot of trouble and tension. So, this girl comes into the picture, feels all the vibes from everyone else and tries frantically to solve all their problems.

Of all the members in this family, she is the first one to seek counselling. She will most likely do that when the eldest daughter leaves home because the second daughter now has to move into the eldest's role of supporting the mother. When she has to move in and become a support to her mother *and* maintain the role of mediator, she goes bananas. She comes to a point where she says, "This is too much for me to bear. I can't handle it any more! Somebody has got to help me!" She is the one who reaches out for help outside of the family.

The Lost Child

The *fifth child* is the *lost child*. This child takes an aloof view of the family. She has a bemused tolerance of all the idiocy that is taking place in the family, and she says to herself, "I don't want to get involved in that." Of all the kids in the family, she is the most likely to end up rejecting faith and never coming back to it because she is just turned off about everything. She has made up her mind a long time ago to find her comfort elsewhere. The family is just too crazy and the signals she receives are too mixed.

There is one more thing we should note about this family. This family tends to be rife with sexual abuse. This sexual abuse can take place on a number of different levels. The older brother and older sister will tend to be involved sexually with each other. As well, the older brother and the mediating sister may be sexually involved. If the roles of the parents are reversed, and mom is elevated and dad is subordinate, the daughter and father can become incestuously involved.

Maybe you have noticed that religious dysfunction and sexual abuse often go hand-in-hand. Witness the number of instances that have been coming out of the woodwork in the Roman Catholic Church in recent years. Notice, too, how often sex and religion go hand-in-hand in many religious cults.

Why is that? The answer is that when you grow up in a religiously dysfunctional home or in an environment that is very repressive, you are not able to be your own person. You are not free to ask questions or work out the things you need to work out. You become another person. You learn to play roles and live up to other people's expectations. That leaves a lot of unresolved feelings that need to be acted out one way or another. Sexual abuse in the family is one common way in which this surfaces. It provides some measure of comfort for what is often a very lonely and repressed individual. The tragedy of this, of course, is that most of it will be so deeply hidden that unless you really know how to look for it, you will never see it. Only when a child leaves the family system and gets empowerment from another source, is it likely to come to light. The shame simply runs too deep.

The Scapegoat

The *last child* we'll add to this family is the baby. Note that she is sitting at her eldest sister's foot and is holding on to her leg. The reason for this is that the mother is constantly tied up with her husband's addiction and so the baby is raised by the eldest daughter. Baby will very likely act out everything that nobody else in the family is allowed to act out. He or she will likely turn into the *scapegoat* when the other acting-out children are gone from home.

• • • • • • • •

Several more observations are in order. First of all, very few people in a dysfunctional family recognize their dysfunction. For example, 50% of adult children of alcoholics will deny that their parents had a drinking problem. Fifty percent! If those adult children are themselves drinkers, the figure rises to an astounding 90%! Those figures hold true for most dysfunctional families.[3]

Secondly, many dysfunctional families are hard to spot. It is true, of course, that there are some who are so obviously dysfunctional that the whole world recognizes them as such. For every one of those, however, there are probably ten others who are just as dysfunctional, but hardly anyone knows about it. I have personally known many families that by any standard of measurement were severely dysfunctional. They had kids who were acting out the dysfunction all over the place. Yet, they were held up as a model Christian family by even their closest friends!

DYSFUNCTIONAL FAMILY RULES

How can that be possible? Because all dysfunctional families operate to a significant degree under the three rules of dysfunction: *Don't talk, don't trust* and *don't feel*. Let's take a look at each of these.

Don't Talk

In a religiously dysfunctional family, life is based on image. The father in the model above does not have a living relationship with God through faith in Jesus Christ. He has a very legalistic understanding of God. He lives in fear. He lives under the law. Consequently, he doesn't experience the saving and healing grace of God in his own life. As a result, there is a lot of insecurity and inadequacy. He doesn't really feel that he measures up. He has a lot of unresolved sin and, usually, many unresolved secrets. He can't afford to talk about these because to admit to them would be to destroy his image. Keeping family secrets is, therefore, very important to him.

So he creates a family atmosphere of "Don't talk." When the children raise questions that threaten to expose his secret fear and lay bare his true condition, they are firmly told to shut up. "We don't talk about things like that here." And for one of these children to blab to someone else what really happens in this family behind closed doors is an unpardonable sin. Like the Pharisees Jesus so often condemns, this man's family is like a white-washed tomb – nice on the outside, but full of dead men's bones on the inside. On the outside, they look like the model Christian family. On the inside, they are full of lust and greed and anger. Understandably, a great deal of energy goes into maintaining that righteous facade. Woe betide the person who betrays that image!

A young man I know grew up in one of these homes. His father would periodically get angry and take out all his frustrations on his children. This has so alienated one of the sons that for years he has wanted virtually nothing to do with his father. His oldest brother, the person I know, has wanted to address this situation for some time and has begun talking about this problem outside the home. Curiously enough, his younger brother, who wants nothing to do with his father on account of his verbal abuse, is absolutely livid with him, as is everyone else, for uncovering the family secret! In a dysfunctional family, if you love each other, you keep the family secrets hidden. This, of course, prevents anyone from getting the help they need to break out of this cycle and it guarantees the transferral of the dysfunction to yet another generation.

I am not suggesting that we talk indiscriminately about everything that happens at home. What I am saying is that in an extremely dysfunctional family you have no place to go with what lives inside you because that is to betray the family secret. The degree then, to which we haven't been allowed to express ourselves about what goes on in our families is the degree to which the *principle* of dysfunction is present.

Don't Trust

You would think that the members of a dysfunctional family would want nothing to do with each other when they grow up. "Glad to get away from the old man!" "Glad to get away from this crazy turmoil." Well, there is truth to that, but only to a certain extent.

Dysfunctional families have, what I would term, a love-hate relationship. They love to hate each other! When they are away from each other, they can't wait to get together. When they get together, they can't wait to leave each other. Each year they can't wait to go home for Christmas; and each year they heave a sigh of relief when Christmas is over and they can go to their own homes again.

Why is that? The answer is because their boundaries are fused. They don't know what it is to be separate persons and so they have a deep need for each other. They have holes in their hearts which they keep wanting family members to fill. Unfortunately, the family members have just as many holes and can't meet those needs. As a result, they are constantly disappointed in each other. That's what drives the love-hate relationship. Their love is an immature craving for each other that turns to anger and hate when it is not satisfied. It flows from boundary confusion which is a common aspect of dysfunctional families that destroys the capacity to trust.

Boundaries

A *boundary* is what defines who you are. Part of growing up is learning that each of us is an individual person with our own personal feelings and tastes. You like red and I like blue. Each of us is allowed to have his or her own personal likes and dislikes. This is represented by the circles in *Figure 5.2*. Note that healthy relationships can have three levels of intimacy: casual acquaintance, closer friendship and intimate relationships. [4]

In a casual relationship, you live side-by-side. What one feels or does has little impact on the other. In a closer friendship, if one person is in a bad mood that is going to affect the other person since their lives are intertwined. In an intimate relationship, what the one feels or does has an even greater impact on the other since their lives are intertwined that much more closely.

What is important to note about normal boundaries in normal relationships is that there is an ebb and flow to the degree of intimacy. In other words, at any given point we can choose to be close to each other or we can give each other space. Dr. Henri Nouwen, the Canadian priest famous for his work with the mentally handicapped in L'Arche community, Toronto, likens it to joining two hands at the fingertips. You can move the palms of your hands closer together or further apart, but your fingertips remain joined. In similar fashion, people who observe normal boundaries can give each other varying degrees of space as the occasion may require, without breaking the bond between them.

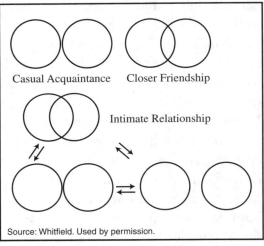

Source: Whitfield. Used by permission.

Figure 5.2
Healthy Boundaries

For example, your opinion may be entirely different from mine. We may disagree vigorously, but we will still be friends and we will remain close in other areas. Or, we may not see each other for a long period of time, but neither of us will get down on the other because we have given each other the freedom to pursue our own dreams. These are normal and healthy boundaries. You come and you go.

What happens in dysfunctional families is that boundaries get distorted. They overlap to the degree that what you think or feel now becomes part of my life. This is represented by the circles in *Figure 5.3*.

Charles Whitfield, in his book *Healing the Child Within*, tells the story of a woman who was so enmeshed with her mother that she literally didn't know what she felt herself until she saw how her mother was feeling when she got up in the morning. If her mother was feeling good, then she could afford to feel good. If her mother was feeling badly, then she felt badly. She was literally an extension of her mother's emotions. [5]

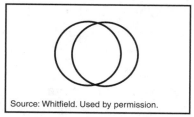

Source: Whitfield. Used by permission.

Figure 5.3
Enmeshed or Fused Boundaries

Take that unhealthy boundary confusion a step further and apply it to a severely dysfunctional family. The result looks like *Figure 5.4*. The big circle represents the alcoholic or the religiously dysfunctional individual. The next size circle represents his co-dependent wife. Note how she is almost completely swallowed up into his circle. She has almost no personal feeling or identity left. Her whole being is identified with his. He has the drinking problem but she feels that she must be the cause of it. Why else must he drink so much? Of course, he is reminding her all the time that if it weren't for the problems she and the kids are causing, he wouldn't have this problem!

The little circle is the child. The child sees mom and dad fighting and says to herself, "I must be the one who is causing all this trouble. I must be a really bad person. Maybe if I was a better kid or if I ran away from home, Dad wouldn't

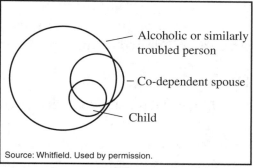

Source: Whitfield. Used by permission.

Figure 5.4
Dysfunctional Family Boundaries

drink so much and there wouldn't be so much fighting." In other words, the child has no life of his or her own. His whole identity is shaped by what is happening with his parents. That is boundary fusion. As one joke puts it: "I'm cold. Go put on a sweater!"

When your boundaries are fused like this, you never learn to develop a healthy trust relationship. How can you? You don't even know which feelings are your own and which belong to someone else. You've been wounded, bruised and betrayed so many times, you become afraid of trusting anyone. Because your skills have not developed properly, if you do choose to trust someone, it is usually someone who is just as dysfunctional as you are and you get hurt again. The result is, that you grow up afraid to trust anyone anymore.

The world is full of people like that. They've been taught and conditioned that they can only trust their own dysfunctional kin. Everyone else is suspect. You can spot them easily because they will reject you before you get a chance to reject them. They will pull you close with one hand and then push you away with the other. And when you allow them to do that, they will turn around and say, "See, I told you so. You can't really trust anybody." Place people like that in relationships and you discover that they haven't the capacity to be intimate. They never quite allow you to get to their true selves, because that is too frightening for them. As a result, many such relationships do not last, and the stage is set once again for the cycle to be repeated in the next generation.

Don't Feel

One of the outstanding characteristics of the dysfunctional family is that it is *predictable* in its *unpredictability*. You never know what is going to happen. You never know if you are going to be hugged or slugged. Yesterday, you did a certain thing and you were complimented for it because your father liked it. Today you do exactly the same thing because you figure that is what your dad wants, and you get yelled at and slapped for it. Yesterday you were allowed to cry and express your frustrations and your parents gave you a measure of comfort. Today you do exactly the same thing, and all hell breaks loose. You get ridiculed and made fun of and told to quit acting like a baby and grow up. When you try to defend yourself, you are told the Bible says to "honour your father and your mother" and not give them any more lip.

What happens when your feelings are not allowed to be expressed naturally? You learn to shut them off. What happens when you shut them off? You stop growing and developing emotionally. You learn other coping mechanisms to deal with emotional pain and before you know it, you are an emotional cripple. You go out into the world and people try to connect with you but there is no one home. You are emotionally absent. Things that ought to bring tears to your eyes and laughter to your mouth, leave you absolutely cold and disinterested. People can't reach you, they can't touch your heart. When you engage in conversation you hide behind clichés, lest your lack of originality be exposed. If you are a religious person, chances are you'll hide behind religious platitudes. Your real heart nobody ever gets to know. Chances are you don't even know it yourself because to face the pain that lives there seems simply too overwhelming.

IN SUMMARY

These then are some of the characteristics you will find in all dysfunctional families. The degree to which they are present will mark the degree to which the family is dysfunctional.

Please note that this cycle of dysfunction runs very deep and is hard to break. The religiously dysfunctional father, in particular, has a hard time giving up his dysfunction. It is like dying to him. It means admitting that he has been play-acting all this time. He doesn't really have a true relationship with God. He hasn't really been motivated by love for God but rather by his own sense of insecurity and inferiority. He's lived like a hypocrite. He's made a mess of his family's life. He bears responsibility for a good portion of his kids' behaviour. That is a bitter pill to swallow! Yet it must be done if we value our children and want to see them grow up in a way that pleases the Lord.

The good news of the gospel is that no matter where we have been or how we have been shaped, by the blood of Jesus we have been *redeemed from the empty way of life handed down to* [us] *from* [our] *forefathers* (1 Pet. 1:18). We can be free! And we can leave a godly legacy to our children.

NOTES

1. Sipa Kessler, "Talk of the Streets," *Time*, 12 December 1994, p. 18.

2. Lisa Beyer, "What Makes a Suicide Bomber," *Time*, 145 (2), 16 January 1995, pp. 50-51.

3. Charles I. Whitfield, *Healing the Child Within* (Deerfield Beach, FL: Health Communications, Inc., 1987) p. 26.

4. I am indebted for these and the following insights to Charles I. Whitfield, pp. 48-49.

5. *Ibid*, p. 33.

PART TWO:

Breaking the Cycle of Dysfunction

From Generation to Generation

6

[The Lord] punishes the children and their children for the sin of the fathers to the third and fourth generation.
Exodus 34:7

A woman in our church came up to me after a service in which I had taught about the three rules of the dysfunctional family that we discussed in the last chapter, and she said to me, "You forgot rule number four." I asked her, "What's that?" She replied, "Don't be."

I asked her what she meant and she went on to explain that, in her family of origin, it wasn't just a matter of not talking, not trusting anybody or not feeling anything. It was also a matter of not being allowed to be who she truly was. She was not allowed to have her own identity; rather, the identity of her parents and others was forced upon her. Understandably, as that particular woman grew up, she experienced a significant number of emotional problems and difficulties. Many of these, by God's grace, are slowly being peeled back as she makes new choices in life and commits herself to being the person Jesus calls her to be.

What we need to understand is that these rules for dysfunctional families are practiced by *all* families some of the time. There are times in all of our families when we say, "Don't talk. Don't put your trust in that person," or we don't allow someone to express his or her legitimate feelings. This doesn't necessarily mean our families are significantly dysfunctional.

In families that are really dysfunctional, these three or four rules are applied unremittingly *all* of the time. When parents do this, they not only cause significant damage to their offspring, but they set in motion a whole series of events that guarantee, apart from God's grace, the passing on of sinful patterns from one generation to another. I call this *generational sin.*

GENERATIONAL SIN

Generational sin is what the Bible talks about in Exodus 20:5-6, when the Lord says:

> *"...I, the Lord your God, am a jealous God, punishing the children for the sin of the fathers to the third and fourth generation of those who hate me, but showing love to thousands who love me and keep my commandments."*

In other words, just as the Lord gives His blessings to a thousand generations of those who fear Him, He also passes the consequences of sin and disobedience of the fathers on to their children to the third and fourth generation.

One of the best ways to understand this is to look at a very common phenomenon in life that most of us will have observed. For example, a young woman grows up in a highly dysfunctional family. Let's say her parents are alcoholics and the family is very unstable. The rules of the dysfunctional family are all in place. The child is just waiting to grow up and get out of the house. She vows to herself that she will never ever marry a man like her father. But what happens when she does marry? Nine times out of ten, she will repeat the pattern established in her family of origin and marry a man very much like her father.

John and Paula Sandford tell the fascinating story of a woman who was raised in a family exactly like that. Her first husband was an alcoholic, just like her father. She said to herself, "This is a bum deal," and divorced him. Then she married another man, one who claimed to only drink socially, but he turned out to be an alcoholic, as well. She got rid of him and married for a third time. This time she didn't want to repeat her earlier mistakes, so she married a man who didn't drink alcohol at all. Imagine her consternation when, after they had been married awhile, he not only turned to drink, but became a full-fledged alcoholic! If that wouldn't make you question yourself and your own sense of judgment, I don't know what would! [1]

You and I look at a person like that and we say to ourselves, "How much bad luck can a person have?" The fact of the matter is, luck has very little to do with it. Rather, it is a pattern of choices that is being passed on from one generation to another. Let's take a look and see how this pattern works.

THE PATTERN AT WORK

Please refer to *Figure 6.1.* [2] What you see there is the interactional pattern that passes dysfunctions on from one generation to another.

Note how the cycle begins with the dysfunctional family rules: *"Don't talk," "Don't trust"* and *"Don't feel."* (see *Step 1*). We can include *"Don't be"* to that, as well.

The *second step* is the development of *a personal pattern of attachment* to one's family. The family members may feel or think, "I am important because I keep the peace in the family;" or, "I allow father to express his anger by taking it out on me;" or, "I am mother's helper and without me and my help, this family would not function;" or, "My parents want me to make them look good in the neighbourhood."

In other words, the child feels he plays an important *role* in keeping the family functioning as it is. This role may not at all be what he or she would have chosen personally. Rather, it is foisted on them by the family.

As we have noted earlier, this is one of the characteristics of dysfunctional families. Roles are foisted on you. In normal families, you have some choice about the role you want to play. If you want to leave home and try to make your fortune, you are free to try to do that. If you want to stay home and work on the family farm, there is opportunity to do that. At the very least, you have the freedom to talk about it.

In a dysfunctional family, that is not usually the case. Your role is determined, not so much by your desires and wants, as by the unresolved needs of the parents. One classic example would be the adult single woman who forgoes marriage in order to provide companionship for a grumpy parent who is terrified of being left alone. Another example would be the lonely teenage girl who has never felt loved and who decides to go out and get pregnant so she can have a little baby that will return her love.

In the model of the family that we looked at in Chapter 5, the super-achiever, for example, may not have had much choice about being the main support for her mom and dad. The role was foisted on her; mom and dad were sick or unable to manage, so she was forced into the role of supporter. But maybe in her heart of hearts, she doesn't want to be this at all. Maybe deep down, she wants to go off to school and become a teacher, but can't because it will disrupt the cycle in the family. And the pressure is on her to perform according to the family rules and expectations – many of which remain unspoken, but are there, nonetheless.

Because children want and need parental love, children tend to want to live up to their parents' expectations. Many people have told me over the years how they have longed for their mom and/or dad to affirm them, to say to them, "Look,

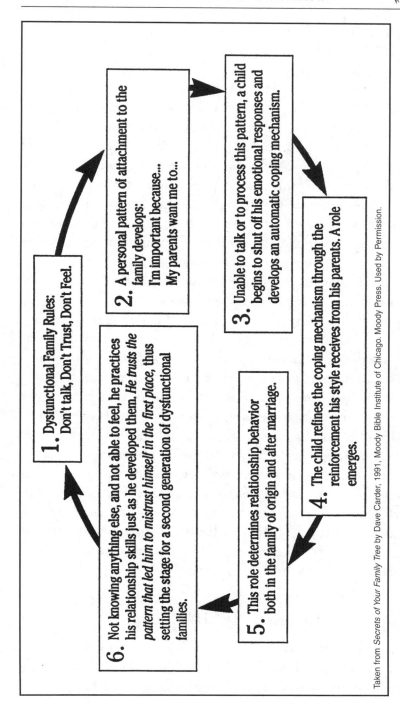

Figure 6.1

The Interactional Pattern That Passes Dysfunction from One Generation to the Next

Taken from *Secrets of Your Family Tree* by Dave Carder, 1991, Moody Bible Institute of Chicago. Moody Press. Used by Permission.

you're a neat kid. I love you and I'm proud of you." This is powerful motivation to continue in the role that best pleases your parents.

But what if that role is not what you or God wants for your life? What if you want to be something entirely different and you chafe over the role that is forced upon you? You're not allowed to talk about it, because that creates family chaos. What do you do now? There is only one thing to do: grit your teeth and bear it. In other words, you shut down your emotions. Pretend that what you feel and think is not important. Go with your parents' interpretation of reality. Failure to do that is to get walloped and branded as a troublemaker. Change your role in any way and you let down the whole family system. That is why, in this family, if you step out of your family role in any way and become a new person in Christ, you let down the whole family system and send it into a tizzy.

It has amazed me over the years to see religiously dysfunctional families in which the teenagers go out bar-hopping and fooling around, and nobody blinks an eye. But these same families are thrown into chaos when their son or daughter comes to Christ, wants to start serving Jesus and rejects his or her old lifestyle. There is chaos, you see, because the teenager's behaviour can no longer be predicted in the family relationships.

When you shut down emotionally at a very early age, what happens? Well, you still have to stay alive and cope with all the inconsistencies of your chaotic family, so you develop survival mechanisms that will help you live in a crazy world without going crazy yourself. These survival techniques are called coping mechanisms (*Step 3*).

COPING MECHANISMS

Coping mechanisms are tools we develop to help us cope with the pain of reality. They have a life of their own and are extremely resistant to change. They become key factors in the trans-generational process of how God visits the sins of the fathers upon the children. Let's look at some of the most common ones.[3]

Denial

The most obvious coping mechanism that we develop is denial. We all use it to one degree or another. Something hurts you or someone says something that is really painful for you. You don't have time or opportunity to process it, so what do you do? Block it out. Just deny it. "It doesn't really hurt or bother me," you say. You can live in denial for a long time.

Some time ago, a woman who had been badly hurt in a significant love relationship came to see me. She had been used and treated very poorly. As she was telling me about it, I said to her, "That must have really hurt you badly." Immediately, her coping mechanism kicked into gear. "Oh no," she said, "it didn't bother me at all!" I knew she was way too glib to be real, so I told her. "I think that's nonsense. You can't go through what you've just been through, and not be hurt by it." After awhile, she admitted that indeed was the case.

Let me give another example: You live in a highly dysfunctional family with all the usual symptoms of dysfunction. Somebody comes to you and says, "You know, your family is strange. Your parents are weird and your brothers and sisters are a little wacko too." How do you respond? Very likely, loyalty will kick in. You may not be able to stand other family members, but when it comes to defending yourselves against the rest of the world, blood runs thicker than anything else. So, you deny there is any problem and will probably get angry with anybody who suggests otherwise.

In Chapter 3, I told the story of a man who remembers as a child being grabbed around the neck by his father, who would hold him until he fainted. After he told me that story with considerable emotion, he then said, "But I don't believe that my family is dysfunctional!" I said to him, "Then what would you call it? It certainly is not normal for fathers to go around choking their sons!" Talk about denial!

I often see that kind of denial in marriages. One partner will be very unhappy and unfulfilled in the relationship and will cry out for help. He, or, more commonly she, will drag or send the spouse for counselling. What you often find is the other partner (usually the man) is totally oblivious to the pain that the spouse is living with almost constantly. "I didn't know she had a problem," is a common response you get. It's no wonder so many marriages are in trouble!

Projection

Projection is blaming others for your own faults. It is attributing to others what really lives in your own heart. I have a good friend who does this all the time to his wife and children. He is a very committed Christian. He is truly anointed of God for ministry. He has a tremendous heart and a passion for the lost. But his family life is so chaotic by times that his family has asked him to leave home. "We can't live with you any more," they have told him.

Why not? Because he keeps projecting his own fears and insecurities onto his wife and children. For example, his oldest girl is entering her teenage years and so, not surprisingly, boys have started coming around. For any parent, that can be scary! Most parents imagine the worst by times, but they eventually learn to live with it, realizing this is part of growing up. Not this father! Time and again he would come down hard on his daughter. Long before she even knew sex existed, he would question her and challenge her motives and accuse her of things she hadn't even dreamed of doing!

Why would he do that to her? He was projecting his own fears and insecurities onto her life. He himself grew up in a very dysfunctional family and made a vow at an early age that he wasn't going to need his parents for anything. He was sexually abused himself, and some sexual issues still remain unresolved in his own heart. As a result, he would read his own thoughts into his daughter's mind and make her life, by times, almost impossible. Mother had to side with the daughter to protect her and keep her safe, and so chaos broke loose in the family. That is projection – attributing to someone else, or blaming someone else, for what lives inside of you.

Reaction Formation

Reaction formation is a variant of denial and projection that produces a behaviour pattern that is directed towards warding off unconsciously forbidden impulses within yourself by trying to stamp them out in other people. A good example would be the virulent anti-pornography crusader who secretly engages in a variety of sexual fantasies and practices, or the latently homosexual anti-homosexual activist. Many otherwise righteous causes are irreparably harmed because people intuitively sense this inconsistency in their proponents.

Displacement

Displacement is a very common coping mechanism. It means that you take out your anger and frustration on somebody and in a place that is unconnected with the original problem. The classic example is when a boss gives a father a hard time, the father goes home and takes it out on the mother, the mother takes it out on the kid, the kid takes it out on the dog, the dog takes it out on the cat and who knows where the cat goes.

Displacement happens in situations where it is not safe for one to voice anger. Displacement takes place in religiously dysfunctional environments because we are all supposed to be so nice and we can't really say what we want to say. So, displacement surfaces in people acting out their frustration in other settings, rather than in the one that caused their anger.

Another good example is the behaviour of kids at school. Teachers can tell you that when a normally well-behaved child suddenly becomes a playground bully, or otherwise unmanageable in class, it usually indicates that the child has a problem. That problem usually has to do with unresolved issues at home and it may come out in the child's artwork or writing. If you have children that constantly express themselves through dark, brooding, violent themes, I would be a little concerned. It may just be a phase they are going through, but it may also be due to a lot of unresolved anger being displaced and coming to expression in these other situations.

A lot of the violence that happens in our culture today, particularly where there is no relationship between the criminal and the victim, can be traced to displaced anger. I can't take my anger out on the situation or person who really deserves it, or who really needs it, so I will find somebody else and vent my anger on them instead.

Idi Amin, back in the 1970s, is a classic case in point. Amin grew up as a member of the Nubian tribe, one of the lowest of the low tribes. Moving all over the place with his mother in this itinerant tribe, Amin never knew who his real father was. He joined the army and decided that he was going to get even with the world.

He became a cruel dictator and personally supervised the destruction of some hundreds of thousands of people. And what was so macabre about it was his perverted delight in tormenting and torturing his victims before he fed many of them to the crocodiles. Adolf Hitler was his hero. Idi Amin was so conceited that he sent numerous letters to the Queen of England offering to be her chief advisor. The last I heard, he was still alive and living in Saudi Arabia. He has never been brought to justice. That is displacement used as a coping mechanism.

Overcompensation

This means an exaggerated striving for any trait which will neutralize and conceal strong feelings of an opposite kind.

When people don't feel safe to express their true emotions, they will often try to cover these up by hiding behind other emotions. For instance, the mascot in the dysfunctional family clowns around to avoid expressing his real hurt.

Michael Cavanaugh, in his book *God's Call to the Single Adult*, tells the story of how, whenever he would get into an emotionally painful situation, he would break into hysterical laughter. He recounts the time when he was talking to a girlfriend, explaining an experiment he had tried as a child. He was supposed to be hatching chicken eggs and they had all hatched but one. He was sitting guard so that when the little chick came out of the last egg, it wouldn't burn itself on the heater. But he fell asleep. The chick hatched, and wouldn't you know, it fell over, hit the heater and burned itself. There it was in the very early moments of its life, struggling in painful woundedness to get to its feet. As Cavanaugh was relating this story to his girlfriend, instead of expressing his true emotion, he burst out in hysterical laughter. The girlfriend (who I don't think remained his girlfriend for very long!) looked at him and said, "What is the matter with you? You're laughing about this!"

He went home and thought and prayed about it, and the Lord brought to mind an incident that had happened in his youth. He had been out on the playground at school and seen the playground bully beating the tar out of somebody else. Michael's heart was tender; he felt so bad for the victim that he wanted to cry. But he knew what would happen to him if he cried in the school yard – he would also become victimized. So, he made up his mind there and then, that instead of giving in to the pain of his heart, he would build his own wall of defense. And he joined the others in laughing hysterically at the abuse being perpetrated on that other child. That became his coping mechanism. Every time he got into a situation where emotionally he couldn't carry it any longer, he burst out in hysterical laughter.[4]

Reactions like this are quite common. Many people behave like this. The situation demands they be serious. Instead, they won't quit clowning around. If you have close friends who are like that, you know how irritating and unsettling that can be!

An equally common example of this is the contrariness that flows out of pain. People whose parents spanked them too much vow, "I am never going to spank my child;" or, "My parents drank too much. I will never drink any alcohol;" or, "When I was a child, we were poor and I always had to wear hand-me-downs. People made fun of me. Nobody is ever going to do that to my child, so I'll go on buying sprees even if I can't afford it, just to maintain the proper image;" or, "As a child, I moved all over the place and never made any friends. I don't want to do that to my child, therefore, I have passed up who knows how many God-given opportunities for advancement in order to give my kids stability."

Ever been there? Not all of this is bad, of course, but if we are still reacting to the past, then we are not responding to the present situation. And yes, maybe you did get spanked too much back then. Does that mean your child will never need spanking? Not likely! The danger of extremes is that one generation swings this way, the next generation swings the other way and the third generation swings back again. God wants us, instead, to maintain a good balance.

Introjection

Introjection means allowing someone else to inject their values or role into your life. Let me give you an example. One woman I know grew up in a family where the parents, at an early age, had been forced to quit school and go to work to help support the family. Quite naturally, her parents expected her to do something similar. And for years that is what she did. After completing her schooling, she went to work and provided abundantly for her parents and siblings.

Now, please don't misunderstand me. There's nothing wrong with helping out your family as long as that is a role you choose to take upon yourself. In this instance, though, it wasn't as much a matter of choice as unconsciously absorbing her parents' expectations and living them out. That's introjection.

Perhaps another example will help. Let's suppose a father is overly critical and constantly belittles his son. When the son absorbs his father's evaluation and accepts that as a true measure of his worth, regardless of his real abilities, that's introjection. He's allowing someone else's views to determine his own even when they are not based on reality.

Repression

Repression means that if you don't like something, you push it away. It is very similar to denial, but it runs deeper. Feelings surface that you don't know how to handle or don't have the time to process, so you just shut them off and push them deep down inside. As in denial, you pretend they were never there. In the meantime, anger is rising up inside you. That anger needs to be expressed in a safe and healthy way but you cannot, or will not vent it. You don't feel it is a safe or prudent thing to do. So you push the angry feelings down. After awhile, you may forget what you were angry about, but the anger itself remains seething below the surface, waiting for an appropriate incident to trigger it and release it. That is repression.

Repression is a very common coping mechanism, and the more dysfunctional the family, the more you need repression to stay alive. It is particularly prevalent in the lives of people who have undergone traumatic experiences, and have not had a safe place, the time, or the energy to process those experiences. Some people are so good at pushing away feelings of pain and anger, they literally forget that anything painful ever happened to them.

How can you tell if someone is suffering from repressed memories? There are several ways of doing so, but one common clue is memory gaps.

Normally speaking, if you have had a fairly protected and safe childhood, you can remember back to early childhood. Wouldn't you agree? Three years of age, give or take a little, is when memory starts for most of us.

For example, my earliest childhood memory is when I was less than 3 years old and was almost killed. My father, brother and I were sitting on a horse-drawn wagon. We had just taken the milk cans to the front of the driveway, unloaded them and loaded the empties onto the back of the wagon. We were coming back down the driveway, which sloped downwards towards the house, when the drawbar came loose from the wagon. The wagon careened off to the side as the horse spooked, and we fell into a very deep ditch filled with water and sewage. Of course, the milk cans came rolling in after us and the horse and wagon almost followed suit. Providentially, the horse's harness got caught on a pole or we would have all been history. As it was, I am told my father had to drag us under water to get us away from the rolling milk cans. My mother, who was pregnant with my younger sister at the time, was standing in front of the house watching all of this happen. She almost had the baby on the spot!

The only part I remember is standing stark naked in the kitchen sink, black as black can be on account of the sewage, being washed down by my mother. That is all I remember of it. I am told that later I got very sick because of the ingested sewage.

Many of us will have memories of this nature. A person who has practiced repression, however, will have gaps in his memory. I know people in counselling who can remember nothing, even good things, before a certain age, until the Holy Spirit comes and restores their memories. Some people can't even remember back to when they were 10, or older. They just don't remember. So, if someone has significant memory gaps, there may be several causes, but repression is often one of them.

Another way in which repression manifests itself is in flashbacks. The repressed, true self wants to come out. Past events need to be processed. The conscious mind works overtime at repressing these memories. And so you get flashbacks. Suddenly, a feeling or a memory from the past will hit you out of the clear blue sky. Usually, it will be triggered by something in the present, and you find yourself having a reaction that is totally out of proportion to what is happening in the present.

Let me give an example. Tabbi was sexually abused in the passenger seat of an automobile. Because the incident was particularly traumatic, this memory was repressed for many years. When it finally surfaced, it surfaced in the form of flashbacks. She would be riding along in a car when suddenly she would be overcome by feelings and memory fragments of the original experience. At first, this was very scary. Later, it helped her come to grips with her past.

Anger, particularly for men, is often an expression of repressed emotions. Things that get stuffed down when the freedom to vent in a redemptive fashion is not there, have a nasty way of coming out in anger. In a lot of very repressive and authoritative families, people are unable to express their emotions, and anger then often becomes the only socially acceptable emotion.

If anger is the coping mechanism for men, depression tends to be so for women. There are many causes for depression and I wouldn't ever want to say that everybody who is depressed is repressed! Far from it. But repression is one of the main causes for a great deal of present day depression. What happens is that your subconscious pours a lot of energy into repressing the things that you cannot handle. You cannot put a lot of energy into forming the person you really are because you are concentrating your energy elsewhere. As a result, you are not free to be yourself and you cannot see your way clear to ever be that, and you feel there is no sense in living. If there is no sense in living, you just turn inward and become more and more dead inside.

HOW ROLES EMERGE

These, then, are some of the more common coping mechanisms. There are more, of course, but these will suffice for our purposes. What we need to understand is that all of these coping mechanisms are *developed* and *reinforced* in a dysfunctional family, whereas in a normal family they are *discouraged*. In a normal family, if a parent sees that the child is denying reality or projecting blame, he or she calls the child to account, provides discipline, if necessary, and thus discourages inappropriate behaviour.

In a dysfunctional family, on the other hand, these patterns are actively *encouraged*. Denial is a way of life. Projection is a normal way of reacting and so on. I am expected to ignore my own instincts and behave in the prescribed way. When I do that, I receive approval. When I don't do that, I am the troublemaker. Out of this emerges my role in the family (*Step 4*).

Let me illustrate it this way. Suppose, for example, that you cope with anger by repression. Your father or mother is angry a great deal. You absorb that anger and learn to keep it all inside. As long as you do that, everybody gets along well because everyone is playing their part. Suppose, however, that one day you decide you don't want to live this way anymore and you start mouthing back. Instead of keeping it all in, you start fighting back. What happens? You cause a lot of trouble. The whole family system is thrown into turmoil because you are not supposed to behave this way. Other people are allowed to be angry, but not you! You will be labelled the troublemaker!

Powerful forces will be brought to bear on you, demanding you to toe the line. Love will be withheld until once again you fit the expected mold. Harmony returns. That reinforces the use of your coping mechanisms as a necessary tool for survival and teaches you that if you want to get along with people, you need to keep all your feelings to yourself.

Soon this is the only way you know how to live and relate. Your true inner self, your true feelings and thoughts, have been ignored for so long that you are hardly even aware of them anymore.

Now roll the clock ahead a few years. You become a teenager. You start dating and get married. What happens in the new social relationships that you contract outside your family of origin? Well, you are going to try to reproduce the dynamics of your known family life. If you are a person who has learned to cope by denial, you are going to try to build a family system that is based on denial. Whenever your spouse raises a problem that could disturb your carefully cultivated peace, you refuse to admit there is any problem. If you have learned to project, you are going to blame other people for your problems. Every time something goes wrong, it is never your fault; it is always somebody else's fault.

Anyone married to an adult child of a dysfunctional family will know what I am talking about. Family of origin patterns tend to be repeated in new relationships with frightening regularity. Even when people make a conscious vow not to, they tend, nevertheless, to repeat the pattern (*Step 5*).

PASSING ON THE PATTERN

What happens when you take the patterns of the past and project them into new relationships? Two things:

First, you try to build new relationships on the basis of your dysfunction. This means you are going to be drawn to other equally dysfunctional people because normal people will not put up with it. The coping mechanisms that work in a dysfunctional family unit where people are geared to take abuse and a whole raft of other hurts, don't work with normal people. For example, a normal person won't tolerate or reward you for your denial. Instead, they will constantly try to make you face the truth, even if that means provoking a crisis to make that happen. Neither will a normal person allow you to make them your whipping post and absorb all your anger and blame. Instead, they will fight back. Unfortunately, in many relationships, dysfunctions don't surface until ten or fifteen years into a marriage because it takes that long to recognize the patterns.

Second, if you contract a relationship with a normal person and that person does not recognize your dysfunction right away, he or she will not be able to adapt fast enough to your coping mechanism. For example, if your role in the dysfunctional family was the clown and you respond to tense situations by joking, your spouse has one of two options. She can accept your behaviour and learn to live with it, in which case she will be buying into your family's dysfunctional pattern and thus setting the stage for the dysfunction to be passed on to the next generation.

Or, she may be unable or unwilling to adapt to your behaviour and insist instead that you change. You, of course, see nothing wrong with your behaviour and resist any such attempts. As a result, the system will grind to a halt and the relationship will collapse.

That is why so many adult children of dysfunctional families experience so many broken friendships and collapsed marriages. The coping skills that worked so well in their own dysfunctional family of origin often do not work in new relationships. Other people simply cannot live with their dysfunctions.

Unless this is recognized and proper help sought, things will likely go from bad to worse. Ironically, it doesn't matter whether or not one is a Christian. These patterns are so deeply ingrained that only God's grace can help us recognize and break out of them. Apart from that, they go from generation to generation, often in subtle ways (*Step 6*).

Witness the example of a man who grows up in an alcoholic family. He swears that he is never going to be an alcoholic, and as he grows up, he never takes a drink. But when you look at the next generation, more often than not, alcoholism re-emerges. Why? Because the father is known as a "dry drunk." He doesn't drink alcohol, but he still has all the unresolved emotions and problems of having lived in a dysfunctional family. And, if he hasn't worked through his dysfunction, he carries these problems and his learned coping mechanisms with him into his marriage and new family.

He doesn't know how to make space for his child's true identity. He doesn't know how to love the child, or what the child's needs are. He just repeats the pattern he learned at home, even though he has tried so hard not to be like his father or mother. That is why husbands and wives, in moments of frustration, say to each other, "You are just like your mother," or "You are just like your father." That usually finishes the conversation for the night!

Are we doomed, then, to repeat the patterns of the past? Is there no escape? Not at all! God in Christ has done everything that is needed to set us free and start a new cycle of blessing and life. The starting point for that, however, lies in clearly understanding the issues that are at stake and learning to apply them to our own lives. More about this in the following chapters.

NOTES

1. John and Paula Sandford, *Restoring the Christian Family* (Plainfield, NJ: Logos International, 1979) p. 196.

2. Taken from *Secrets of Your Family Tree: Healing for Adult Children of Dysfunctional Families* by Dave Carder, 1991, Moody Bible Institute of Chicago, Moody Press. Used by permission.

3. I am indebted for many of these insights to Dave Carder, "Passing the Torch: The Multigenerational Transmission Process," *Secrets of Your*

Family Tree: Healing for Adult Children of Dysfunctional Families (Chicago: Moody Press, 1991) pp. 67-91.

4. Michael Cavanaugh, *God's Call to the Single Adult,* available from Mobilized to Serve (7245 College St., Lima, NY 14485).

7 | Facing Yourself

*Search me, O God, and
know my heart!*
Psalm 139:23

In June of 1994, the blood-soaked bodies of Nicole Simpson and Ronald Goldman were found outside her plush condominium in Los Angeles, California. Shortly thereafter, her ex-husband, O.J. Simpson, was charged with both murders. In the sensational murder trial that followed, one of the first witnesses to come forward was a former L.A. policeman by the name of Ronald Ship. Ronald Ship professed to having been a friend of O.J. and Nicole. He claimed in court that after their much publicized fight on New Year's Day of 1989, he met with O.J. and Nicole separately to talk with them about the issue of wife battery. Here is what Ship said at his court testimony: "I showed each of them a textbook profile of a typical wife-beater. Nicole said all the descriptions applied to her husband, but Simpson saw little that resembled himself in the profile. Simpson said, 'Maybe I'm a little jealous, but that's all.'"

When I first heard that story, I couldn't help but reflect how typical this is in dysfunctional relationships. It is ever so much easier for other people to see our dysfunction than it is for us to see it ourselves. Nicole had no trouble seeing how her husband fit the wife-beater profile. O.J. looked at the same profile and saw nothing resembling himself. That happens a great deal, doesn't it? It is so much easier to see the splinter in the eye of the other person than to see the log in your own eye. Why is that?

COPING TO SURVIVE

The answer lies in the coping mechanisms that we develop to keep pain manageable. As I pointed out in the last chapter, whenever we are confronted by painful realities, the tendency is to develop coping mechanisms to make the pain bearable. We have looked at seven of these: denial, projection, reaction formation, displacement, overcompensation, introjection and repression.

What we need to understand about coping mechanisms is that they are a means of survival. They are a way of staying alive in the midst of very painful situations. You think, "If I do not deny the pain in my life, then the pain will overwhelm me. I can't stand that, so I have to pretend it doesn't exist. If I really face the fact that I am the one with the problem and it is not caused by others, then I have to look at myself. If I do that, I will have to face all the rest of the garbage in my life too. I never bargained for that." So, I blame others or adopt one of the other coping mechanisms. The point is, I want to stay alive. The urge to survive is the strongest of all biological urges. When pain consumes your life, you'll do anything to make it go away so you can survive.

Therein lies the problem. When you get raised in an unstable environment where the rules of "Don't feel, don't talk and don't trust" are being applied on a regular basis, this way of life becomes normal. When something becomes normal, it becomes the standard by which you measure everything else in life. And when dysfunction becomes normal, it is very hard to recognize as abnormal. That is why it is so hard to see the log in our own eye. As far as we are concerned, there is nothing wrong with us. It is the rest of the world that is out of tune. For example, if we were raised in a world where the sky was green and the grass was blue, that would be normal. And if somebody else were to come along and say it was the other way around, we would say he was crazy! That is why the more the world falls apart, the harder it is for people to understand the difference between "function" and "dysfunction," and "normal" and "abnormal."

Just recently, I saw a comic strip that illustrates this truth perfectly. In *Between Friends,* Maeve and Helen are talking and the one says to the other, "I am surprised you are seeing Arthur again." The other woman says, "Why?" The first answers, "Because you said that it bothered you that he had been married twice and had four children." In the next frame, the other woman responds, "Yeah, well, I decided that I was being too judgmental. And besides, with all the pressures and stress we have to deal with in our modern day world, dysfunctional is about as normal as it gets!" How sadly true that is!

OPENING OUR EYES

If understanding generational sin is the first step in breaking free from the patterns of the past, the second step is having our eyes opened. We need to see what we are really like and where we are dysfunctional, so that we can go to God and have those cycles broken through faith in Jesus Christ. Psalm 139 puts it this way: *Search me, O God, and know my heart; test me and know my anxious thoughts. See if there is any offensive way in me, and lead me in the way everlasting* (vs. 23-24).

If you look at the context of these verses, you see that God is an omniscient God – He knows everything. He is also omnipresent – there isn't any place where we can go that God isn't already there. Consequently, there isn't any fig leaf that we can put in place to hide our true selves that God doesn't already know what is behind it.

I am dismayed sometimes at our perversity. We think we can hide our true condition from God. That is so foolish. Even the darkness is not dark to God. There is nothing He doesn't know and nothing He doesn't wish to bring into the light. And the reason for that is not so He can club us over the head with our sin, but rather so we will recognize it and thus turn to Him for healing and forgiveness.

Let's take a look then at some of the vehicles God uses to open our eyes and speak truth into our lives.

God Speaks to Us Through the Scriptures

Your word is a lamp to my feet and a light for my path, says Psalm 119:105. Verse 104 says, *I gain understanding from Your precepts; therefore I hate every wrong path.*

We live in a day and age where, increasingly, moral values are thought to be relative. Nothing is absolutely right or wrong. It all depends on the situation and the circumstances. "If it feels good and doesn't hurt other people, do it," is the motto of our age. It doesn't take a lot of wisdom to figure out that when this kind of relativism holds sway, moral confusion begins to abound. Darkness starts to look like light, and dysfunction is considered normal.

A good example of that is the increasingly wide-spread acceptance of homosexuality today. Time was, not that many years ago, when homosexuality was considered something sinful, an aberration. Even people who didn't particularly consider themselves Christians felt that way. All of that has drastically changed in recent years. In 1973, the American Psychiatric Association (APA) voted to delete homosexuality as a medical term from its lists of abnormalities. Though only about a quarter of the APA members were present at that meeting to vote on the proposed change, this vote and its subsequent news coverage have given the homosexual community a platform from which to proclaim their lifestyle as "normal."

Even people who call themselves Christians get in on the act. When, on June 9, 1994, the Ontario legislature refused to accept the much-debated NDP Bill 167, which proposed extending same-sex spousal benefits to gay and lesbian couples, the Rev. Brent Hawkes of the predominantly gay Metropolitan Community Church in Toronto led the protest from the public gallery. The *Toronto Star* said, "When the vote was announced [he] stood up in the public gallery and shouted: 'This is an absolute outrage! Shame! Shame!'" [1]

God's Word, says the psalmist, *is a lamp to* [our] *feet and a light for* [our] *path*. No matter how times may change and people's understanding of truth changes, God never changes. He holds to eternal standards of truth and righteousness and He continues to communicate these standards through the pages of Scripture.

For that reason, if we want to know what "normal" is, we need to read and study the Scriptures. This is where God reveals His own character and nature and teaches us how He wants us to live. As we read and study the Scriptures with a view to honouring and obeying God, He will let His light shine into our lives and show us what the truth is.

Needless to say, that truth is not always pleasant. There are people who think that reading Scripture or coming to church ought to be primarily a "comforting" experience. It should make them feel better. And yes, it is true that the Holy Spirit is the Comforter. And yes, many times as we read Scripture we will be comforted and strengthened as God's children. But my experience has been that long before He brings comfort into our lives, He will first bring conviction. He'll show us areas in our lives that are not pleasing to Him and that, therefore, need changing. For that reason, reading

Scripture or going to a worship service where Scripture gets expounded and applied to life can sometimes be very painful.

I was at a Bible study one time years ago where we were studying 1 Corinthians 13 – the great love chapter. As we were going through the chapter verse by verse, looking at the definition of love – *Love is patient, love is kind. It does not envy, it does not boast, it is not proud....* (1 Cor. 13:4) – a friend of mine suddenly burst into tears, slammed her Bible shut and cried, "I don't like this at all!" What was happening? The Scriptures were speaking to her. She was going through a difficult time in her relationship with her husband and was coming under conviction.

Scripture will do that. In a world of changing values, God's truth stands firm. It shines like a light in a dark place. It exposes our short-comings and our sins. Scripture says, *The word of God is living and active. Sharper than any double-edged sword, it penetrates even to dividing soul and spirit, joints and marrow; it judges the thoughts and attitudes of the heart* (Heb. 4:12-13). It shows us what "normal" is from God's point of view.

When it does that, we can do one of two things: We can reject the light and hold on to our view of reality because we like it better; or, we can embrace the light, allow it to expose our sin and dysfunction and turn to the Lord for help in changing our lives. That is the purpose of Scripture – to make us men and women of God, equipped to serve Him. Paul, in 2 Timothy 3:16-17, puts it this way: *All Scripture is God-breathed and is useful for teaching, rebuking, correcting and training in righteousness, so that the man of God may be thoroughly equipped for every good work.*

God Speaks to Us Through Modelling

A second way in which God will help us to understand dysfunctional patterns in our own lives is through what I call modelling. Rather than just telling us what we are doing wrong and how we should change it, the Lord will bring people into our lives who can actually model or demonstrate for us how we should live.

This modelling can be one of two kinds: *direct* or *indirect*.

Direct Modelling

Direct modelling is seeing in somebody else's life or family a pattern of behaviour that is very much different from your own and thus opening up for you whole new possibilities.

Let's suppose, for example, that you are raised in an alcoholic family. All the dysfunctions normally associated with this kind of family are part of your experience; you never know whether you are going to get hugged or slugged, complimented or yelled at, comforted or ridiculed. You have learned to live in denial because to give in to your feelings is going to be way too painful, and there is a lot of fighting and a lot of conflict and everybody just sort of does his own thing.

Now the curious thing is that when you grow up in this kind of environment, that is all you know. You think this way of life is perfectly natural. You think that everybody lives that way. But then you go over to a friend's place and their family life is entirely different from your own. They say grace at the table. They actually talk nicely to each other and say please and thank you. They seem to enjoy each other's company. They treat each other with dignity and respect and allow each person to express himself in fitting and appropriate ways.

A young man whose home I know to be rather dysfunctional because of his father's anger told me recently, with amazement in his voice, what a wonderful summer he'd had staying with relatives. "They didn't just boss me around," he said. "They actually asked me nicely if I would be willing to do things for them." That was an eye-opening experience for him. He'd never seen that in his relationship with his own father.

Many of us, I'm sure can identify with experiences like that.

When I was a kid, Saturday nights at our house were a time when the adults would retire to the living room and the rest of us, after our baths, would gather in the kitchen. We would roll up the carpet and have a whole group of friends over and go at whatever we felt like doing. Sometimes it would be games or wrestling matches. Other times it would be some construction project we had in process. We'd get out a hammer and saw and go at it, making an incredible ruckus and an awful mess. Remember now, this was Saturday night, when traditionally everything had been cleaned up and readied for Sunday.

Some years ago, I got to reflecting on this and I said to myself, "How in the world did my mother ever put up with all that?" So I asked her. Here is what she said: "I would rather have you in my kitchen where I can keep my eye on you than out in the street where I don't know what is going on." She was prepared to sacrifice the neatness of her house for the well-being of her children.

Years later, one of those neighbourhood friends who used to come over on those Saturday nights came to my mother as an adult and thanked her for the way he had been included in our family. He told her what an eye-opener it had been for him to see another family at work as opposed to his own and how that had served as a model for his family now. That is *direct* modelling.

Indirect Modelling

Modelling can also be *indirect*. By indirect, I mean primarily *story-telling* and *dramatization*. In the church I presently pastor, we occasionally use short dramatizations of real-life situations in our worship services to set the stage for the message. As with so many things, when we first started to use these dramas, the response was two-fold: Many found themselves powerfully moved and ministered to as they saw their own lives acted out; others were deeply offended that the dramatic arts should be brought into church and saw it as a sell-out to the world.

I, for one, appreciate that kind of concern because it is all too easy for the Church to compromise its message in an attempt to remain culturally viable. At the same time, I believe that if the message of the gospel is to be communicated effectively, it must be communicated in a culturally relevant way. That's what story-telling and dramatization have done throughout most of history.

The World

Ask yourself the question, "How does the world impart its values to the majority of people today? What makes a Hollywood culture the dominant cultural force even in many third world countries?" Story-telling and dramatization, that's what! Seldom does the mass media preach in the traditional sense of the word. Seldom do they challenge Christian values and truths head on. Instead, they portray life in such a way as to create a demand for Western secular culture all over the world. And anyone who has ever lost a child to the world will know how hard it is to fight the subtlety of it all. Along the way, fact often gets confused with fiction and people start living in a fairy-tale world that doesn't really exist.

A friend of mine tells the story of a woman who came to church and stood up during prayer time to request prayer for a girl named Rachel. "Can we please pray for her?" she asked. "She is seriously ill." Tears were streaming down her face. Dutifully, the pastor and the congregation invoked heaven's blessings on poor Rachel, only to discover later that Rachel was not a real person at all! She was merely the star of a television soap! That shows the power of drama, doesn't it? People remember far more of what they see and experience than what they merely hear.

Jesus

You can see this method very clearly in the ministry of Jesus. Jesus was certainly one of the most effective teachers in history. If you look at His ministry, you will find that a great deal of it involved story-telling. His parables are often held up as models of effective communication. Not only that, but each miracle He performed, in its own way, was an acting out of His message and His ministry. Indeed, His whole incarnation, His coming into the world in human form, was a matter of the word being made flesh.

The Prophets

The same things can also be said of the Old Testament prophets. They not only spoke the word of God, they modelled it. Take the prophet Hosea. Chosen by God to call a spiritually adulterous nation back to Himself, Hosea not only spoke the message, he lived it. At the instruction of the Lord, Hosea married Gomer, a prostitute, and in their life together acted out God's grief towards an adulterous nation. Or take the prophet Jeremiah. Jeremiah is known as the weeping prophet because his heart was broken over the sins of the nation. At the Lord's command, he went and buried a loin cloth at the Euphrates River. Later, again at the Lord's command, he went and dug it up, only to find it spoiled. This then became an object lesson for Israel to show how her sin had spoiled her usefulness and glory before the face of God. Examples like this could be multiplied many times over. The prophet Ezekiel was commanded to get a brick and act out the upcoming siege against the city of Jerusalem and so on. All of these are examples of the biblical use of drama.

The Church Today

Drama has an ability to get into our lives through the back door. Because it bypasses the mind to some degree and engages the emotions, it gets around all the defenses we have built up against biblical truth. Those of us who have gone to church a lot and listened to many sermons, have often learned to tune out biblical truth to a remarkable degree. We just don't hear it anymore. If we do still hear it, we have a whole series of rationalizations to help us explain away our disobedience.

Effective story-telling and dramatization often gets around that. Because they employ more senses than just hearing, they touch us in ways the spoken word alone often cannot. Many times, I have seen people moved to tears because the slice of life they have seen modelled was such an accurate reflection of their own life's experience. That in turn makes them that much more open to the clear presentation of the gospel.

God Speaks to Us Through Life's Experiences

It would be wonderful if every time God spoke to us by His Word or Spirit we would all listen. In truth, that is seldom the case. Our coping mechanisms are simply too well developed for us to give up our independence and trust in the Lord instead. They are, after all, a means of survival. If I give up my denial, then I have to face reality. And reality may well be overwhelming. If I stop projecting my blame on to you or my cat or my dog or whomever, and take responsibility for my own problems, then my fear is that I will be overwhelmed by all of the pain. I don't want that to happen, so I keep on going, no matter how much my dysfunction may hurt myself or other people. To stop and face the pain of dysfunction at the core of my being is simply more than I can bear. So I screw up my courage and keep on going and going and going until I can simply go no more.

Often that is when God steps in. He knows that if I am to bear significant fruit in His Kingdom, sooner or later I will have to stop running. I have to face reality. And so, in His providence, the Lord will sometimes pull the rug out from underneath us. Suddenly the coping mechanisms I have developed to get me through life don't work anymore. Trouble and heartache overtake me. In my despair, I cry to the Lord and, slowly but surely, He starts to deliver me from the old, destructive patterns that were so much a part of my life. He replaces them with patterns of behaviour that bear good fruit. The psalmist said, *It was good for me to be afflicted so that I might learn Your decrees* (Ps. 119:71).

The temptation for each of us, of course, is to just push the problems aside and keep on pushing on. We keep busy with our work, we throw ourselves into more relationships, into drugs or whatever to keep the inner pain at bay, hoping that someday we will wake up and the pain will be gone. That is seldom the case. Sooner or later, unresolved issues catch up with us and bog us down.

The Tractor Pull

Figure 7.1
Tractor Pull

I was discussing this recently with someone who lives in denial. The analogy that came to my mind was that of a tractor-pull. Tractor-pulls are very popular in some parts of the country. They involve the pulling of a special sled called a "drag" behind a tractor or some other souped-up vehicle. The drag usually consists of a flatbed trailer that has wheels at the back and a skid at the front. Positioned over the rear wheels is a big block of concrete that is attached to a chain which is geared to the rear wheels. As the drag is moved forward by the tractor, the block of concrete moves forward on the flatbed, increasing pressure on the front skids. Eventually the weight of the concrete produces so much drag that the tractor either stalls or spins out. The idea of a tractor-pull is to see who can go the furthest distance. (See *Figure 7.1*).

They are fun to watch (and expensive to operate, I might add, because equipment breakdowns are common – and costly). The thing about tractor-pulls, of course, is that they are self-defeating. It doesn't matter how much horse-power or speed you have, eventually the weight in the back will catch up with you and drag you to a halt.

And that is the way it is with unresolved issues from the past. We can ignore them for a long time. We can pretend they don't exist. But eventually, they will catch up to us and drag us to a halt.

How Unresolved Issues Surface

For some people, this will show up in *depression*. They are overtaken by a deep sense of futility and aimlessness. A woman I know well called me on the telephone one day and said, "I don't know what is the matter with me. I am so depressed." And she asked me what I thought was the cause of her depression. I said to her, "Do you really want to know?" She said she did. (One advantage of being at the end of your rope is that you have nothing more to lose).

So I gave her my opinion. I said, "The reason I believe you are depressed is because you have tried so hard to live up to your husband's expectations that you have lost your own identity in the process." That really clicked with her. Her husband is a very strong man. He has very strong opinions and has definite expectations of what she ought to be like and what she ought to do. For years she had ignored her own sense of right and wrong and, out of a mistaken notion of biblical submission, had tried to go along with him. She had learned early on in the marriage that she couldn't ever win an argument, so she had just quit trying. She figured she was wrong anyway, even though her own sense told her there were times when she was right. In the process, she lost her own soul. She lost her own identity. And that's why she was depressed. Years of not being understood or appreciated finally caught up with her and dragged her to a halt.

So I said to her, "If you want to regain your life, you will have to repent of your idolatry. You will have to confess that what your husband thinks of you has become more important than what God thinks of you. And you have to choose once again to be and become all that God has made you to be."

As you can imagine, that set off some real fireworks at their house. No matter how dysfunctional our relationships may be, they nevertheless provide us with a measure of security and predictability. Thank God, she had the courage to persevere and several weeks later she called me again. "You wouldn't believe all that has happened," she said. And she went on to describe how the joy of the Lord had overwhelmed her and how finally she was on her way to becoming the person God meant for her to be. That doesn't mean all her troubles were over. Subsequently, she and her husband went through a very difficult time sorting out all the changes in their relationship. Gradually, God has been reworking and rebuilding their lives. But it took a crashing halt to make them stop and think.

Broken relationships is where the problem shows up for other people. Many people stand aghast when suddenly, after many years of marriage and church-going, a relationship breaks up. "Isn't that sad," they'll say. And yes it is. Broken relationships almost always cause a great deal of pain and often leave long-term scars. But break-ups don't occur in a vacuum. They are usually the result of accumulated hurts and frustrations that have not been resolved. Eventually the weight of the baggage exceeds people's ability to cope and relationships fail.

For others, it takes the form of a *nervous breakdown*. There are, of course, many reasons why people have nervous breakdowns, but one is that unresolved past issues drag the system to a halt. One woman I know grew up in a highly dysfunctional family. Because of this, she made some very unwise choices growing up as a teenager. Eventually, the guilt and the shame of it all caught up with her and she was hospitalized with a nervous breakdown. No longer able to cope with even the simplest functions, she was finally forced to stop and process all the accumulated garbage in her life. As she worked through her whole backlog of guilt and anger and turned them over to the Lord Jesus Christ, she was finally able to get the monkey off her back. And though circumstances of her life since that time have been everything but easy, she has remained strong and secure in the Lord.

IN SUMMARY

So, the second step in breaking out of the cycle of dysfunction is a realistic self-assessment. We must face who we are. Only as we frankly face our fears and our weaknesses, can we turn them over to the Lord and find forgiveness and healing. That's not always easy to do. The desire to cover up and present a better appearance than what is really warranted goes as far back as Adam and Eve's attempt to cover their nakedness with fig leaves. Thank God He is not content to leave us in our pitiful condition. Instead, He searches us out, pulls the rug out from underneath us if need be and shows us what our real needs are. Only then can we turn to Him in trust and faith and find the forgiveness and healing we all crave.

NOTES

1. Peter Edwards and Jack Lakey, "Irate Lesbians, Gays Protest MPP's Vote: The Community is Seething With Anger," *Toronto Star,* 10 June 1994, p. A10.

8 | Core Issue 1: Idolatry

You shall have no other
gods before me.
Exodus 20:3

Core issues are conflicts or problems which occur repeatedly in our lives, consciously or unconsciously. They originate from unresolved areas in our past which need to be addressed and worked through. If these core issues are not resolved satisfactorily, we continue to carry these conflicts with us into the present, thereby distorting our world and life view and affecting our behaviour.

Let me give you an example. George is what I call a "runner." Whenever George finds himself in a tight spot, he literally runs away! If his boss puts too much pressure on him, George is out of there. If his wife gives him a hard time, he's gone – sometimes for a few hours, occasionally for days at a time.

Why does he do that? Because he's never learned how to handle his feelings. When he was a child, his father would beat him to within an inch of his life if he misbehaved. He learned at a very early age that it was better to avoid painful situations than to face them. And so he became a runner. And even though as an adult he knows intellectually that this is not a very satisfactory way of coping with a problem, he has very little control over it. Once the tension builds up, his old coping mechanism kicks into gear and George is out of there.

That is a core issue. Core issues are very common to adult children of dysfunctional families and over the years, psychologists have been able to isolate a significant number of them.

Charles Whitfield, in his book *Healing the Child Within,* identifies thirteen such core issues that people from dysfunctional families have to be able to recognize and resolve satisfactorily if they are going to break the dysfunctional cycle:

1. Being too controlling;
2. Difficulty trusting others;
3. Handling feelings;
4. Being overly responsible;
5. Neglecting your own needs;
6. All-or-nothing thinking or behaviour;
7. High tolerance for inappropriate behaviour;
8. Low self-esteem;
9. Difficulty in being real;
10. Grieving ungrieved losses;
11. Fear of abandonment;
12. Difficulty handling conflict;
13. Giving and receiving love.[1]

For our purposes in this book, we are going to re-organize these thirteen core issues into four broad categories: Idolatry, Handling Grief, Handling Emotions and Shame-based Addiction.

In this chapter, we will deal with idolatry. In subsequent chapters, we will deal with the other core issues.

IDOLATRY

Idolatry, in its simplest definition is looking to something or somebody other than God to meet our needs and thus living to please them. Idolatry was probably *the* besetting sin of Israel in the Old Testament, particularly in the days of the prophet Hosea, who was called to bring Israel back to the Lord. Here is what he says in Hosea 14:1-3:

> Return, O Israel, to the Lord your God. Your sins have been your downfall! Take words with you and return to the Lord. Say to Him: "Forgive all our sins and receive us graciously, that we may offer the fruit of our lips. Assyria cannot save us; we will not mount war-horses. We will never again say 'Our gods' to what our own hands have made, for in You the fatherless find compassion."

The context of this passage is that Israel was unfaithful to the Lord her God. Instead of looking to Him for all her needs, she looked instead to the Baal gods, those Canaanite fertility gods the Lord so despised. Then, when that didn't work out, she made military alliances with Assyria and Egypt, pagan nations that hitherto had been her enemies. Needless to say, God was not too pleased and He brought judgment on His people because of their persistent idolatry.

I believe that idolatry remains to this day one of the besetting sins of human-kind. And while it is true that all of us, apart from God's grace, are guilty of idolatry to one degree or another, I believe it is particularly true of people who have been raised in dysfunctional families.

Let me try to explain it in this way: The biblical picture of reality is that God is the overflowing Source and Fountain of all of life. He loves His creation and wants everyone, particularly His children, to look to Him for all of their needs and to trust Him to provide for them. According to the level of maturity we have attained, God expects us to have that kind of confident trust.

Now, because we are all sinners, this is difficult for all of us. None of us naturally trusts God nor looks to Him. It is especially difficult, however, for people raised in dysfunctional families. In normal families, parents serve as a vehicle for God's grace to flow into the lives of their children. And children learn what psychologists call "Basic Trust." They learn that they are fundamentally accepted for who they are and that people will look after their legitimate needs.

Love Deficit

In a dysfunctional family, parents are often too busy looking after their own needs to have time and energy to look after the needs of their children. This produces a condition I would term a "love deficit." A "love deficit" is a hole in one's heart that cries out, "Won't somebody love me? Won't somebody understand me? Won't somebody really take care of me?" In other words, the child does not learn Basic Trust. (See Chapter 18 for more details on this.) His capacity to believe that other people will love him and provide for him is damaged. The severity of this depends largely on the degree of abuse suffered as well as the resources provided for the child during this time. As a general rule, the earlier the wounding, the more severe the damage.

Now, what happens when you have a hole in your heart? You want to fill it, of course. Ideally speaking, we should fill it with God. People have great difficulty understanding this, but from God's point of view, even a child, to the extent to which he is able, should be looking to God to defend and provide for him. Would we be able to do that, then God Himself would be our shield and defender. Scripture makes that very clear. Psalm 27:10 says, *Though my father and mother forsake me, the Lord will receive me.*

The problem is, of course, that we live in a fallen world. Even as wounded and frightened adults, we often find it impossible to have that kind of trust in God. Imagine how difficult that is for children who have nowhere to turn! As a result, we tend to look to other sources to fill the hole in our hearts. That is idolatry in its essence: Trying to find life outside of God and living to please someone or something other than God.

Parents as Idols

To what kind of idols do we turn? For children, parents are a common idol. A child has the right to expect his parents to love him unconditionally and provide for his needs as they are able. The problem is, dysfunctional parents are not able to provide adequately for the child's needs. Nevertheless, the child still wants love and still wants it from the parents who are unable to oblige. It is at this point that the child begins to assume his *role* in the family. He becomes what he thinks his parents want him to be. He thinks, "If only I act a certain way, or behave in a particular fashion, then my parents will love me and provide for me." So instead of living to please God and finding his security in the Father's perfect love, he is living to please his dysfunctional parents.

The problem is that dysfunctional parents have their own struggles. In their own woundedness, they are not consistent in their demands. What they demand today may be different from what they demanded yesterday or will demand tomorrow. They are not acting in their child's best interests but rather their own. And so the child who keeps anxiously trying to please such parents will find himself on a never-ending treadmill of failure because their demands change constantly. No matter what he does, it is never good enough. He loses his own sense of identity in the process. Unless he manages to break out of the cycle, he may be seriously and perhaps irreparably damaged in the process.

This idolatry can be very subtle in its manifestations. Let's suppose, for example, you have a child whose father wants him to steal. Ideally, what the child should do is say, "Stealing dishonours God. I don't want to dishonour Him. Much as I love you, father, I won't oblige you in this matter." Should he decide to do that, chances are very good the father will withdraw his love from his son. For the son that is difficult to bear, because he wants his father's approval. And so what commonly happens is that, in order to remain in his father's good graces, the child will oblige the father and steal. That is idolatry. It is putting loyalty to parents ahead of loyalty to God.

Other Idols

There are many other idols we latch on to as well. Suppose that for all our loyalty to them, our parents are still not meeting our needs. Then what? Well, very likely we will try to latch on to other significant people: friends, teachers, counsellors, even demons – anyone, or anything, who will help us fill the void in our heart. The problem is, each of them is less than perfect. They all have needs of their own. They all demand something back and, sooner or later, apart from God's grace, there comes pay-back time. When push comes to shove, they will choose their own interests over mine and I will again be left high and dry. The world is filled with people who have naively given their heart to others for safe keeping, only to have it shattered and broken in the process. That is why there are so many people who refuse to trust anyone. They become their own god. They become hard as nails. Nobody is going to mess around with them. The downside, of course, is that nobody can get really close to them. They keep everyone at arm's length.

As Oswald Chambers so aptly observes, "If we love a human being and do not love God, we demand of him every perfection and every rectitude, and when we do not get it we become cruel and vindictive; we are demanding of a human being that which he or she cannot give." [2]

That is why it is so important to have no other god but the Lord God Almighty. He is the only one who loves me perfectly. He is the only one who has my best interests at heart and will always act in love towards me, enabling me to fulfill my God-given purpose and destiny.

How do I know? Because He loved me enough to give His Son for me. The Bible says, *For God so loved the world that He gave His one and only Son, that whoever believes in Him shall not perish but have eternal life* (John 3:16). As I lose my life for Him, paradoxically, I gain it.

That is why, if we are really serious about being healed and breaking the pattern of generational dysfunction, the first thing we need to do is return to the Lord. That is what Hosea was trying to tell the people of Israel so many years ago:

> *Return, O Israel, to the Lord your God. Your sins have been your downfall! Take words with you and return to the Lord. Say to Him: "Forgive all our sins and receive us graciously, that we may offer the fruit of our lips. Assyria cannot save us; we will not mount war-horses. We will never again say, 'Our gods' to what our own hands have made, for in You the fatherless find compassion"* (Hos. 14:1-3).

RETURNING TO THE LORD

Notice that Hosea outlines the following process of returning to the Lord:

We Must Become Aware of Our Sin

Return, O Israel, to the Lord your God. Your sins have been your downfall! (Hos. 14:1)

Ever since Adam and Eve fell into sin, we have all had the tendency to blame others for our problems. That is especially true once we start to understand the concept of generational sin. It becomes so easy to say, "If my mother had been more caring or if my father hadn't been such a hot-head, I wouldn't be where I am today." And that may be true. When we think about the hurts we have received, real or imagined, it is easy to become very angry and to let the anger dominate our lives.

What we need to remember, though, is that we cannot change what has been done to us by others. Neither can we blame them for all the problems we have experienced. How our lives turn out isn't simply a function of the pain or abuse we have experienced. There are many who have gone through unspeakable abuse, who nevertheless, by God's grace turn out to be caring, responsible individuals. What makes the difference? It's how we respond to the pain we have experienced. If we bottle it all up inside and fill our lives with anger and bitterness, the abuse will certainly destroy our lives. If, on the other hand, we honestly face it and turn it over to the Lord, taking responsibility for our own wrongful responses, God can certainly turn it around for good.

Steve and Annie Chapman have a song that goes like this:

Two Children

Two children, a brother and a sister,
born to a father who was a slave to wine.
They do remember their younger years of sorrow,
how their daddy used to hurt them time after time.

But somehow they grew to be so different,
their lives turned out to be like day and night:
One lives in peace up in Ohio;
one was full of hate until she died.

I wondered what could make the difference
in the two of them;
both had reasons to be bitter, but one was so sweet.
How could one live in peace and not the other?
Not long ago the answer came clear to me.

I saw the brother at his daddy's grave.
Placing flowers there his eyes were filled with tears,
as he said, "Daddy once again I do forgive you,
for the way you made us suffer through the years."

Now I can see how the two could be so different,
How their hearts turned out to be like day and night:
He lives in peace up in Ohio;
she was bitter till the day she died.

He lives in forgiveness up in Ohio;
She was bitter until the day she died —
a bitter heart was the reason that she died. [3]

That doesn't mean we absolve other people of their responsibility; nor does it mean we turn a blind eye to the injustices that have occurred. What it does mean is that we trust the Lord to take care of those issues. We are not responsible for the choices other people make. We are only responsible for the choices we make. These we need to face up to before the Lord. We need to say to Him, "Lord, show me where I have not trusted and obeyed You. Help me to face my own rebellion and unbelief and help me to turn away from it."

That is hard to do. Everything inside of me says it was all the other person's fault. And perhaps it was. But dwelling on that will not solve my problem. It'll just make me more angry because chances are the other person either cannot or will not admit to their sin. What I need to do is face up to my own short-comings in all of this, my own failure to trust and obey. If I am in a right relationship with God, then God will take care of all the other matters in His own time and way.

We Must Confess Our Sins to God

Take words with you and return to the Lord. Say to Him, "Forgive all our sins...." (Hos. 14:2).

To confess our sins means to agree with God that we have been wrong. Many people find that hard to do because to admit that we are wrong is to get ourselves into trouble. For that reason, many people would rather blame others than accept blame themselves.

Christians, however, can afford to admit to being wrong because they understand the nature of grace. No one can live up to God's perfect standards. But when we accept Jesus into our hearts, we come to understand that He died for all the bad things that we have done and ever will do. It means that we can afford to admit and confess our sins because we will be forgiven. That's what grace is – knowing we aren't perfect, admitting our faults and accepting God's healing and restoration in our lives.

The story is told of a little girl who was maybe 5 years of age when her parents took her and her little brother, who was a year-and-a-half old, to the beach for the day. For whatever reason, the parents had to leave for a little while, perhaps to visit someone else at the beach or to get some supplies. Whatever the case, they only thought they would be gone for a little while. Unfortunately, they were gone much longer than they had planned.

Before they left, they instructed the little girl to be sure to look after her little brother. Make sure, they said, he doesn't go out to the sandbar, because when the tide comes up, he won't be able to get back in to shore and he'll drown.

Well, you can imagine what happened. The little girl got busy on the beach building her sand-castle. She forgot all about her little brother as well as the rising tide. The little lad wandered out to the sandbar, the tide came in and the little boy drowned.

Can you imagine the guilt and the grief this young girl felt? All through her growing up years she felt she had been responsible for the drowning death of her little brother. Eventually, this bothered her so much that she got weighed down with a heavy depression. Nothing she did could shake her out of the conviction that she had caused her little brother's death. In an attempt to alleviate her depression, she went to counsellor after counsellor. They all told her the same thing: "You were little, you didn't know what you were doing. You must forgive yourself and get on with your life." She'd go home and try to follow their advice and promptly fall into depression all over again!

Finally, she found a Christian counsellor. Like all the other counsellors, he listened sympathetically to her story. When she finished, he looked her square in the eye and said to her, "It is true. By your negligence you contributed to the death of your little brother. You have reason to feel guilty because you are guilty. No matter how young you were, or how wrong your parents were to leave you in charge like that, you did disobey your parents even while you knew better. You are guilty." Those were hard words for her to hear, even though in her heart she had known all along that they were true.

But the counsellor didn't stop there. He went on to say, "Now that you have faced the guilt and the shame of it, there is a place for you to go with it." And he pointed her to the Lord Jesus Christ and His sacrifice on the cross. And for the first time in her adult years, the woman was finally set free from the heavy load of guilt and shame that she was carrying. The psalmist put it this way:

> *When I kept silent, my bones wasted away through my groaning all day long. For day and night Your hand was heavy upon me; my strength was sapped as in the heat of summer. Then I acknowledged my sin to You and did not cover up my iniquity. I said, "I will confess my transgressions to the Lord" – and You forgave the guilt of my sin* (Ps. 32:3-5).

I am afraid that much of the Christian community is way too glib about confession. You have heard the prayers and I have too: "Lord, forgive all our many sins for Jesus' sake. Amen." When I hear people pray like that, I always want to ask to which particular sins they are referring. We don't sin in generalities, you see. We sin in specifics. And for confession to be meaningful, we need to confess our sins specifically. We need to say, "Lord, in this instance, I committed spiritual idolatry. What my spouse wanted was more important than what You wanted. Pleasing my children was more important than pleasing You. Gaining the approval of my friends was more important than gaining Your approval. Living for myself was more important than living for You. And Lord, it was wrong. I repent of it and I ask You to wash it away by the blood of Jesus." That is what confession is. It needs to be done thoroughly and without haste.

We Need to Renounce Our Idolatry

Assyria cannot save us; we will not mount war-horses. We will never again say 'Our gods' to what our own hands have made, for in You the fatherless find compassion (Hos. 14:3).

To renounce means to break off. It is not good enough to confess our sins and say, "Lord, I am sorry for all of these things that I have done." If we are really sorry for our sins, there is also a desire to make a clean break with them.

I believe each of us needs to do a periodic house-cleaning of our idols. As the old hymn says:

> *The dearest idol I have known,*
> *whate'er that idol be,*
> *Help me to tear it from Thy throne*
> *and worship only Thee.*[4]

That means, first of all, *naming* our idols and then *renouncing* them. We need to say, "Lord, I have lived to please my spouse. I have lived to please my children, or my neighbour, or my friend or whomever it may be. I have put their wishes ahead of Your wishes and that has been wrong. I have done it because I was afraid that if I lived for You, they wouldn't like me anymore and would withhold their love from me. I could not bear the thought of that. Lord, that fear is very real. By times it truly paralyses me. But You have told me I am not to have any other gods before You. You want me to trust You and You alone. And so therefore, I renounce all false gods that I have looked to for life and comfort. From now on I want to live for You and You alone." That is renouncing.

The results of that are often astounding. A woman came to see me one time, suffering from a heavy-duty case of depression. As we talked and counselled, it became immediately obvious that her depression stemmed from emotional and physical exhaustion. This was brought on by her trying to be too much for too many different people. As we dug into her family background a little bit, it became evident that the relationship between her parents had been pretty rocky throughout her childhood; so much so, that the burden of trying to keep them together and the family free from tension had fallen on their daughter's shoulders. Instead of being a carefree little girl, she had been saddled with the responsibility of keeping her parents happy. As you can imagine, that was a pretty heavy responsibility. In looking after everyone else's needs and living to please them so that in turn they would love her, she lost her own sense of identity and almost her sanity. Only by renouncing the false need she had to please her parents and other significant people in her life was she able to overcome her depression and start on the road to recovery.

As we face our fears and renounce our idols, God's grace is truly able to meet us and provide us with courage and strength that we never thought we had before. It also simplifies our lives immeasurably. Instead of living to please half a dozen different people, all with their own agendas, I now only have to live for the Lord. And because His love towards me is perfect, He enables me to become the true person He has created me to be. That is freedom!

We Need to Serve the Lord Jesus Christ

Take words with you and return to the Lord. Say to Him: "Forgive all our sins and receive us graciously, that we may offer the fruit of our lips" (Hos. 14:2).

The phrase, *We will offer the fruit of our lips,* in the original Hebrew really says, "We will render the bull of our lips." That's really a reference to a thanksgiving sacrifice in which a bull was slain before the Lord. What it means is that as we repent of our sin and renounce it, we are going to offer to the Lord a sacrifice of thanksgiving.

It is never enough to simply break off the negative. It needs to be replaced with a positive. Nature, in the spiritual as well as the natural, abhors a vacuum. If we renounce all other idols, we also need to rededicate ourselves wholeheartedly to serving the Lord Jesus Christ.

Very specifically that means two things:

First, we need to *commit ourselves to trusting the Lord* for time and for eternity.

I don't know about you, but I find that very hard. I find that human nature doesn't mind trusting the Lord in the areas where it is not really important, but to trust Him with my life? To step out in areas where I am completely at His mercy, where I have lost all sense of control, is a most frightening thing. That is why many believers keep one foot in the world and one foot in God's Kingdom. We will go along with the Lord so far, but we want to keep the bridges to the past intact just in case it doesn't work out. Then we can always high-tail it back to where we came from. We call that wisdom. The Bible calls it unbelief!

I believe there needs to be a time in our lives when we get down on our knees and say, "Lord, I want to trust You in every part of my life. I repent of the unbelief that I have. I repent of believing the devil's lie. Give me a revelation of Your Father heart and help me to understand that all Your actions towards Your children are gracious all the time."

Second, we must *learn to obey*.

Maybe you've never noticed this in your own life, but my experience is that when you make a commitment to the Lord to follow Him, He starts talking to you! Through His Word and Spirit, He starts pointing out things you are to do or not to do. Have you ever noticed that?

What does He start talking to you about? Usually about things you are really not very interested in doing! Isn't that true?

I remember when the Lord became real in this way in my own life. The first thing He did, and I remember this so very clearly because I found it so difficult to do, was to convict me of the need to go see my mother and apologize for some of the misdeeds of my youth! In the cosmic scope of things, I suppose it wasn't such a major thing. But it was for me. It became for me a very practical test of who was going to be Lord of my life. Was I going to follow Jesus or was I going to follow my own wisdom? I am sure that if I could somehow have squirmed my way out of that one, I would have done it, but the fear of God was too great. And *the fear of the Lord*, says Scripture, *is the beginning of wisdom* (Prov. 9:10).

I suspect you will find the Lord leading you in the same way. You will find that the Holy Spirit will put His finger on the area of your fear. He will say to you, "Alright, you have failed to express your opinion over the years because you thought other people were going to ridicule you and could do it better anyway. Now is the time for you to step out in faith and utter the words that I am going to give you." And everything inside of you says, "If I do that I will die! I won't know what to say. People will make fun of me. Here I am, Lord, but send Larry!"

Have you ever been there? I bet you have. We fight with the Lord. We hope if we just ignore Him, He will go away. But sometimes He proves so miserably persistent that at long last we give in because we'll only be more miserable if we don't. And when we do, what happens? We discover that in the Lord we can do a whole lot more than we ever thought we could! We discover that God is setting free and cultivating the treasures He has entrusted to us in Christ so we can bear fruit for His glory.

NOTES

1. Charles Whitfield, *Healing the Child Within* (Deerfield Beach, FL: Health Communications, Inc., 1987) p. 67.

2. Oswald Chambers, "The Discipline of Disillusionment – July 30," *My Utmost For His Highest* (New York: Dodd, Mead & Co., Inc., 1935).

3. Steve and Annie Chapman, "Two Children," Dawn Treader Music, 1986. SESAC. Used by permission.

4. William Cowper, "O For a Closer Walk With God," 1772.

Core Issue 2: Grieving Our Losses

9

*My tears have been my
food day and night.*
Psalm 42:3

Grief is the emotion we experience when we suffer loss. It is, of course, a perfectly natural human emotion. Even the Lord Jesus Christ, for all of His divine attributes, is said to be *a man of sorrows, and acquainted with grief* (Isa. 53:3, RSV). Grief is a very complex emotion. It involves facing our pain, reliving the memory and processing our grief. Hopefully, in time, we will be able to leave the grief behind us and become whole again.

If you were raised in a reasonably normal family, then you had the opportunity to grieve your losses as you were growing up. Think back, for example, to the time when you fell down and skinned your knee, or a local neighbourhood bully beat the tar out of you. You went running home in tears. What did your mom and dad do? They were there for you. They wrapped their arms around you, wiped away your tears and kissed you better. They gave you an opportunity to vent your pain and they bandaged you up, if not literally, then symbolically. That enabled you to pull yourself together, learn from your experience and face the future unafraid.

Or think back to the time when your favourite pet died. I had a pet turtle when I was a child. It was a great little turtle and required very little care. (That is why I had it!) It lived a good, long, healthy life, but eventually it died. When it did, I grieved its loss. On a more serious note, perhaps you remember the death of a grandparent, or a brother, or a sister or maybe even a parent. Remember how there was opportunity within the family situation to talk about the loss. You were allowed to cry out the pain. Chances are you thought the tears were never going to end, but eventually they did. You grew up, and though the memory is still there, it hasn't significantly scarred or wounded you for life. That is grieving your losses. It is an important part of growing up emotionally.

If, on the other hand, you were raised in a dysfunctional family, you grew up in a family where the three rules of the dysfunctional family were applied: *don't feel, don't trust, don't talk*. Chances are, you never had the opportunity to grieve your losses. If you were born into, or raised in a family where you were not allowed to feel anything, then your feelings of pain or loss were never authenticated. They were either ridiculed or ignored. And if you weren't allowed to express emotion, then your tears were not allowed to flow freely. You had to go cry in a corner, where no one would be bothered by your tears.

If you were not allowed to talk at home or anywhere else either, there was no way to grieve your loss. You lived with the pain.

A woman in our church told me the following story not long ago about one of her childhood memories. She recalls waking up with a tremendous scream early one Saturday morning because of a fearful nightmare that she was having. She dreamed that her feet were on fire, when in reality, she had pinched a nerve and they were just asleep. Her father was trying to sleep in that particular Saturday morning and was not at all thrilled to be awakened so early. Instead of going to her room to find out why she was screaming and to comfort her, he went there fully intent on disciplining her for being so inconsiderate. When she saw him coming, she saw the look in his eyes and knew what was going to happen. She jumped out of bed to try to get away from him. He chased her into the hallway, and she found herself cornered at the head of the stairs. There she lay, weeping and whimpering, wondering what he was going to do to her. Her mother, now awake, took her to the kitchen and tried to get her to drink some juice. Then she said this: "Now look at what you've done. You've gotten your dad all upset! Apologize to him!"

Can you imagine that? This is an example of a child not being able to grieve her losses. Is it any wonder this girl grew up suffering significant psychological disorders that only Jesus Christ proved able to heal?

Most of us may not have been raised in such a sadly dysfunctional household. Chances are, though, living in a sinful world as we do, we all have had some tears we were not allowed to cry and losses we were not allowed to grieve. These are ungrieved losses.

FAILURE TO GRIEVE

What happens when we cannot grieve our losses? Well, we develop coping mechanisms. Coping mechanisms, as we saw in Chapter 6, are devices we develop in order to minimize the pain and enable life to continue with some measure of normalcy. Suppose, for example, I have suffered a serious loss. What's my first reaction likely to be? Denial. I pretend it never happened. To face that it happened is simply too painful and so I learn to block it out. That way it doesn't bother me.

We all do that to some degree, don't we? When things hurt too much, we push them aside and pretend they never happened. That way we don't have to worry about getting bogged down in our pain and perhaps even going crazy. The more traumatic our experiences have been and the less opportunity we have had to work through our losses, the more apt we are to do that. Very often we can do this so effectively that we forget the very memory of the pain.

The problem, however, is that the pain is still there inside us. Contrary to what many people hope and think, ungrieved pains do not leave by themselves. They remain and fester and surface to wreak havoc in new situations and relationships. Psychologists have determined that:

Past losses and separations
have an impact on current losses, separations
and attachments.
All of these factors bear on fear of future losses
and our capacity to make future attachments.[1]

What that means is that our unresolved losses from the past become a part of our lives in the present and will affect our future. An illustration from biology will help us understand what I mean.

Let's suppose you have a festering sore or an untreated broken bone in your body. In the course of time, it will try to heal itself. What sometimes happens, though, is that outwardly the wound will heal, but inside the infection will continue. What happens then, of course, is that either the whole system gets ill with the poison that is being pumped into it, or else the poison will periodically erupt and break through in the form of another infection.

That is precisely what happens psychologically when our psychic wounds are not tended properly. They will go underground and poison the whole system in unexpected ways. They will most commonly surface through a series of symptoms that are intended to serve as a warning signal that there are problems that have not been resolved.

SYMPTOMS OF UNRESOLVED GRIEF

Let me give you some examples of how this pain commonly surfaces. [2]

Chronic Anxiety

Chronic anxiety is an undercurrent of anxiety that never quite leaves. You fear the ball is going to drop at any time, but you have no idea why you are so anxious.

A few years ago, I spoke at a retreat for another congregation. After one of the sessions on inner healing, an older man came to me with tears in his eyes. He told me, among other things, that stress is a significant factor in his life. He talked about his high blood pressure and things like that. Then he told me some of his life story.

He told me that as a young man, he hadn't done very well in school. At one point, the principal of the high school had come to his father and told him, "Your son is not a good student. We recommend a lower course of education instead of the higher one that he wants to pursue." So his father was disappointed in his son and told him so.

Well, that did it. Of course he didn't want to disappoint his father. He wanted to prove he was just as bright a student as everyone else, and so he threw himself into his school work. And wouldn't you know it, within just a couple of years he managed to push himself to the front of his class hoping in this way to gain his father's approval. That, however, proved not to be so easy.

Though he grew up to be a very determined man and a genius in his field, in his youth he had a habit of starting things he never managed to finish. His father would constantly criticize him for that. One day he wanted to prove to his father that he could do it and he told him he was going to build a model boat in a bottle. Instead of encouraging him and building him up, his father said, "We will see about that when you get it finished." So the young man poured hours of labour into building this model, anxious for his father's approval. When he had completed it, do you know what his father said? His father hemmed and hawed and then said, "Well, what practical use is it, anyway?"

Fifty or sixty years after the fact this man told me this story with tears streaming down his face. Is it any wonder that most of his life he has had to contend with chronic stress? He could never just be who he was. He always had to prove to himself and to everyone else that he was just as good as the next person. That pushed him to the top of his chosen profession but at what price?

Tension

Tension and fear are often the fruits of unresolved pain. Not very many people know this, but for years – until fairly recently, as a matter of fact – I used to get a knot in my stomach when I attended meetings of our church council. Going to council meetings is a regular part of my professional obligation and so having knots in my stomach was not a very helpful thing!

Why did I get such a knot in my stomach when I had to go to council meetings? For the very simple reason that for a number of years at a particular church I pastored, council meetings were not a pleasant experience. The church was going through some considerable growing pains that left some members very dissatisfied, and this would understandably surface at council meetings. From month to month, I never knew what was going to hit me next or from where it would come. In many instances, the issues were personalized and everyone's frustrations would get dumped on me. I didn't particularly like that! In retrospect, I probably should have done some things differently and not accepted that kind of abuse.

The memory and the fear of pain readily fill our lives with tension and make us fearful long after the reason for the fear has been removed. To this day, I prefer not to sit with my back to a large open area. Why? When I was younger, one of my brothers used to come up behind me and wallop me unexpectedly. Imagine then the fear of people who have experienced truly traumatic experiences.

Anger and Resentment

Some people are angry a lot. I know a man who, almost every time you meet him, seems angry. Why? Because he was hurt in the past. He, too, felt he couldn't please his father. He, too, feels people are always giving him a raw deal. And so he responds in anger. There are many like that. Anger usually flows out of a sense of injustice. I wasn't treated right. Nobody understood me, stood up for me or defended me. And I'm angry about that. Unresolved issues of hurt will commonly surface in a stream of anger that can defile people for generations to come. Witness the intractable conflicts that rage in many of the world's trouble spots. Almost all of them are fuelled by an historic sense of injustice that keeps feeding a fountain of anger.

The Quebec independence movement in Canada is a good case in point. Though sovereignty association was narrowly defeated in the October 1995 Quebec referendum, it continues to be a popular notion among many Quebec Francophones. Why? Because it is fuelled by an historic sense of injustice. Up until the Battle of the Plains of Abraham on September 13, 1759, Quebec had belonged exclusively to the French. It was their country, their culture, their way of life. After their defeat by the British, they increasingly felt themselves to be a conquered people at the mercy of their erstwhile enemies. As Canadian historian Susan Mann Trofimenkoff observes in her book, *A Dream of Nation*, "Conquest is like rape. The major blow takes only a few minutes; the results, no matter how well camouflaged, can be at best unpredictable and at worst devastating." [3]

History clearly bears that out. Unless these historic injustices are addressed and laid to rest, anger and resentment will continue to be the order of the day.

Confusion, Guilt, Shame

One of the difficulties we all experience in times of pain is the question of "Why?" "Why did my father die?" "Why did I lose my child?" "Why is my life coming apart at the seams?" While many times we may not be able to arrive at a satisfactory answer, the fact remains that we must work through the why's associated with our trauma. Unless we have some sense of understanding what happened and whose fault it was, our lives will be filled with confusion, doubt and blame. We wonder, "Is God trying to punish me? Should I have done something differently? *Could* I have done anything differently?" That robs us of confidence and makes us hesitant to face new challenges.

Suppose, for example, that I have just gone through a painful divorce. Unless I have worked through the issues involved, understand what I did wrong and what my partner did that contributed to the failure of our marriage, I cannot in good confidence establish a new relationship. If I do, as do so many, then the ghosts of the past will likely haunt the new relationship, possibly causing untold hardships, if not irreparable damage. People who haven't satisfactorily resolved past issues of hurt tend to become insecure and fearful because their personal sense of identity has been fractured.

Sadness, Emptiness, Lack of Fulfillment

The world is full of people who have a sadness that pervades their whole being. They laugh sometimes, but even during the laughter, and in moments of privacy and intimacy, there is that big, love deficit hole inside that cries, "Does anyone love me? Does anyone want me? Does anyone think that I am a significant person? Do I have any significant contribution to make throughout the rest of my life? If I would die, would anyone miss me?"

Now, perhaps we all feel this way upon occasion, but a person who feels that way most of the time is a person who has been deeply wounded and has not had the opportunity to grieve his or her losses.

No Feelings At All

Some people pride themselves on the fact that they are "Oh, so stable." They never get excited about anything, they never really get depressed about anything. They just have a cold wall of protection in place all around their heart, and nothing ever significantly appears to fizz on them. People like this are often proud of their ability to withstand pain. If you have ever lived with that kind of a person, or if you have ever tried to be friends with that kind of a person, then you know the incredible energy this relationship requires, because you can't have real relationships with people who are dead inside. They are numb, and numbness is one of the body's reactions to pain. There are people who can turn off their bodies, minds and personalities until they "feel no pain." I know many people like that. They feel virtually no pain under certain circumstances. They can almost completely turn off. That is usually not a healthy sign. It usually means there is unresolved grief in their lives.

Psychosomatic Illnesses

Full-blown emotional, physical or psychological disorders can flow out of unresolved grief. In extreme instances, of course, unresolved grief results in disorders, such as *anorexia nervosa,* which is essentially a modern-day phenomenon. Anorexia hits young women primarily and usually young women raised in achieving families. These young women struggle with personal issues of trying to be what they are expected to be. Often anorexia is a mask for pain.

Closely related to anorexia is *bulimia*. If an anorexic starves herself to death, a bulimic gorges on food and then self-induces vomiting in order to relieve stress and pain on the inside. In addition to these two conditions, there are many other ways in which people can be engaged in very painful and self-destructive, learned behaviour, which they use to avoid dealing with pain and grief.

· · · · · · · · ·

Now, I don't want to suggest that everyone suffers from the above disorders, or that everyone who has high blood pressure, or any of the other symptoms mentioned above necessarily harbours a lot of unresolved pain and grief. Nor am I suggesting that you put this book down and begin navel-gazing, saying to yourself, "I wonder what is wrong with me and I wonder what I can straighten out in my life?"

I believe Christians need to focus on the issue of obedience. We want to be men and women who desire wholeness, who can love God with all of our hearts, souls, strength and minds, and who can love our neighbours as we love ourselves. That is why Jesus died, rose and poured out His Spirit.

In the process of trying to live out this Spirit-filled life and growing into Christ-likeness, we discover sometimes that we come up against a ceiling. We can go no further. We're stuck. There just are certain things we cannot do, though we know we should. For instance, there are certain people we just cannot love. There are certain situations that paralyze us with fear and keep us from being obedient.

When that happens we need to seek the Lord in the context of the Christian community. We need to say to the Lord and to one another, "Is there an ungrieved loss that has kept me from growing up emotionally? Help me to understand what is going on so I can be all that the Lord wants me to be."

You see, most people think if you can just put the unresolved past behind you, it will go away. The fact of the matter is, as we saw in Chapter 7, it is like that trailer behind the tractor in the tractor pull – the further along you go, the heavier the weight becomes until your wheels spin out or your engine stalls (see *Figure 7.1* on page 136). Many people approach life like that. They figure if they can just pour enough energy into living, they can out-run the weight they are dragging behind them. They forget, of course, that the weight is attached to them and keeps moving forward until even the strongest of us either stall or spin out.

How can we avoid crashing like that? I believe there are three things we need to do: 1) We need to identify our losses; 2) we need to relive the pain of our losses; and 3) we need to learn to grieve properly.

In the remainder of this chapter, we will look at identifying our losses. In the chapters that follow we will look at reliving the pain and learning how to grieve properly.

IDENTIFYING OUR LOSSES

The first step in working through our hurts from the past is learning to identify them. We need to get a handle on what ungrieved losses we have experienced in life. For most of us, this is very difficult to do, for two reasons: First of all, our most significant losses will often have occurred in our childhood years. For that reason, these losses are old history and hard to remember. Secondly, and even more significantly, we have a vested interest in not remembering the pain.

Pain is one of the greatest threats we have to life and health. Therefore, when we are overwhelmed with pain, particularly emotional pain, everything inside us wants to escape the pain. Understandably, this gets in the way of identifying our losses. The moment we start to think about our losses, the pain we have so carefully pushed away surfaces. Immediately our automatic coping mechanisms kick into gear and we cannot and/or will not remember the losses we have so painfully experienced. For that reason, losses are hard to access rationally.

Psychologists tell us that only about 12% of our knowledge and experience is on a conscious level. Some 88% is on a subconscious level. What that means in practical terms is that when you start trying to remember the pain of yesterday, it is very hard to recapture the feelings and the emotions directly.

For that reason, God will often use a much more indirect way to flush our hurts out into the open.

One of the ways in which He does that is through *music*. The church I presently pastor has an extensive music program. Very often, people who are new to our church especially, will cry their way through the worship time, sometimes to the point of being embarrassed by it. We always tell them not to worry about it because that is one of the functions of music. It bypasses the rational to some degree and helps us get in touch with our emotions. That allows us to open up and receive God's healing grace.

Another way the Lord does this is through *story-telling*. At a recent conference held at our church, one of the speakers, herself the victim of incest, shared some of her story. Sitting in the audience, I could just sense the pain of memories that were surfacing in the lives of people. The Holy Spirit will often use other people's stories to flush our own pain out into the open.

Still another way to help identify our losses is through *listening prayer*. We have found that to be very effective. Many times in ministry we will meet people who have run into some roadblock in their spiritual development. They just cannot seem to get beyond a certain point. What we will do most commonly is spend some time in prayer together, asking the Lord to uncover the roots of the problem. We ask the Holy Spirit to shine light into the pain of that person's heart. Time and again, the Holy Spirit – who is everywhere present, from whom no one can hide, and for whom time has no meaning – will put His finger on the root cause of the person's problem. Not infrequently, these are ungrieved losses.

Don Bloch, who was a farmer before God called him and his wife Anne into a healing ministry, tells the story of a man who for most of his life had this real sense of guilt and unworthiness. At one of their earlier conferences, a number of lay people had been assigned to pray with this individual. They asked the Lord why this man was feeling so guilty. As they were praying in that fashion, the Holy Spirit gave one of them an image of a little boy sitting at the bottom of the steps crying and crying.

So they asked the man if this rang any bells with him. As happens so often when the Holy Spirit's time has come in a person's life, this grown-up man immediately began to weep bitterly. Through his tears, he said, "I am that little boy." He went on to relate that when he was a young child there was a time when he was standing at the bottom of those steps calling for his mother to come. In response to his plea for help, his mother had come to the top of the steps, but something happened. She fell down the steps and landed on the floor right in front of him, unconscious, with blood all over her face.

In ways that children so often do, he felt he was responsible for her fall. After all, if he hadn't called her, she wouldn't have fallen. Ever after that the little boy felt guilty and thought he was the cause of his mother's injury. This had haunted him all his adult life and caused him to harden his heart to the gospel. It wasn't until that prayer session that he could finally see what had really happened and receive healing for his wounded heart.

Let's take a look now at some of the common losses we experience.

COMMON LOSSES WE EXPERIENCE

Loss of an Important Person

Probably the most significant loss anyone can experience is the loss of a person with whom we have had a close or meaningful relationship. Examples would include separation, divorce, rejection, desertion, abandonment, death, abortion, stillbirth, illness, geographic moves and children leaving home.

Let me zero in on several of these:

Separation or Divorce

One of the most painful losses anyone can ever experience is the loss of a spouse through separation or divorce. Ask anyone who has gone through it and they will tell you that it rivals or perhaps even exceeds the pain of the death of a family member. Divorce and separation often involve an element of rejection that death does not. A loss like this is not easily forgotten or, for that matter, overcome.

Death

This would include the loss of a parent, friend, brother or a sister through death. Erin was one of a set of twins. When the twins were 15, it was Dana's turn to do the paper route, but Erin took her turn instead. Erin was killed by a passing automobile. You can't begin to imagine the emotional and mental anguish that has since ruled Dana's life. Not only did she suffer from having her twin taken away, because as many twins are, they were incredibly close, but she also suffered from living with the guilt that, "It was my turn to do the paper route." In addition, the whole family, of course, suffered intensely after Erin's death.

Abandonment and Rejection

While it is true that separation, divorce and death all include elements of abandonment and desertion, there are many instances of abandonment and rejection that we don't readily identify as such. Let me give some examples:

An unwanted child: Scientific research has established beyond any shadow of a doubt that if an expectant mother goes through an extended period of emotional turmoil, that can significantly affect the life of the fetus. Interestingly enough, short-term stress poses no effect on the baby. Long-term stress associated with an ill-timed or difficult pregnancy can cause immense problems in the life of a child.[4] Imagine how vulnerable an unborn child feels when the most significant people in his life don't want to have him around. That is rejection!

Being born of the wrong sex: For some families this is a big issue. A parent wanted a boy or a girl and the child that is born is of the opposite sex. Most parents adapt to that pretty quickly and are happy just to have a healthy child. Some, however, resent the child. Consequently, the child faces rejection from very early in life. That can be a very painful rejection indeed. There is, after all, nothing more fundamental than being male or female. To be rejected for our sex leaves us little reason for living.

Early instances of hospitalization: My wife and I have a good friend who, when we first met her, was one of the coldest persons you could ever meet. She is a beautiful young woman, but her heart was cold. She had an emotional wall that kept significant relationships at a distance. She had a tremendous hate and anger towards her father and did not have a good relationship with her mother either.

We began to seek the Lord for some of the root causes for her hurt and anger and asked Him to heal that. The Lord brought to her mind an awareness of the fact that when she was born she needed to be hospitalized for two weeks, and the bond between her and her mother was significantly broken. While it is hard for us to sometimes appreciate or understand it, the spirit of a child in that situation can easily make a vow. The child says, "The world is not a very safe place. I don't ever want to love anyone, because loving someone is going to cause me too much pain."

That is why people become cold. We often think people are stuck-up and have their noses up in the air. Not really. They are afraid to be loved, because they fear if they allow their heart to be open to love, someone could run right over it and destroy them. That is why they will reject you before you get a chance to reject them.

Loss of Part of Yourself

We not only lose significant people in our relationships, but we can also lose a portion of our own being. Examples of this include: Body image, illness, accident, loss of function, loss of control, self-esteem, independence, ego, expectations, lifestyle needs, culture shock, job change, etc. Again, let's look at several of these in more detail.

Body Image

We all wish we were born with perfect bodies. Most of us learn sooner or later to make do with what we have. For some people, however, that is more difficult than it is for others. I am thinking particularly of people with significant disfigurement, due to surgery or accident. You don't know how important it is to look "normal" until you don't look normal. It is very painful to discover that you have to go through life missing a limb or looking odd. Not only do you experience the pain and the physical limitations associated with that loss, but you also go through the emotional turmoil of fitting in a world that takes pride in physical beauty. This is particularly true for adolescents who receive radical medical treatment, such as chemotherapy or radiation. Their hair falls out, their skin breaks out in a rash and they feel sick and ugly. That can be pretty tough to handle! As a result, many handicapped people develop an attitude of self-sufficiency that is geared at keeping other people at bay. Robbed of self-confidence, they need to prove to themselves and the world around them that they are not any less than anyone else.

Loss of Function/Loss of Control

Two years before my father died at the age of 56, he had a stroke which significantly limited his ability to work for a period of time. Though eventually he was able to return to the farm work he loved so dearly, he was but a shadow of his former self. That was extremely difficult for him to face, particularly since he had grown up in a culture where one's ability to perform physical work was the mark of a man. He would, upon occasion, regale us with stories of the physical contests he and his friends would engage in during their youth. To lose that ability was very difficult for him. That was a loss that needed to be grieved.

Many people go through that, particularly when illness or old age brings us face to face with limitations we never experienced before.

Job Change

The end of the 20th century has been characterized by an unprecedented upheaval in the market place. Gone are the days when a person could count on holding the same job for the better part of his or her life. Gone are the days when loyalty forged a strong bond between employers and their employees. Instead, downsizing, rapidly-changing technology and global competition have thrown hundreds of thousands of people out of work, long before they were ready to retire. Such losses and changes are often very traumatic for the people involved and their families. So much of our identity is often tied up with what we do, that to be no longer wanted is like losing a part of yourself.

Childhood Losses

Because they are especially dependent on the significant adults in their lives, children's losses can be particularly devastating. Parental failure to sustain and protect them emotionally and physically, loss of special objects such as a blanket or teddy bear, loss of childhood innocence and the death of a parent or a sibling are all examples of childhood losses.

Let me elaborate particularly on the loss of one's childhood. Many people raised in dysfunctional families never really had a childhood. They were never allowed to play. They were never allowed just to be kids who could trust the significant adults in their lives to exercise the necessary responsibility both for their own lives and that of their children. Instead, they ended up having to exercise responsibility for their parents and their siblings.

Loss of childhood is especially true of people who have suffered sexual abuse in their childhood years. While all abuse is traumatic, sexual abuse is especially traumatic. It robs children of their virtue and thus their sense of identity. Relationships become sexualized and many normal emotions and feelings cannot develop properly because of the self-loathing and shame that gets attached to their personhood. For that reason, many victims of sexual abuse suffer from significant psychological problems. They tend to suffer from low self-esteem, frequently become sexually permissive and often try to commit suicide. Loss of innocence is serious business and needs to be grieved properly.

Loss of Hopes and Dreams

Why do some people have a *mid-life crisis*? Why do some people suddenly throw away everything they have ever worked for and risk it on a crazy gamble? Well, one reason is that suddenly in mid-life they realize that their hopes and dreams are not likely ever going to materialize. They have to re-adjust their ambition and their goals, and settle for what is, rather than for what they have dreamed.

For some people that may not be very difficult. For other people, that comes as a rude awakening that fills them with discouragement and depression. Not many people recognize this as a loss that needs to be grieved, but it is.

Loss of External Objects

This includes things like money, property, sentimental objects, collections and so on.

Anyone who has ever lost property such as a business or a home or even a car will know how painful such a loss can be. Other people can tell you, "It is only a material thing." And that is true. But even material things can hold a significant emotional attachment for us. That is especially true if we have put a great deal of ourselves into it. It has become an extension of ourselves and to lose it is like losing a portion of ourselves. The same is true for things that hold a sentimental value for us. Other people may say, "It's only a piece of junk." In our eyes, it is a valuable symbol of a significant relationship and to lose it is to lose something very precious. Even material losses can cause a deep and lasting grief that needs to be worked through.

NOTES

1. Simos, 1979 as quoted by Charles Whitfield in *Healing the Child Within,* (Deerfield Beach, FL: Health Communications Inc., 1987) p. 89.

2. I am indebted to Charles Whitfield, *Healing the Child Within,* for many of these insights.

3. Quoted by Rudy and Marny Pohl, "Healing Canada's Wounds," *Intercessors for Canada Newsletter – Special Edition*, April/May 1996. A book by Rudy and Marny Pohl on this topic is available from Peacemakers Canada, 12-1165 Meadowlands Dr., Nepean, Ontario, K2E 6J5.

4. Thomas Verny and John Kelly, *The Secret Life of the Unborn Child* (Don Mills, ON: Collins Publishers, 1981) p. 13.

10 | Facing the Pain

When you pass through the waters,
I will be with you.
Isaiah 43:2

We saw in the last chapter that grieving our losses starts by identifying them. You cannot grieve for what you do not know. For that reason, when the Lord starts bringing wholeness into our lives, He will most commonly start by bringing to memory the losses that we have experienced. We begin to understand what we have lost.

That brings us in this chapter to the second step of working through our grief: We need to relive the pain of our loss. That is to say, we need to relive the agony and the emotion of the original experience.

Now, many people have a lot of trouble with this step for the simple reason that we all hate pain and have spent the better part of our lives trying to avoid it. To willingly dredge up old pains seems ridiculous. Only a masochist would engage in such foolish behaviour!

Christians in particular often have a considerable resistance to having to re-live the pain of the past. We often have a magical notion that God should just wave His wand and take our pains and problems away. After all, didn't Jesus die for all our sorrows and aren't we healed by His stripes?

Yes, that is true. That does not mean, however, that God will just wave a magic wand and make all our problems disappear. If that were true, then Christians should not have any problems. As one who spends the bulk of his time working with Christians to help them through their problems, let me assuredly tell you this is not so! Rather, the pain has to be faced and worked through in the strength of the Lord. When the Holy Spirit begins to work healing in our lives, He doesn't just make the pain go away. He helps us to face the pain squarely. Only in that way does true healing come.

Let me try to describe how the process works.

UNDERSTANDING THE PROCESS

Let's look again at the issue of abandonment. I mentioned in the last chapter that when a child is abandoned, or is afraid of being abandoned, he undergoes a numbing and often life-changing experience. You can imagine how scary it is to be left all alone with no one to protect you or make you feel safe. To be at the mercy of forces that frighten you or harm you when you have no way to defend yourself is paralyzing indeed. For that reason, we push those terrible feelings away, hoping against all hope that if we don't think about them anymore they will go away and leave us alone. As we have already seen, that is seldom the case. They resurface in flashbacks, nightmares and all kinds of irrational feelings. This is especially true when the Holy Spirit has heard our cry for wholeness and is thus flushing them to the surface where we have to deal with them.

So what happens now is that all the emotion associated with the original abandonment comes rushing back, filling me with unspeakable dread and confusion. I suddenly have this totally irrational fear of being left alone. Whereas most of the time I am quite capable of being by myself and am quite willing to let my spouse or friend go off and do their own thing, I am now suddenly seized with a dread of aloneness that cannot be described. I know in my head that it is irrational, but there is nothing I can do to stop it. I feel just like a child and desperately crave for someone to hold me and let me know I will be safe. Waves of fear and other emotions associated with abandonment come rolling over me, threatening to swamp my little boat.

People who have never gone through flashbacks have a hard time understanding them or identifying with the emotions involved. All of us, though, go through this to one degree or another in our lives. Think, for example, of the most painful feeling or experience you have ever gone through. What happens when you start to think about that pain, particularly if you haven't taken the time or had the opportunity to properly grieve it? The pain comes rushing back into your life threatening to swamp you. Most of us know how to shut it down pretty quickly and walk away from it. For that reason, many people who have gone through traumatic experiences cannot and will not talk about it. The memories are still too vivid and dwelling on them only brings them out into the open. That is re-living the pain. It is a very unpleasant experience, but absolutely critical if we are to come into real wholeness.

Let's suppose that as a child you were shamed. Others made fun of you. They said you were stupid. They did things to you that were painful and bad and left you filled with shame and embarrassment. When you got old enough, you decided to put these shameful things away and you chose to forget about them.

Now, years later, you have asked the Holy Spirit to fix up your life and, true to His nature, He starts to flush the episodes of ridicule and shame and anger back out into the open. What happens? All the original pain and emotions come back to you, and they are often as fresh as the day when they happened. They haven't healed at all. They've just been cov-ered over, pouring their hurt and pain into your whole system.

Interestingly enough, they will often be triggered by events similar to the original event. For example, the person who has been abandoned early in life will suddenly experience this over-whelming sense of abandonment when somebody close to him or her has to go away. I know of several people who are absolute-ly panic-stricken when someone close to them has to leave for even an overnight trip. Logically, it makes no sense; emotional-ly, it ties into unresolved childhood fears of abandonment.

The same thing can happen to a person who was deeply shamed or ridiculed in childhood. A new experience of shame or ridicule will trigger all the old feelings.

Dr. Fred Downing tells the rather humorous story of the time when he took a group of young people to the Arrowhead Stadium in Kansas City to watch a football game. At half-time, he had to go to the washroom. When he got to the washroom, it was unlike any washroom he had ever visited. He recognized none of the plumbing. Instead of the usual fixtures normally found in a washroom, all he found was a trough-like affair with a spouting water fountain sitting in the middle of the room. He said to himself, "Now that is kind of strange." But the more he thought about it, the more he could see the possibilities. "I think this could work," he said to himself. So he proceeds to go to the bathroom in this trough-like affair.

While he is going to the bathroom, in walk three other men. They look at him in a kind of funny way, but make no comments. He notices though, much to his surprise, that they go through the room he is in, through a door and into anoth-er room. Then, when they have gone through that door into the other room, he hears one say to the other in a loud, bois-terous voice, "Hey, did you see what that guy was doing out there where you wash your hands?"

Well, as Dr. Downing relates the story, the shame of his stupidity just flooded over his being. As he walked from the washroom back to his seat in the stadium, his whole life of shame passed before his eyes. Every stupid incident that he had ever been involved in throughout his life came flashing back to him. He says that when he sat down, shame exuded through the whole section of the stadium. By the time he was done pondering his shame, he says, the whole stadium was filled with his shame.

We work very hard at pushing away those times of pain and shame, because they can be so excruciatingly hurtful. I have been with adults facing the pain of their past, and seen them literally sob and convulse with the pain. They cry bitter tears of what seems like unending pain.

Pain within the heart can be incredibly overwhelming. When it overwhelms you, everything inside of you says, "I want to shut it down." That is how a lot of people go through life. They will never talk about their painful experiences. Survivors of concentration camps often use this coping mechanism. You won't hear them cry about the things they really went through. They will push it far, far away from memory, because the horror is too unspeakable. But, in the meantime, this coping mechanism locks you up on the inside. It keeps you from becoming free in the Lord to try new things and to become all that God is calling you to be.

So the question is, "How, then, can I face the pain of my failure? How can I look the stupidest thing I have ever done square in the face and know I can get through it, and leave it far behind so it no longer colours me for the rest of my life? How can I take the most wounding experience of my life, experience all its painful emotions to the core of my being and not feel I am being destroyed in the process?"

Here are some suggestions.

Decide to Face the Pain

First, we must make a conscious decision to face the pain squarely and work it through with God. We need to tell God that we are afraid to face the pain but that we are determined to do so because we want to be everything He wants us to be. We need to tell Him we are making a conscious choice to allow Him to tear down all the internal walls we have built for protection and to uncover the things that have hurt us the most. We will face what we need to face so that we can truly be whole again.

The reason this is so very important is that anything less than a conscious decision to work through the pain for God's sake will cause us to back out when the pain becomes too intense. Very often, we decide to face our losses by relying on our own will power and because we want to feel better. The problem is, when we start facing our losses, we will often feel worse before we feel better. What happens then is that when the pain becomes too much or the process takes too long, we decide to bail out. The feelings are too intense, family and friends are not sufficiently supportive and we give up. It is not worth the pain to us.

On the other hand, when we make a conscious decision to become whole for God's sake, bailing out is not an option that is open to us. There may be times when we have to shut things down because we feel overwhelmed, but we know we can't stay there. We want to be well and so, no matter how much time it takes or how much pain we may have to endure in the process, we are committed to recovery for God's sake. Besides, we know that God has promised that He won't give us more than we can bear and so we can lay hold of His promises until He does for us what He said He would do.

I often say to people in our church, "You are going to experience pain, whether you go God's way or Satan's way. The difference is when you go Satan's way, in the end there is nothing to show for it but destruction. When you go God's way, in the end there is life." *For the wages of sin is death, but the gift of God is eternal life in Christ Jesus our Lord,* says Paul in Romans 6:23.

Know That Christ is With Us

Second, we need to understand that Jesus Christ is with us in our pain. The Bible says, in Isaiah 53:3-5,

> *He was despised and rejected by men; a man of sorrows, and acquainted with grief; and as one from whom men hide their faces He was despised, and we esteemed Him not. Surely He has borne our griefs and carried our sorrows; yet we esteemed Him stricken, smitten by God, and afflicted. But He was wounded for our transgressions, He was bruised for our iniquities; upon Him was the chastisement that made us whole, and with His stripes we are healed* (RSV).

Why did Jesus come into the world? He came into the world to take our place. The Bible says He was tempted in all things, just as you and I face temptations. He experienced the totality and the agony of hell. He never shrank from the will of God. And because Jesus faced and overcame it, the Bible says, He is a merciful high priest at the right hand of God, ever living and making intercession for the children of God.

When, by faith in Christ, we become the children of God, Jesus Christ has promised to be with us always, even unto the end of the age. That means when shame, pain and anguish come flooding into our souls, and it seems we are never going to be able to live and survive, Jesus Christ is there to help us. He will walk through the waters with us so that we can come out on the other side, knowing we will not be consumed by the fire.

> *When you pass through the waters I will be with you; and through the rivers, they shall not overwhelm you; when you walk through fire you shall not be burned, and the flame shall not consume you. For I am the Lord your God, the Holy One of Israel, your Saviour* (Isa. 43:2,3, RSV).

Note the emphasis on passing *through* the waters and *through* the fire. As I mentioned above, one of the misconceptions we often have as Christians is that, if God loves us, then He will take away our problems and difficulties by somehow waving His magic wand and undoing all our past and woundedness.

God is indeed a miracle-working God. He can do anything that He pleases! And yes, there are times in the lives of God's people when God supernaturally comes along and takes incredible injury, damage and pain, absorbs it into Himself and sets us free. We feel like there was never pain in our lives before.

But I think that for every individual who experiences this healing in an instant, there are many who have to face the pain and step out in faith, trusting that though the waters try to overwhelm us, Jesus is with us in the water. Though our emotions may seem to be all over the place and the pain too intense, He will be with us in the middle of our suffering. He will take us through the fire, He will bring us out on the other side, and we will be more than conquerors.

In ministry, we often deal with people who have been really hurt at some point in their life. We have found that one of the most effective ways the Lord has given us to help these people through their valleys is to invite Jesus to reveal Himself as He stands with them in their pain. When we do that, Jesus often reveals His presence in unique ways. Very often He will reveal Himself in visions or in the mind's eye and show them the reality of His love. He wraps His loving arms around them and shows unmistakably that He was with them even in their most desolate and forsaken moments. He assures them both of His desire and power to bring healing to their most wounded areas. This often encourages people to step out in faith trusting that He will see them through their difficult moments.

Here is a story that was given to me by a survivor of sexual abuse. Note how Jesus demonstrated His presence in the midst of her pain.

A Child Reborn

In a dark bedroom sits a little girl, numbed by the horrors of her life. Her head is bowed as she fidgets with her hands in her lap. Scrawny legs hang limply over the edge of the bed barely reaching the floor. She is alone now.

Her life is a picture of pain. Rumpled sheets reveal the struggle that rages within. The darkness that presses in examplifies the suffering of her soul. She is lost in thought and seems to forget where she is.

Confusion is written across her downcast face. She wants so much to be special and feel happy; yet her visitor, who promised, "It would feel good," made her feel so dirty and unwanted. Now she feels so desperately alone. A single tear trickles down her cheek as she cries out for someone to hold her.

The room brightens ever so slightly, and shadows that loomed now slink away. A soft, lulling voice, filled with compassion and love, encourages her to look up. Slowly, hesitantly, two little green eyes peer up towards the voice. Her face lights up with joy.

Before her stands her Friend. Hands reach down to grasp her own. Those hands, so gentle, beautiful and kind, bear scars that equal her own. Understanding lights the dullness of her eyes, and no longer hesitant, she jumps into His arms.

Delight is written across her face. She feels special, forgiven, and oh, so clean. She is laughing and plays securely in His loving arms. He smiles at her freedom, and whispers in her ears that with Him she is no longer alone. She smiles and nods as He quietly closes the door to her pain-filled life. And off she skips, with her hand in His, to glory and joy unseen.

I was there when this revelation happened. I can tell you, it was not a figment of her imagination. It was the powerful love of Jesus reaching into the pain of her existence, getting beyond all the walls and all the defenses, into the core of her heart. Jesus healed what nothing or nobody could ever heal before.

That is why I get excited about the Christian message. It is indeed the power of God unto salvation. What nothing or nobody can do, Jesus Christ has already done by His death and resurrection. When by faith we turn to Him, we'll find He's there just as He promised, through both the good times and the bad times.

Seek Spiritual Parents

The third important aspect of re-living our pain is having spiritual parents there to walk us through our journey of pain. Paul writes in 1 Corinthians 4:15, *For though you have countless guides in Christ, you do not have many fathers. For I became your father in Christ Jesus through the gospel* (RSV).

What is a spiritual parent? Someone who embodies the love of Jesus and carries you in his or her arms just like parents do with their children. Someone who serves as a vehicle of God's love and grace. It is a wonderful thing that Jesus Christ Himself is immediately present with us in our pain. But if you have ever gone through extreme pain, then you know that sometimes it is not enough to know that spiritually Jesus is with you here. You need somebody of earthly flesh, blood, skin and bones to wrap their arms around you and love you with the love of Jesus.

Somebody once told me, "The problem with re-living emotions is the fear of going totally out of control and absolutely berserk." She likened it to a fire-hose which has escaped the grip of the fireman. It whips all over the place dangerously. It can cause a great deal of damage because of the force behind the water.

Many people who have suffered through very painful experiences, which have become deep-rooted and hidden in their subconscious, fear that if they were ever to let go, nothing and nobody could contain their rage. They will either destroy or be destroyed. That is why they keep putting the lid on their feelings. That is why they keep on screwing up their courage and cranking up the power of their tractor, so to speak, so they can keep on dragging that weight behind them.

For such feelings to be released then, it must be safe. That is where spiritual parents come in. We need somebody who will keep us safe when we fear for our own sanity. We need someone to love us, be there for us, hold us in their arms and be a vehicle of grace through whom God's love flows into our pain. We need someone who will help us cry our tears, verbalize our anguish and put us back on our feet, so we can grow and become whole men and women who can live for the praise of God's glory.

This is not an easy task. It is almost akin to parenting in the natural, only much more difficult, because a small child is much easier to handle than a big child. The demands made on a spiritual parent or community by one who is in pain are very intense and difficult. Such a person, therefore, needs to exhibit sufficient maturity, emotionally and spiritually, to be able to handle the load.[1]

Let me describe some of those characteristics that I believe need to be present in such a person:

A Measure of Personal Healing

A spiritual parent needs to have worked through his or her personal dysfunctions to a considerable degree. A fire-hose that is flopping all over the place can be very irrational and inconsistent. People who are in pain often don't have a lot of emotional strength and energy left over to be nice to anyone else. They probably have spent their whole life trying to be nice, and have discovered in the process that they have lost more and more of themselves, because their lives haven't been rooted in the grace of Jesus.

Unconditional Love

Unconditional love is love without conditions. It is love freely given, regardless of whether the person in question deserves it or not. It's the kind of love God had for us when He sent His son to die for us while we were yet sinners.

The reason unconditional love is so important is that people in pain have a difficult time believing anybody else really cares for them. Accordingly, whenever someone gets close to them, they will do their best to drive them away. When they succeed in driving them away, they say, "See, I told you. Nobody really cares for me." They will continue to use that then to keep their masks in place and their shame covered. The only thing that can break that is unconditional love — love that refuses to take no for an answer, love that refuses to give up, love that is not scandalized by the most shameful revelations.

Over the years in my capacity as pastor and counsellor, I have heard countless confessions entailing deep shame and embarrassment. I can tell you from first-hand experience that when people first tell you their story, they watch your every move. They read your body language and wait for you to show shock on your face. They are just waiting for you to lower the curtain or put up the wall and say, "I don't want to hear any more of this. This is too sordid for my liking." The minute they sense condemnation or rejection, they will shut down and keep their shameful secrets to themselves. That is why counsellors need unconditional love.

A Personal Faith

Anyone who has ever seriously sought to be used of God in helping other people with their problems will know how easy it is to become overwhelmed. The mountain can be so high, the valley so deep, the horror so great that you want to throw your hands up in despair and say, "What's the use anyway? We'll never get through it." When we who try to help others feel that way, imagine how the people going through this must feel? That's why there are so many hopeless and cynical people in the world.

That is why spiritual parents must be persons of faith. Scripture says that *faith is the assurance of things hoped for, the conviction of things not seen* (Heb. 11:1, RSV). It is an ability to keep hoping and believing that God, for the sake of Jesus, cares about us and will involve Himself in our affairs. And while it is true God requires that faith of each of us, for Scripture says that *without faith it is impossible to please God* (Heb. 11:6), the fact remains that for people going through a hard time, that can be very difficult indeed. What we need then is others around us who can believe even when we cannot.

Do you remember the story in the gospels about the four men who brought their sick friend to Jesus? Jesus was teaching in someone's house and the crowds were so great they couldn't get their friend to Jesus for ministry and healing the regular way. So what they did was go up on the roof, opened up the roof tiles and let their friend down by ropes until he was right at the feet of Jesus. That's what spiritual parents and counsellors sometimes need to do. They need to take their sick friends to Jesus and do the believing for them. The curious thing about that story is that the Bible says, *When Jesus saw **their** faith, He said, "Friend, your sins are forgiven... get up, take your mat and go home"* (Luke 5:20,24).

A lot of times, when people are suffering, they no longer have faith to believe life is ever going to be any different. Spiritual parents or other brothers and sisters in the Lord need to be there to help them carry the load. They need to believe with them and for them, and help and encourage them. *He who began a good work in you will carry it on to completion until the day of Christ Jesus* (Phil. 1:6).

A Good Listener

Most people are not good listeners. Rather, they are anxious to give advice. Have you ever noticed that? When you share your heart with a friend, or in a small group, the first thing many want to do is tell you how to solve your problem.

That is not all bad, and a lot of times, I am sure it is well-intended. However, most of the time most of us aren't so much looking for advice and solutions as a little understanding.

A good listener is one who listen empathetically, or with understanding and sympathy. He or she needs to be able to draw out the person who is talking, actively ask questions for clarification and show an accepting attitude.

Very often, when people come to see me, the very first thing they say is, "I don't know why I am here, and I don't know where to begin." (I usually suggest they start at the beginning!) The reason for that is that for most people, feelings are very hard to put into words. Most of us have never talked about these things before and so it is difficult to find words to express what is deeply hidden inside our hearts. Accordingly, we are very hesitant to speak lest it come out wrong and we are misunderstood. Or worse yet, our deepest secrets may be exposed to the whole world.

Good listening, therefore, is *active* listening. It is helping someone put his or her thoughts into words. It is asking for clarification in such a way that people don't feel stupid or foolish. It is reflecting back to them what you think they are saying. Very often, for example, when someone talks to me, I will ask, "Is this what you are saying?" Or I will try to give them clear feedback that I understand what they are trying to say. That often comes as a tremendous relief for people because the fear of being misunderstood is so very great. Usually this stems from well-meaning, but insensitive people who are dispensing advice before they have really listened to the pain behind the complaint. Good listening is a tremendous asset!

An Ability to Keep Confidentiality

Next to wanting to be understood, most people crave confidentiality. None of us likes to have his or her dirty laundry aired in public. That is especially true when we are still in the early stages of processing our pain and shame. Later, when we have worked through the issues, it is no longer part of our lives in the same way and we're not so fearful of having other people know about it. But while we are still going through it, it is pretty tender and needs to be treated with the utmost respect.

That is why, when I share stories in speaking or writing, I'll do so only with the permission of the people involved. When that is not possible, I try to make sure the facts are disguised sufficiently that no one can tell to whom it actually refers. Mind you, even that can backfire. More than once people have been sure I was talking about them when I was actually referring to someone else!

These then, are some of the qualities that should be present in those who wish to be spiritual parents. It's not an easy task. People who have undergone a great deal of rejection will often do whatever they can to reject us before we reject them. Yet it is absolutely critical they have someone in their lives who can stand above all that and patiently walk them into wholeness through faith in Jesus Christ.

The church community especially needs to be this kind of community – a safe place where people can come with their wounds and hurts and be loved back to life. Only then will we be a light to the nations and a fitting channel of God's marvellous grace.

NOTES

1. For additional insight on this topic see Henry Cloud and John Townsend's book, *Safe People* (Grand Rapids, MI: Zondervan, 1995).

11 | Good Grief!

Weeping may tarry for the night, but joy comes with the morning.
Psalm 30:5

There is an old saying that goes, "Laugh, and the world laughs with you, weep and you weep alone." There is a lot of truth to that, because all of us would much rather laugh than cry, and most of the time we would much rather be with people who make us laugh, than with people who are sad and make us cry. Nevertheless, sadness and grieving, crying and pain are very much a part of life. Even the Lord Jesus cried out in agony to God, *"My God, my God, why have You forsaken me?"* (Mark 15:34). The psalmist said, *"O my God, I cry by day, but You do not answer; and by night, but find no rest"* (Ps. 22:2, NRSV).

As we have seen, grief is our emotional response to things or persons we lose. Grieving properly involves: 1) identifying our losses; 2) re-living the pain of our losses; and 3) learning how to grieve properly. It is this third point we are now going to consider in this chapter.

Grief, like all human emotions, is a very complex emotional experience. It can be long-term or short-term; it can be intense or very superficial; and it can occupy any stage in between all of these extremes. But whatever form it takes in our lives, there are particular stages of grief that we go through. It is helpful to analyze these stages to understand where we are in the grieving process. It also helps us to be compassionate towards other people who are grieving. It is so easy, either because of ignorance or lack of sensitivity, to try to shut other people down when they are grieving or to otherwise hurry them along. What we need to do is let them grieve appropriately so their hearts can truly heal.

THE STAGES OF GRIEF

Here then, are some of the commonly accepted stages of grief: [1]

Continuing, Intermittent and Lessening Denial

What is the first reaction we have when we experience a significant loss in our lives? It is shock, followed closely by denial. Denial says, "This doesn't really bother me. This doesn't really hurt me. This has not really happened to me."

A friend and colleague of mine, Dale Evenhouse, told me about an automobile accident he had been in many years ago. It was a fairly serious accident but neither he nor others suffered any significant damage to life or limb. He related how he was amazed to discover the power of shock and denial. Even while he was speaking with the investigating officer immediately after the accident, everything inside him was already pushing away the pain and the memory of it. Only with the greatest effort could he make himself recall the particulars of the accident.

As we were talking about this, he said to me, "If that happens in something relatively minor like this, you can well imagine what happens when people experience a trauma that is much more severe." Alarm, shock, denial – they all kick in to try to hold the pain at bay.

Gradually though, as time goes on, our denial lessens. The shock wears off, and we allow ourselves to come face to face with what has happened. As we do, the memories come flooding back, and with them the pain of our traumatic loss. When that becomes too great, denial kicks in once again. We push it away until such a time we are ready to face it once more. And so through a series of stages, shock and denial gradually become less.

Pain and Distress

When denial wears off and pain comes home with a vengeance, we discover that pain can be one of two kinds – physical or emotional.

Physical pain occurs when the body relives the original trauma. For example, a victim of sexual assault will sometimes relive the actual physical pain of the attack. I have been with people when they were going through this and it is very, very scary. Their bodies convulse with a pain that appears to have a life of its own. The tendency, of course, is to want to run away from that pain because it is so intense. Yet, it needs to be re-experienced so that it loses its power over the person.

Pain, of course, is also psychological. For example, consider the pain of questions like, "Why did these things happen to me? What is wrong with me that all of this came into my life?" There is much pain in remembering the actual loss or rejection. That pain can remain fresh for a long period of time.

Emotional pain will manifest itself intermittently, much like a roller coaster. Grieving people for that reason are very inconsistent. One moment they are smiling and appear happy, and they are doing all right. Then, all of a sudden, something triggers a memory and they are overwrought. Tears flow, and all the pain of their loss comes flooding back. This can happen for a long period of time after the actual event takes place.

I recall the story of a mother whose little boy had drowned in a neighbourhood pond. A long time after his drowning, she was cleaning the house and found his little shoes. With that sudden and unexpected reminder, all the memory and pain of her loss just came flooding back into her soul. The pain was so intense, she wondered if she would ever get through it again. That is very common as we experience grief. For a long time afterwards, certain events, sights or sounds will trigger the old painful memories and we find ourselves in serious distress.

The temptation, of course, is for comforters and counsellors to say, "You've cried enough. Pull yourself together. Get on with life." And there is a time when we have to stop grieving and get on with life. But it has to be the right time. To do that too early is to cut short the grieving process and that in turn will cause problems of unresolved grief later on.

It is particularly important for Christians to understand that, I think. We readily admire people who are strong, particularly in difficult circumstances. Sometimes we give the impression that to be a victorious Christian is to exhibit a smiling face even in the midst of the greatest tragedy and pain. But that is hardly biblical. Even Jesus wept. We should not try to be more spiritual than He is. Weeping can be an important part of the healing process. We need to give ourselves and others permission to feel the pain without trying to shut it down too early.

Searching Behaviour

We feel we need to try to regain the loss we have experienced. When we have lost "something" and are in the middle of grieving, we think we want that "something" back. We try to fill that hole.

We do this in a number of different ways.

We can be preoccupied with thoughts of the loss. If ever you have lost a loved one, or even an object very precious to you, then you know that for a time, your mind just goes around and around, thinking about your loss. You can't get rid of those thoughts. You think about it when you go to bed. You think about it when you get up in the morning, and in between you dream about it all the time.

Along with that comes a compulsion to speak of the loss. Talking about our grief is one of God's methods of helping us work through our grief. It gets it out of our hearts and into the open so that we can learn to understand it and process it. That's not always easy to do. It can hurt a lot. Other people will sometimes do a one-upmanship. ("You think you have it bad? Let me tell you about what happened to my Uncle Joe!") But speaking of it is a necessary part of healing.

Then there is also the compulsion to actually retrieve that which has been lost. One way we try to do that is by replacing the lost object by another. For instance, if our marriage fails, we will commonly try to marry again, often on the rebound, to avoid the pain of failure. If we have been abandoned as a child we will often latch on to some father or mother figure who will fill that hole in our hearts. If we lose a child through miscarriage or death, we will often try to replace it as soon as possible with another child. That is not necessarily all bad. But it can become a very compulsive cycle that short-circuits the grieving process. It can also make survivors feel they are a substitute for the person who has been lost.

For that reason, I question sometimes the practice of naming a new child after a previously deceased one. In some cultures, that is quite common. When a child dies, the next child born of the same sex will carry the name of the deceased child. I suppose that wouldn't hurt if the parents were able to love the second child in his or her own right. Unfortunately, what often happens is that the second child feels he or she is a substitute for the child that has been lost. As a result, he ends up absorbing a great deal of grief associated with the previous loss.

Further ways in which searching behaviour can manifest itself include the following:

- A sense of waiting for something to happen.
- Aimless wandering and restlessness.
- A feeling of being lost.
- Not knowing what to do.
- Inability to initiate any activity.
- A feeling that time is suspended.
- A feeling that life can't be worthwhile again.
- Confusion and feeling that things are not real.
- A fear of going crazy.

The last one, "A fear of going crazy," is a common tool the Enemy uses to keep us from grieving properly. I know all kinds of people who need to come to grips with some pretty significant losses in their lives. But they are afraid to do it. Why? Because they fear that if they open the can of worms, their emotions will get out of control and they'll have an emotional breakdown.

And that is not an unrealistic fear. Some people do have breakdowns when they start processing the unresolved pain of the past. What is helpful to understand is that it is not the Lord who causes the breakdown. Rather, the breakdown is the accumulated fruit of unresolved issues. The way to avoid such breakdowns is not to avoid the grief but rather to deal with it in a proper and timely fashion.

Crying

Tears are part of God's solution to our grief. Psalm 56:8 says, *You have kept count of my tossings; put my tears in Your bottle!"* (NRSV). There is some interesting historical background to this verse. In ancient times, there was the practice of gathering one's tears in a little bottle. The idea was that in this way, God could keep track of our grief and reward us accordingly.

Crying relieves and releases tension. I don't profess to understand all of the biology of it, but I have heard that tears release certain chemicals in the body which help us relax and cope with pain. Those for whom tears come easily know what a tremendous relief it can be to be able to cry when the pressure simply becomes too much. Those for whom tears come with more difficulty will testify that they often wish they could cry and thus release the pain and frustration. Weeping is a normal human emotion. We don't have to be embarrassed about it nor try to hide it from each other. Healthy community allows for healthy weeping. Even Jesus wept. As someone has said, "Weeping allows us to clean our windshields so we can see more clearly!"

Anger

This is surely one of the most common of human emotions. You cannot face a significant loss in your life without experiencing at least some anger. That anger can be directed towards God, other people or yourself. For God's people, it is often directed towards God. The reason for that is that as Christians we know God is absolutely sovereign. He's in charge of all things. Things that go wrong, therefore, must ultimately be God's responsibility. After all, He could have stepped in and prevented it from happening. Of course, we don't often consciously admit to this reasoning. But that doesn't mean it isn't there.

My wife and I once knew a couple who, for most of the years of their marriage, were not able to get along very well with each other. They were both somewhat dysfunctional, and when two dysfunctional people marry and try to run a household, sparks fly. Their relationship was so difficult that upon approaching their 25th anniversary, they seriously considered not having a celebration, because as they said, there wasn't too much to celebrate. Nevertheless, they went ahead, in the certainty that God really wanted to heal their relationship.

For years there wasn't much evidence that anything was changing for the better. If anything, there were times when things seemed to get much worse. But they persevered and kept looking to the Lord to heal them. Eventually, they experienced a remarkable breakthrough. Their relationship became everything they had ever dreamed and hoped it would be. That lasted about six months. Then suddenly the husband died. He had a fatal heart attack as they were visiting the home of one of their children.

When I talked to his wife later, one of the cries of her heart was, "How can God allow this to happen when finally it looked like we were getting it together?" She went on to explain how much they had finally looked forward to their retirement and the plans they had been making for a new house. Now all the dreams were gone. You could sense her pain and also her frustrations with life and with God. Thankfully, she worked through it pretty well, but it was tough.

Christians sometimes are so concerned about anger being sin that the moment someone expresses a rebellious or angry thought, we try to shush them because, "Anger is not good." But that is not biblical. The Bible says, *Be angry but do not sin.* It also says, *Do not let the sun go down on your anger* (Eph. 4:26). We need to understand that God is big enough to handle our anger and that it is all right for us to have a good fight with Him. Even the psalmist struggled with God. You don't come to a real resolution of the agonies of your life unless you have worked out your anger. Many people have told me that they have never been angry with God. I question if they have ever really been crossed by God, or by other people. Anger is a necessary part of the process that we will go through at this stage of grieving. [2]

Guilt and Shame

You can't face the past without some awareness of failure on your own part. Even if 99% of what has happened to you is a result of what other people, situations or circumstances have done to you, you can't escape the reality of the guilt and the shame you feel about your own level of involvement in the situation. Very often, we have been part of what made it happen, if not in reality, then at least in our own imagination.

Let me give you an example. Suppose a husband asks his wife to pick up a pack of cigarettes. In the process of going to the store, she is killed in a traffic accident. That man has to live, not only with the grief of the loss, but also with the very real guilt that it was he who asked his wife to run the errand. That can be a very painful experience.

Or suppose a teenager has a fight with his parents, and frustrated and angry, he goes out and commits suicide. Things like that happen. Not long ago, there was a story in the news just like that. A 14-year-old young man from the Vancouver, B.C. area was on a Caribbean cruise with his parents. For one reason or another, they got into a hassle. What did he do? He left his shoes and glasses on the deck, and then jumped overboard. At least, that is what everyone thinks he did. They searched the ship high and low but were not able to find him anywhere. If he wanted to get even with his parents, he chose a very good way of doing so. Talk about guilt and shame!

Or what about siblings who fight, and their parents eventually split up? Each child lives for many, many years with the question, "Was it my behaviour that made the marriage fall apart?" Children have a unique way of personalizing the failure of a marriage. You can tell them all you want that they had nothing to do with it, but in their heart of hearts, they often feel they are to blame for what happened. Kids have this amazing ability to connect things that bear no logical relation.

I recall my parents telling me the story years ago of how my paternal grandmother died of a heart attack. As they recounted the story, they mentioned how the night she died she had told the story of someone else who had died unexpectedly. Can you guess what conclusion I reached from that in my childish mind? I said to myself, "If she had not talked about the other person dying the night before, she wouldn't have died either." Now, is that logical or not? Of course not! But that is how children's minds work and unless they have opportunity to get their perceptions straightened out, they can go through life feeling guilty and ashamed for things that are not their responsibility.

Regression

Regression is a return to behaviours and feelings of an earlier age. An adult assuming a fetal position is an extreme example of regression.

All of us have had moments of regression. Let's assume, for example, that you have spent the better part of your life trying to escape from the clutches of some dominating adult. You are tired of father or mother bossing you around. You've finally grown up and become your own person. You've learned to make your own decisions. Now you decide to go back home for a visit. You're confident you can handle it. You know you can stand up to your mom or your dad. But what happens when you are back home? You feel like a little kid all over again, isn't that true? All of the old dynamics of what took place years ago kick in and before you know it, you are once again the child. All the feelings of helplessness and powerlessness that you felt as a child come rushing back at you. You want to kick yourself, and you say, "I am an adult and I don't have to listen to them," but you can't escape it. It's an automatic response. That is regression.

In its more severe forms, regression will actually enable people to revert back to an earlier age in which they will manifest many of the characteristics that they experienced at that particular time. This is very common in trauma counselling. People will actually re-live the traumatic experience. I have personally witnessed this on several occasions. People revert to feeling and behaving just like a little child. It can be pretty scary for someone who is going through it. Yet it is a normal stage of grieving.

Hopelessness and Despair

This is the most critical stage of grief. People can live through almost anything if they see light at the end of the tunnel. Give people hope that one day the situation will change and they will be motivated to endure. Take that hope away from them and they will likely be overtaken by feelings of hopelessness and despair. *Hope deferred makes the heart sick,* says the book of Proverbs (Prov. 13:12). This can readily lead to suicide. The alarming climb in the rate of suicide among young people can largely be traced precisely to this hopelessness. They see no light at the end of the tunnel.

When we encounter people like that, the tendency for many of us is to try to encourage them with many words. "Look at the bright side," we say. "Life could be so much worse. Think of all the people who are worse off than you," and so on. Most of the time, that has very little effect. What people need is not so much a "pep talk," as someone who will just walk through their suffering with them – someone who can let them know they are not alone and who can gently point them to Jesus, who suffered the loss of everything that we might have eternal hope. *Weeping may tarry for the night, but joy comes with the morning* (Ps. 30:5, RSV). Eventually, there comes a time when the pain begins to decrease and the capacity to hope and cope increases. That is the beginning of true healing.

Just as God has instituted principles for the healing of our bodies, if they are properly taken care of, He has also made provision for the healing of our souls. If we will but identify our losses, allow ourselves to re-experience the pain and allow the Holy Spirit to take us through the grieving process (always pointing us to Jesus), then, though *weeping tarry for the night, joy comes with the morning.*

Healing may not always come instantly or dramatically. As a matter of fact, most of the time it won't. But slowly and sure-ly, the grief begins to wear off. The crying spells become less frequent and the memory less painful. The grief begins to abate and with it there rises in our hearts a longing to make a new start. Having learned from our losses, we now start planning again for the future. We dare dream again. Eventually, we learn to integrate our losses into our new life. We may even become appreciative of the losses that we have experienced because they have been used by God to make us better and stronger people. Deepened in our own walk with God, we now are much bet-ter able to praise Him and bless other people. That is why the psalmist ends as he does:

> *You who fear the Lord, praise Him! All you descendants of Jacob, honor Him. Revere Him all you descendants of Israel! For He has not despised or disdained the suffering of the afflicted one; He has not hidden His face from him but has listened to his cry for help* (Ps. 22:23,24).

NOTES

1. I am indebted for these insights to Charles Whitfield, *Healing the Child Within* (Deerfield Beach, FL: Health Communications Inc., 1987).

2. For a thorough study of righteous anger, read Dr. Christopher M. Schrader's book *Righteous Anger: Christ's Expression as a Model* (Belleville, ON: Essence Publishing, 1996).

12 | Recovering From Our Losses

You have turned my
mourning into dancing.
Psalm 30:11

ho hasn't felt the pain of grieving for that which was? Who hasn't longed for a better life and a better world? When a person experiences the kinds of losses and griefs we have looked at in the last few chapters, then it is easy to wonder, "Will life ever change? Will the tears ever stop? Will I ever be happy again?" The psalmist puts it this way, *I am weary with my crying; my throat is parched. My eyes grow dim with waiting for my God* (Ps. 69:3, RSV). The answer is yes. *Weeping may tarry for the night, but joy comes with the morning* (Ps. 30:5, RSV).

When we cry out to God in desperation and brokenness, when the disciplines of God have fulfilled their purpose in our lives, and we have been driven to our knees in repentance and faith and have renounced all of our idolatries, there will come a time when we meet God in a new way. We discover, in that hour, that God reaches into our lives in a way that only He can. He brings healing and restoration.

That is what Hosea talks about in Hosea 14:4-7:

I will heal their faithlessness; I will love them freely, for my anger has turned from them. I will be as the dew to Israel; he shall blossom as the lily, he shall strike root as the poplar; his shoots shall spread out; his beauty shall be like the olive, and his fragrance like Lebanon. They shall return and dwell beneath my shadow, they shall flourish as a garden; they shall blossom as the vine, their fragrance shall be like the wine of Lebanon (RSV).

There are three things in these four verses that God promises to His people as they finish their grieving, repent of their idolatries and return to the God of their salvation: 1) Healing; 2) Prosperity; 3) Status. Let's take a closer look at each of these.

He Promises To Heal Us

What happens when we repent from turning to false gods for our happiness? God meets us with healing: *I will heal their faithlessness; I will love them freely, for my anger has turned from them* (vs. 4).

Healing is a very broad topic. When God heals His people, there are at least three kinds of healing we can expect Him to undertake:

Spiritual Healing

Spiritual healing is restoration in our relationship with God. Why is there so much grief, trouble and difficulty in the world? One reason, the Bible says, is that we are alienated from God through our sin. We have no meaningful relationship with God. We haven't learned to build our lives on His Word. As a result, the consequences of our sin have overtaken us.

When God begins to heal, He begins very often by healing our relationship with Him. He helps us to understand that when Jesus died on the cross He absorbed into Himself all our grief and sin and that when He arose from the dead, He raised us with Him. The result is that through faith in Jesus our sins are no longer held against us. We are considered righteous before God and, instead of turning His back to us, God now turns His face towards us in love.

Emotional Healing

Emotional healing, as the name implies, involves the healing of our damaged emotions. As we have turned away from God and sin has done its damage, we have died emotionally. That is to say, our capacity to feel, trust, love and care has all been damaged to varying degrees. As we turn to Jesus and allow Him into the core of our hearts, He starts to heal our emotions as well. He helps us to accept our losses. He dries our tears. He gives us a new purpose in life. He also gives us the ability to forgive whoever or whatever has contributed to our hurt in the recognition that God has taken even the bad things that have happened to us and turned them around for our good.

Physical Healing

Psalm 51:8 says, *Fill me with joy and gladness; let the bones which Thou hast broken rejoice* (RSV). Scripture is filled with many examples of God's healing power. Jesus, during His ministry on earth, healed many who were blind, lame or sick by the Holy Spirit's power. His disciples also performed many miracles. Even in the Old Testament, God used His healing power to heal many, including Namaan, who was cured of his leprosy after dipping himself in the Jordan River seven times.

Now, what I would like for us to note in Hosea 14 is that when God gives His blessings, He does so freely and generously: *I will love them freely, for my anger has turned away from them* (vs. 4). That is to say, God is going to lavish His love upon His children.

In our more cynical moments, we think God is stingy. Don't you feel that sometimes, when your prayers are not being answered, your tears are not being dried and nothing much changes in your life? Don't you sometimes see God as someone who just really isn't very sensitive and not very caring? And if He does give you something, it is almost done grudgingly, because He wouldn't want you to become too happy or too blessed. That is often the image we have of God. But that is not what the Scriptures say God is like. God says He will love His children freely. Paul puts it this way in Titus 3:5-6: *He saved us... in virtue of His own mercy, by the washing of regeneration and renewal in the Holy Spirit, which He poured out upon us richly through Jesus Christ our Saviour* (RSV). Look at the generosity of God and how He runs the world. When it rains, it pours. When God makes wild flowers, He doesn't just make one or two of them, He splashes the countryside with them. And God delights in pouring out His healing.

One of the characteristics of the Kingdom throughout all of Scripture is that as people repent and turn away from their pain, grief and sin and return to the Lord, then God will move among His people. As He does so, He takes our wounds, pain, hurts, broken relationships and broken bodies, and He breathes new life in us so we can live for the praise of His glory. Hosea says this is God's promise to His people. God says, *"I will heal their faithlessness; I will love them freely."*

He Promises to Bless Us With Prosperity

Hosea goes on to say, *I will be as the dew to Israel; he shall blossom as the lily, he shall strike root as the poplar; his shoots shall spread out; his beauty shall be like the olive, and his fragrance like Lebanon* (vs. 5-6). Let's take a look at each of these phrases:

I will be as the dew to Israel.... This imagery, of course, is of moisture descending out of the night air, watering vegetation and making life possible in the dry areas of the Holy Land. From a New Testament perspective, we know this is symbolic of the outpouring of the Holy Spirit. God has promised to pour out upon His people the early rain and the later rain – symbolic representations of the water of the Holy

Spirit. And when, through faith in Jesus, we are restored to God, and God washes away our tears and heals our lives, He is not just content to put us back together so we can limp on through the rest of life. He opens the windows of Heaven for us and pours out whatever we need to prosper in the growth that He has for us. He fills us with a light and a life full of the vitality of Him.

If you read through the book of Isaiah, for example, you would find instance after instance of God promising to pour out rain for His people, making the barren wilderness come to life, bringing healing for His children.

He shall blossom as the lily.... This lily is the fragrant white lily that grows wild in the Holy Land without any kind of cultivation. It is a very fruitful lily. One plant can produce as many as fifty bulbs from a single root. Its imagery here illustrates how God promises to make His people fruitful.

Why has God made us? So we could be *oaks of righteousness, a planting of the Lord for the display of His splendour* (Isa. 61:3). I don't know about you, but I find it so tremendously exciting that God, in Jesus Christ, can come into our hearts and lives, take all the hurts, garbage and woundedness of our past and pour out His love upon us. He makes us fruitful so our lives can reflect His glory.

He shall strike root as the poplar.... Literally, the Hebrew text says, *He will strike roots like Lebanon.* This imagery is of something very deeply rooted. Roots, of course, serve two functions. They provide nutrients for the tree and they also anchor the tree against the storms of life. When Hosea says, "He shall strike root as the poplar, or strike roots as Lebanon," he is saying, God will provide stability for His people. He will enable us to sink our roots deeply into His love and power. It doesn't matter how many storms rage in life, God's people will stand secure, because their God sits upon His throne, and nothing and no one can ever hurt, wound or destroy us contrary to the will of God.

His shoots shall spread out; his beauty shall be like the olive, and his fragrance like Lebanon.... If roots are downward and indicate stability, then shoots are upward and indicate growth and maturity and beauty. As I have said before, I cannot tell you how excited I get when I see God move in people's lives after they have been broken by sin, (sometimes by their own and sometimes by that of other people), and their life has been without hope and purpose. Jesus comes along, washes away their sin and pours His Holy Spirit into their hearts and into their lives. He lifts away all the garbage that has weighed them down. He quickens their spirits and anoints their personalities, which have been squashed and distorted by sin. They have been afraid to live, to speak out, to *be*, because it was never safe. Then God comes along and breathes life into them, takes them by the hand, and they step out and begin to blossom like a rose.

Recently, I saw a young woman who had been wounded in her past, and I said to her, "You look nice today." I did that because I really believed it and I really believed she needed to be encouraged. She went on to tell me that she was really doing well in drawing, and was entering a national contest. I said to her, "If you ever get a chance, show me some of your drawings." My heart just leapt with joy at seeing God take hold of her life. He is beginning to develop her abilities and her talents, when instead, her life could have so easily gone in a whole different direction.

God says that *His shoots shall spread out; his beauty shall be like the olive, and his fragrance like Lebanon.* God is so generous that He doesn't just settle with blessing us with the absolute necessities and nothing more. No, the promise here is that we will have the beauty of an olive, the lasting useful qualities of olive trees and a fragrance like Lebanon.

He Promises to Restore Us to Our Status and Position

They shall return and dwell beneath my shadow, they shall flourish like a garden; they shall blossom as the vine, their fragrance shall be like the wine of Lebanon (vs. 7).

What is God's purpose for His people? It is to demonstrate His glory and His love to all the nations of the world. When God pours into our lives something of His healing and presence, He doesn't just do that to make us feel good, or because He delights in blessing us. He does it so that through us, the blessings can flow to the nations of the world. God's promise for His children is that, as they serve the Lord, He will lift them up. He will establish them in their inheritance, and people from all over the world will be drawn to God's children because God is in their midst, and the glory of God is seen upon their faces.

This is one of the things that has been happening in recent years at the Airport Christian Fellowship (formerly Airport Vineyard) in Toronto. Airplanes filled with people from all over the world are coming to see what God is doing there. When God works in our lives, He wipes away our tears, integrates our losses and puts us back together. He takes the very losses which we have experienced and builds this into the life and ministry He has for us.

Let me end this chapter with a story. I was talking with a woman, who in the course of her growing-up years, experienced considerable pain and, in the middle of that pain, remembers crying out to God as a little child, saying, "God, please protect me, please don't let anything happen to me tonight." And the heavens remained like brass, and God didn't seem to be there. Her pain went on and on and on. Part of her struggle in growing up was her question, "How can I now trust God with my life when I called on Him and needed Him as a little child and He wasn't there?" We talked about that, and I told her I didn't know all the answers to the struggles she was going through in this issue. All I knew was that the heart of God breaks in the pain of our hurt and agony and He longs to heal and restore us. But as we were talking, the light went on, and it became clear to her and to me that one of the reasons God sometimes doesn't take us out of our pain is that He uses the pain to prepare us for a greater weight of glory. Did you know that?

Paul said, *"I consider that our present sufferings are not worth comparing with the glory that will be revealed in us"* (Rom. 8:18). He also says that when all has been said and done, these present momentary afflictions are preparing for us a weight of glory that is beyond understanding (2 Cor. 4:17). I believe that when the curtain is pulled back and we see clearly, we will discover in that hour, that the grief, pain and agony we dreaded the most have been transformed by God in our lives, used of God to make us that much stronger, so for all eternity we will be filled with greater glory. In some ways, the greater the pain and agony that we have suffered – certainly on His behalf and in His name – the greater will be the measure of His glory and blessing in our lives.

On a much smaller scale, you already see this happening in the world today. Who are the most compassionate counsellors? Who are the best at comforting people who are grieving? Who are the most skilled in reaching out to people stuck in the dregs of life, for whom faith has been lost and life has no future? Aren't they the men and women who have "been there" – men and women who haven't "stayed there," but who have experienced the touch of God and experienced His salvation? God has healed their brokenness and woundedness, and now His grace flows through them like a river. They are able to do things that many of the rest of us cannot do, because they have paid the price. That is how God heals our lives.

Core Issue 3: Damaged Emotions

13

> [We] *opened wide our hearts*
> *to you.... As a fair exchange...*
> *open wide your hearts also.*
> 2 Corinthians 6:11-13

One day after I had been doing some teaching on what normal grieving is in a family, a woman from our congregation came up to me and said with wonderment in her voice, "Is that really the way it is supposed to be in a normal family?" She went on to relate that in her family of origin, she never thought of going to her mom or dad with a scraped knee when she was a little girl. She would either ignore the scrape, or if it was bad enough, she would put a bandage on it herself. But never would she go to her mom or dad. The reason for that, she said, was that she could predict what their reaction would be. Their reaction would be, "It's a little thing. Don't worry about it. Don't cry. Be a big girl. Big girls don't cry."

As I reflected on her story, it struck me how aptly it illustrates one of the characteristics of emotionally unhealthy families: *Parents who haven't been able to resolve or deal with issues of pain or grief in their own life, cannot accept or tolerate pain or grief in their children.* It reminds them too much of their own unresolved pain and, as a consequence, they will either minimize it or ridicule it in the lives of their children. In either case, this can cause serious distortions in the lives of their children as to what is or is not normal emotion. Let me illustrate.

I have a good friend whose name is Art. Art is a Dutchman by birth and an aggressive man by nature. Apart from God's grace in his life, I wouldn't want to meet him in a dark alley! How did he become so aggressive? Well, undoubtedly, part of it is genetic. The Dutch have a certain reputation in this regard! (I can say that since I also was born in the Netherlands!) Part of it was environmental. Art tells me that as he was growing up, aggressiveness was a quality that was highly prized by his father. If, for example, he came home with tears running down his face because some neighbourhood bully had beat him up, he soon learned not to expect sympathy. Instead, he was marched out the door with a wooden shoe in his hand and instructions to find the bully and get even.

Now, I think I understand what his father was trying to do. He didn't want to raise a son who was a wimp. Tender emotions had not been allowed in his life when he was growing up and they weren't going to be allowed in his son's life either. Is it any wonder that until the Lord Jesus got hold of my friend's life, he was a fighter that few would dare cross?

This story illustrates how unresolved emotional issues in the lives of parents can cause distortions in the lives of their children. That, in turn, just perpetuates the cycle of dysfunction from one generation to another.

For that reason, when the Lord sets about healing generational sin, one of the areas that He wants to heal is the area of damaged emotions. He wants to make fathers and mothers strong in righteousness so that they can leave a godly inheritance for their children – children who by God's grace will be capable of loving God above all and their neighbour as themselves.

With that in mind, then, let's take a look in this chapter at the subject of emotions and how they can be healed.

Psychologists who have studied dysfunctional family patterns for a long time have discovered that there are certain patterns common to people who have been raised in abusive situations. Let's take a look at some of them.

COMMON DYSFUNCTIONAL FAMILY PATTERNS

All-or-Nothing Thinking

All-or-nothing thinkers tend to see the world in black and white; there are no shades of grey. Everything is either really good or really bad.

All-or-nothing thinking expresses itself in many different ways. For example, all-or-nothing thinkers see friendships in black or white terms: Either we are the very best of friends or we cannot stand each other; there is no middle ground. We are either intensely loyal to each other, or else we are always tearing each other down. There is no ability to recognize that the best of us have some bad spots, and even the worst of us have some good spots.

It also comes to expression in how we work. An all-or-nothing thinker either throws himself into work with all of his being, or else he won't get involved at all. Again, it's all or nothing. There are no shades in between.

All-or-nothing thinking comes out of being raised in an environment where your value is determined by what you manage to accomplish. When you accomplish things, you are loved, cherished and valued. But if you do not measure up to standards (which often change), then you are rejected and considered no good, whether in reality or in your own imagination.

People raised in that kind of an environment learn to only set about tasks in which they are going to be successful. If they can't be successful, then they don't want to engage in that kind of activity at all because they know, or they feel, that they are going to be rejected for not doing it "right."

Control

A person raised in a dysfunctional family will have a tendency to control his or her own world. The reasons for that are fairly obvious, because one of the characteristics of a dysfunctional family is that it is predictable in its unpredictability. You never know which way the wind is going to blow. You never know when the standards are going to change. What you did yesterday is not always what you are expected to do today. This unpredictability causes tremendous emotional pain because you don't know if you are going to be hugged or slugged. You don't know if your father is going to be sober when you get home or whether he is going to be in a drunken rage. You don't know if your mother is going to be there when you get home from school, or if she is home, whether she'll be in a good mood or a bad mood. So you learn that the way to minimize pain is to try to control your environment so you can dull the impact of being at the mercy of other people's shenanigans.

Control can be *direct* or *indirect*. An example of *direct* control is when a husband tells his wife or children what they should think or feel. For instance, the wife will say, "I feel tired or discouraged today." Or the child will say, "I feel sad and I want to cry." The father who hasn't learned to deal with his own emotions can't deal with their emotions, so he minimizes them. "You don't really feel that way." "You're not really tired." "Big boys don't cry."

Don't you hate it when people do that to you? Our feelings may be right or wrong, our thoughts may be right or wrong, but they are still our thoughts and feelings. We need the space to be allowed to own our own thoughts and feelings. Only then can we give them to Jesus and ask Him to renew them so they can line up with His will.

Another example of exercising direct control is when a person dominates a conversation. Perhaps you will have noticed this at parties or in other social settings. There are certain people who always want to have the last word. If you tell a story, they will have a story that is so much better. If you tell a joke, they will tell two jokes. If you mention an accomplishment, they will try to beat you at that as well. That's one-upmanship. It often comes under the guise of wanting to give love and protection, but it is actually a form of control. It keeps others in place so that your own position of security is not threatened.

Indirect control is, of course, much more subtle than that. That is why there is a lot more of it and it is much harder to spot. An example of indirect control would be when a parent has a certain career in mind for his teenager and offers to pay his way to a particular college on the condition he follows a specified course of studies. However, the parent refuses to pay a cent if the teenager goes to another college to study the career of his own choice. That is indirect control.

Likewise, a person who tries to control others by his or her moods is exercising indirect control. For example, someone who radiates disapproval, either through silent treatment or other forms of ugliness, is exercising indirect control. He is using his moods to try to get someone else to toe the line. Some people can radiate disapproval in a way that intimidates others, even though nothing has been said. The tendency is to want to accommodate such a person, particularly if their love and support is important and needed.

Faked illness can be another way of exercising indirect control. My father, who was an exceptional storyteller, told the story of a woman who was a bit of a hypochondriac. I think she had a bit of a breathing problem or something like that. One night, her breathing was really bad. It was stormy outside and she had no medicine left. So she asked her husband if he would please go to the doctor and get some medication. Well, her husband was concerned with her well-being and, thinking she was on the verge of dying, put on his coat, got out his bicycle and went to the doctor for the medicine.

"Well," says the doctor, "I am sorry to have to tell you, but I don't have any of the medicine left that I usually give her. But here's what we will do."

With that, he got a little bottle, went to the tap and filled it up with water! Then he said, "Usually I add a little food colouring for effect, but I don't have any of that left tonight. Just give it to her plain. I guarantee you, this will fix her up."

The husband put his coat back on, got on his bicycle and pedalled all the way back home. He gave his wife the medicine, and she took a tablespoon of it, and then another. Immediately, she started feeling so much better!

As my father used to relate the story, the husband got so angry he refused to ever go see the doctor on her behalf again.

As a rule, controlling people are very unhappy and angry people. The more they feel they are losing control, the angrier and more upset they will be. Increasingly, it consumes a tremendous amount of energy because nobody can control other people indefinitely, and no one can control the whole world. And so, controllers constantly live in fear of losing control.

The remedy, of course, is to turn our control over to Jesus and to recognize that God alone is in control. As I yield my life to His control, not only will He take care of me, but He will give me a healthy ability to manage my own life in a way that pleases Him and respects other people's boundaries.

High Tolerance of Inappropriate Behaviour

High tolerance of inappropriate behaviour means putting up with behaviour by other people that is not appropriate to the occasion. For example, allowing your drunken husband to verbally or physically abuse you or the children is tolerating inappropriate behaviour. So is allowing other people to take advantage of your kindness or generosity.

This is a common characteristic of people raised in a dysfunctional environment, and it is not hard to see why. Children commonly believe that what they grow up with is normal. If you grow up in a family where people are at each other all the time, or where your father or mother is never home, or it isn't safe to talk about your feelings, then you believe that is all very normal. You think everyone lives this way. It is not until you get out into the wider world and see that other people live differently, that you begin to question the way you were brought up. The problem is, by then a lot of behavioral patterns have already been programmed into your life, and you have a hard time recognizing them, let alone getting rid of them. As a result, many of these are reproduced in subsequent relationships.

That is one reason why a girl who grows up in an abusive family will so often marry an abusive husband. All logic asks, "Why in the world would you want to do such a thing?" You'd think she'd want to marry a man who was totally different from her abusive father. And she does. The problem is it feels "normal" for her to be treated this way. Bad attention is preferable to no attention. Consequently, she gravitates towards relationships that will treat her the same way. If she is not being treated in this way, she feels there must be something wrong and she may even, consciously or subconsciously, provoke her partner to treat her badly.

I have known many people like that. They grew up in situations where they were treated like dirt. When they started looking around to form relationships with other people, guess what? They gravitated towards those who treated them in the same way.

I have known girls who had opportunities to break out of that cycle and choose boyfriends who would treat them with dignity and respect. But the moment a young man began treating them with dignity, they ditched the relationship and went back into an abusive relationship, because somehow or another, it felt more "normal." They didn't know how to handle themselves in different situations. It filled them with dread and insecurity.

They didn't think they were worthy of a good relationship and felt instinctively that they would never be able to hold on to it. So they gravitated towards people whom they perceived to be lower on the social scale than themselves. Predictably, such relationships would invariably be rocky.

Fear of Conflict

People in normal relationships experience times of tension and conflict. You cannot become intimate, in the true sense of the word, with another human being without occasionally being frustrated by what the other person says or does, or doesn't say or do. Healthy relationships can tolerate disagreements. You can have a good rip-roaring fight, clear the air and know your relationship is going to be better as a result. You learn the skills you need to resolve the issues you face.

But if you live in a dysfunctional family, you don't have that kind of luxury. In a dysfunctional family, a fight gets out of control. If mom or dad have a fight, it might be the breakup of their marriage, or at the very least, it will cause some very unpleasant pain and difficulty. Those who have grown up in an environment where there was a lot of fighting, therefore, tend to avoid conflict altogether.

You can easily spot these people. As soon as there is tension in the air, their hearts begin to beat out of their chests. They are afraid everything is going to blow up and no one will have life under control anymore. They surface as the mediators when others become engaged in a disagreement. They try to slip into the relationship and keep the warring parties apart. Often they are quite prepared to be treated inappropriately and take others' pain themselves, so that the tension in the relationship can be alleviated.

Not all of that is bad, of course. The gospel calls us to be peacemakers. Jesus says, *Blessed are the peacemakers* (Matt. 5:9). The danger comes in when our peacemaking stems from unresolved needs in our own lives rather than from a commitment to truth. When we sacrifice truth, we do not have what the Bible calls a true and biblical peace that lasts. We have merely covered up the problems and empowered evil to carry on and do its dastardly deed in the next generation.

A classic example historically, is that of Prime Minister Chamberlain of England, before World War II. He was elected in 1937, and in 1938, he had an extensive meeting with Adolf Hitler. They signed the *Pact of Munich*. In the *Pact of Munich*, Chamberlain conceded Czechoslovakia to Hitler. When he came back to England, the headlines proclaimed, "Peace in Our Time." How long did the peace last? Days maybe, or weeks at best? Soon Hitler's army charged into Czechoslovakia and took the portion of the land that had been deeded to him. But it did not stop there. He continued to cause anguish and death for millions of people, and the anguish continued long after peace was declared.

When God makes peace, He makes peace on the basis of truth. True and lasting peace in our lives and relationships is founded on the truth of what God says ought to happen.

Fear of Giving and Receiving Love

One of the greatest blessings of being alive is that of having an intimate relationship with a friend, spouse or child. We have been made in the image of God. We are not meant to be alone, but are meant to be able to see heart-to-heart, eye-to-eye and life-to-life with someone else. To know there is someone who loves you, cares for you and with whom you can share your heart safely and securely is one of the most wonderful blessings in life – blessings that we often, in so many ways, take for granted until we lose them.

If you have been raised in a dysfunctional environment, you tend to feel it isn't very safe to either give love or receive it, because there is a dark side to love. Whenever you open up your heart to someone else and share your innermost thoughts and feelings, you become vulnerable. They now have the power to hurt and betray you. They know where your weaknesses lie, and they can exploit them if they so desire. That can cause you pain like nothing you have ever known before.

For that reason, people raised in a dysfunctional family tend to go to one extreme or another when it comes to giving and receiving love. They will either become too permissive, too open, perhaps even promiscuous in accepting or receiving love from whomever seems to offer it; or, they will go to the opposite extreme and close their hearts off altogether.

In her book, *Released from Shame: Recovery for Adult Children of Dysfunctional Families*, Sandra Wilson tells the story of a bright, attractive, Christian woman who was raised in an abusive family. When she found herself pregnant, she said, "I just knew the minute I met him that I could trust him completely. He was older than me, and so wise and kind. He said he loved me too and would marry me as soon as he settled some minor personal problems. I never asked the details because I didn't want him to think I didn't trust him. When I told him I was pregnant and would like to get married right away, he laughed and told me I was too naive for my own good." [1]

After one goes through that treatment a couple of times, what happens? You build up all kinds of walls. You don't allow other people to love you or get close to you. The world is filled with people who are not capable of forming intimate relationships with others.

Again, they are not hard to spot. You will seldom hear them talk about how they really feel or what they really think. Oh, they will talk, but only superficially, about things, issues and other people, but they won't talk about what lives in their heart. When the conversation gets too close to home, they change the topic because they don't want to reveal what lives inside their hearts. They are the kind of people you become good friends with, and then all of a sudden they just disappear because they feel they need to reject you, before you ever get a chance to reject them. They are people who always want others to pour experiences into their lives, but they have nothing to give in return.

Can you imagine what happens when you grow up in that kind of an environment, where your parents aren't mature enough emotionally to look after your needs?

Dr. Fred Downing, tells the story of when he was 8 years old and started going to church on his own. He heard the pastors saying in their sermons that unless you were worshipping, you would probably be lost and go to hell and die. Fred got scared for his mom and dad and tried to get them to go to church. He didn't want them to go to hell and felt it was his responsibility to help save them. He said he went to church for the eight o'clock morning service, then would skip Sunday School, rush home, go into his parents' bedroom, pull their covers off and demand they get up and go to church. But he said they never did go. (I don't know how they felt about his coming in and pulling their bed covers off all the time, but that isn't the point of the story!) The bottom line is, in so many relationships, the child becomes the parent, while the parent becomes the child. [2]

These, then, are some of the emotional distortions common to those who grow up in a dysfunctional family.

BREAKING FREE FROM THE PATTERN

How do we break out of these distortions? How can we be truly healed so that God can fill our whole being and we can once again reflect His glory?

Here are some suggestions:

Accept Our Emotions as God's Gift to Us

It has been my experience that a lot of us don't like our emotions. Emotions have a life of their own and are like that proverbial fire hose that can bang around out of control. We get angry and don't know what to do with our anger. We feel sad and don't know where to go with our sadness. We feel alone and don't know what to do with our loneliness.

Consequently, a lot of people have learned to shut down their emotions as one of the best ways to exercise control. I believe that is particularly true for people who are, in fact, emotionally sensitive and have been raised in an environment where it was not safe to express those emotions.

The problem is that when you shut off the negative, you also lose the positive. That is to say, if you close your heart because the hurt is too great, you also lose the corresponding ability to feel the joy of living. Haven't you ever noticed that? Some people you meet are the deadest people you could ever imagine. You feel like there is "no one home." You can't connect with them. They have no passion, they don't get excited, nor do they get angry. They don't know how to really live; they just sort of float along, because they have shut off their past. That makes it easy for them to cope with life. The problem is that other people around them constantly have to make up for their emotional deficiency. I know of wives, for example, who are starving emotionally, because their husbands just have no idea how to relate to them on an emotional level. The wives end up pouring energy for both parents into the lives of their children and don't get anything in return. Is it any wonder that many such wives turn to adulterous relationships to fill the hole in their heart?

God has not made us to be void of emotion. Emotions are one of God's gifts to His people and His Church, so we can express and relate to God and one another in an appropriate way. The way to experience that, is not to rebel against God by denying the way He made us, but to go to Him with our emotions and say, "Lord, I receive my emotions as a gift from You. I know my emotions have been distorted by sin, I know they often get in the way and I don't know what to do with them. But, God, I acknowledge that You have made me a man (woman, boy, girl) with feelings, and there are things that feel good, and there are things that feel bad. I accept the fact that You have made me with a particular temperament and a certain set of feelings."

What happens in many cases is that people are afraid of becoming like certain other people whose ways they don't like. Many of us have a fear in the back of our minds that says, "If I really let my emotions become real, I will be a blubbering idiot, just like the people I have rejected." This is particularly true if you grew up in an environment where your mother or father was not very strong emotionally, and you decided that you would never be like that. So you made vows to rebel against the way God has made you.

We need to understand that God made each of us unique. He has made each of us with feelings. When those feelings are yielded to Jesus, and He lives in them by the power of the Holy Spirit, God will help us to control our feelings and channel them into ways that make life exciting and pleasurable. Can you imagine what a dull and boring place this world would be if none of us ever felt emotions or could experience feelings of love, hate or anger? We need to accept our feelings as a gift from the Lord.

Give Our Feelings to Jesus for Healing

Scripture says, *Love the Lord your God with all your heart and with all your soul and with all your mind and with all your strength... Love your neighbour as yourself* (Mark 12:30-31). While it is true that love is far more than emotion, it certainly also includes emotion. The Lord wants us to be passionately in love with Him and with one another. That means our whole being, including our emotions, needs to be set free to serve Him and one another.

Ever since the enlightenment, Western civilization has emphasized the rational over the emotional and spiritual. That has also affected how the Christian Church has sought to express her spirituality. Often we have become rational at the expense of the emotional. The result is that enthusiastic passion is considered normal everywhere except in church! We can be enthusiastically fanatical at a sporting event, talk with great enthusiasm about our new job, car or what have you, but let someone get too enthusiastic about his relationship with the Lord, or too expressive in Christian affection, and he is immediately branded as radical or weird. It's just not the "cool" thing to do.

That's a distortion of biblical reality. To love the Lord our God with all of our being means we are to love Him with our emotions too. That means we need to give our emotions to Him and ask Him to heal us so that we can truly love Him and others in a God-glorifying way.

Many years ago, when Billy Graham was holding some of his first crusades, he was criticized in some circles for the emotional element of the altar calls. People would say, "When Cliff Barrows leads the choir to sing 'Just As I Am' for the invitation, it creates an emotional environment in which people are propelled forward by their emotions, but there is no lasting reality of their stirred emotions."

I will never forget Billy Graham's response. He said, "It may be true that people's emotions are stirred, but what do you expect to happen when people encounter the living God for the first time in their lives?" Should we not expect there to be some demonstration of emotion when people come face to face with their sin, repent of it and turn their lives over to Jesus Christ?

Likewise, should there not be some demonstration of emotion in the way God's people interact with one another? Some people have a very difficult time expressing affection or love for one another. I know men who seldom speak affectionately to their wives, and parents who have seldom hugged their children. I know people whose only acceptable emotion is anger. All others are a sign of weakness to be avoided and shunned at all costs. All of these need to be surrendered to Jesus.

The big fear people have, of course, is becoming something other than they are. But that is part of Satan's arsenal to keep us locked up. The Lord doesn't make us into something other than we are. He sets us free to become what we have always been intended to be. He removes the restrictions that keep us from bearing the kind of fruit that we have been destined to bear for His glory. *"By this my Father is glorified,"* said Jesus, *"that you bear much fruit, and so prove to be my disciples"* (John 15:8, RSV).

Practice Our Emotions in the Obedience of Faith

Paul says in 1 Corinthians 13:11, *When I was a child, I talked like a child, I thought like a child, I reasoned like a child. When I became a man, I put childish ways behind me.*

This passage is significant in that it clearly demonstrates the process of growing to emotional maturity: *When I became a man, I put childish ways behind me.* The phrase, *put childish ways behind me,* as Dr. David Seamands points out so capably in his book, *Putting Away Childish Things,* is the Greek word *katargeo.* It is a very strong word which means, "break its hold, finish off, be done with it." [3]

Just because we have come to Jesus and He has come to live in our hearts does not mean we are delivered from all the fear, pain and agony of our past. Many of these are so deeply ingrained in our hearts, that they will surface again and again. That is why so many thoroughly committed Christians can act so miserably immature at times! The spirit is willing but the flesh is weak.

When, however, we have made a commitment to Christ and He has come to live in our hearts by His Holy Spirit, He is no longer content to leave us that way. Our sins not only grieve God, they hurt other people around us. Having committed ourselves to Kingdom living, He now calls us to put off the old and to put on the new. Ephesians 4:22-24 says: *You were taught, with regard to your former way of life, to put off your old self, which is being corrupted by its deceitful desires; to be made new in the attitude of your minds; and to put on the new self, created to be like God in true righteousness and holiness.*

The way that works is that the Holy Spirit starts to put His finger on areas where we are not yet mature in faith and He says, "Put off childish ways and put on the new man you are in Christ." To the person who wants to operate in a world that is black and white and can't live with shades of grey, He says, "I want you to learn to see good in the worst, and the worst in the best, and to understand that life isn't always clear-cut black and white, but has shades of grey; and I will give you the help and wisdom to know which is which."

For the person who always feels he has to control everything around him, whether directly or indirectly, God sets it up so that he loses control. And God says, "Just learn that I am in charge and know how to look after you better than you know how to look after yourself."

To the person who is used to accepting any type of inappropriate behaviour, the Holy Spirit will come along and tell him, "Enough is enough. Now is the time to stand up, let the truth be made known, and let people know that this is how far they can come, but no further," and know you are doing it by the power of the Holy Spirit.

God allows the person who is afraid of conflict to be placed in a situation of conflict that he cannot avoid, and God teaches him how to walk through it and discover that he can come out on the other end intact and safe in relationships built up in Christ. To the person who says, "No one is going to get close to me, no one is going to know my real heart and no one will get under my skin," the Holy Spirit comes along and says, "Alright, now is the time to step out and let down your guard. You are going to try to form a friendship with a person you have never been friends with before, and you are going to trust me, as I walk with you through the pain, and know that I am there to hold you. I will teach you and help you to sustain the relationship."

Now, that is very scary business. Stepping out in the area of our vulnerability feels like dying a thousand times over. In fact, many people prefer death to the pain of having to step out of their comfort zone into a walk of faith, particularly as that relates to their emotions. That is why many of God's people shrink back at this stage of their lives. As a result, they short-circuit God's process of sanctification. They remain stunted in their growth, not able to give and receive the full measure of love that God has intended for them.

Those who do pay the price, however, those who, by trial and error, learn to step out in faith and trust God, discover the rich reward of their inheritance. Gifts and abilities they never thought they possessed are now set free. Emotions that were kept tightly under wraps are now free to flow. And everywhere they go they spread the blessings of the fragrance of Jesus Christ. The following story is a clear testimony of this.

Maria's Story

Maria's life is a good illustration of God's redemptive power. Born the fifth child in a family of eight to parents who themselves had considerable unresolved issues, she decided very early in life that she could not afford to be her own person. When her siblings were rebellious, she vowed to never put her parents through that grief. When one played a certain instrument, she decided she wouldn't, lest she infringe on the other's space.

As a result, she slowly began to die. Life became one series of devastating blows after another. She had on-going health problems. A serious four-year relationship with a man she was deeply fond of was terminated without as much as an explanation. She was in a car accident and suffered amnesia.

Another ex-boyfriend committed suicide. Her father died suddenly and she and her brother discovered his body and tried to revive him.

Eventually, she married. Far from taking away her pain and giving her the soul-mate she had longed for, marriage only increased her pain and accentuated her loneliness. She withdrew even more from life. She felt that if she was to ever fit in, she must become even less. She stopped painting, writing, playing her flute and exercising. What she had feared most of her life was becoming a dreadful reality. She became a living nothing.

That's when God met her in a fresh way. Through some books she read and some friends who counselled her, she came to see that God's aim in life was not to destroy her, or reduce her to nothingness as her experience in life had seemed to indicate. His aim was to give her life and that more abundantly. And so she faced her deepest fear – that if she let go of all the coping mechanisms she had developed to minimize the pain, she would shrivel up and die – only to discover that God was there to love and protect her. Far from wanting her to be nothing, in Christ, He had destined her to be somebody. As she said in a recent testimony:

> *"He made me who I am. He made me a woman, He gave me passions for living, a life to express; He made me intense, He gave me talents, He wanted my analytical mind; and to let anyone else have the power to define me and make me apologize for who I am is to apologize for what God made. He made me a visionary which doesn't always sit well with logical rational thinking but it's His life in me and He'll figure out all the angles and outcomes, and fill me in on the ones I need to know.*
>
> *"I'm re-learning a lot. I need to live the fruit of gentleness and love. I'm experiencing emotions again which I can't explain. I'm learning to accept my emotions and not be afraid of them controlling me. I'm an adult learner in social graces that others have spent a life-time learning. I'm living again, slowly getting involved in people's lives, in feeling*

things (although other people's pain is still overwhelming to me). I'm playing my flute, sewing, going for walks. My marriage is a new creation.

"I'm finding that when I jump off the cliff of faith, hoping He'll catch me, He not only puts my feet on solid ground which I can feel and experience as true but He gives me wings to fly into experiences I never had the eyes to see with before, places I never knew were a part of reality too. I can go places I couldn't go before. I'm free and am learning to claim more of that freedom all the time."

That's the paradox of the gospel – as we face our deepest fears and step out in confidence that God is true to His Word, we discover He's there to bring us into greater freedom than we ever imagined possible! To God be the glory!

NOTES

1. Sandra D. Wilson, *Released From Shame: Recovery for Adult Children of Dysfunctional Families,* ed. Gary R. Collins (Downer's Grove, IL: InterVarsity Press, 1990), pp. 138-139.

2. Dr. Fred Downing, "The Family Disease – Part 1," *The Family Systems Workshop,* video.

3. David A. Seamands, *Putting Away Childish Things* (Wheaton, IL: Victor Books, 1982), p. 5.

14 Stepping Out in Faith

*Without faith it is
impossible to please God.*
Hebrews 11:6

We were looking in the last chapter at the importance of stepping out emotionally in obedience to the Lord Jesus Christ. If ever you have done that, then you know how very difficult it can be. It often feels like you are walking on water. Things are no longer under your control and that can be scary. At least in our dysfunction, life is at least predictable in its unpredictability!

For that reason, there are multitudes of people who appear quite content to remain where they are, despite the fact that their woundedness is causing damage and injury to themselves and other people. Though initially they embrace the message of the cross with great zeal and enthusiasm and are eager to follow Jesus, their joy evaporates when they hit the first hurdle. "This isn't what I bargained for," is their cry and, given half a chance, they revert back to their old way of life.

Walter's Story

Let me tell you a story which for me personally has been a real heart-breaker. My good friend Art, whom I mentioned in the last chapter, has a heart of love and compassion, especially for the weak and those who cannot defend themselves. A number of years ago, he befriended a man named Walter. Walter was a little man who hardly ever talked. He was definitely socially and economically disadvantaged and not the kind of person most people would want to befriend. There didn't seem to be "anyone at home" when you met Walter. That is how wounded he was. Nevertheless, Art became his friend.

In due time, Walter came to know Jesus and his sins were washed away. The Holy Spirit came into his life, and wouldn't you know it, his life began to change dramatically. I remember seeing him in a prayer meeting smiling from ear to ear, talking about how good God is. I couldn't believe how much that man could talk!

As he pursued his walk with Jesus, the Holy Spirit began to stir things up in his life. There were some fears that he had to address. One day in a prayer meeting (I wasn't there), as Walter was receiving a prayer, the Holy Spirit pointed out to him a deep-rooted sin in his life that he needed to surrender, because it was standing in the way of even further freedom in Jesus.

To this day, I don't really know all that transpired, but I was told that in the middle of that prayer session, panic hit Walter's soul and he high-tailed it out of there, never to come back. He broke off his friendship with Art, which up until that point, had been as dear to him as life itself. Walter left the church and went back to his old friends. The last I heard, he was living in some old age home, all by himself, reverted back to the meek, closed-in person he was when Jesus first found him.

Now, I am hopeful that Jesus will complete the work he began in Walter's life, if not in time, then in eternity. The Lord is so much more gracious than we often think. In the meantime, however, there are wasted years in his life. The witness that he could have been, the glory he could have given to Jesus – none of these have materialized.

I have reflected about that a good deal over the succeeding years, wondering what all must have transpired for Walter to make that decision to run from Jesus. Several things stand out:

1) The light may have been too bright. If you have lived in the darkness for a long time, and then someone shines a floodlight in your face, you can't take it. You want to run because it seems so wrong and frightening, whereas the darkness is so normal.

2) A demonic component may have been involved. I think the devil saw that Walter was going to move forward with Jesus and be a testimony to Jesus in the Kingdom, so somewhere along the line, the devil hit him with a load of something and Walter high-tailed it out of there, never to come back.

But I think there was more at work here than just these two elements. I believe that in the core of Walter's heart, there was a dual root of evil and unbelief that kept him from going all the way with Jesus.

The root was *evil* because when the Holy Spirit began to shine His light into the depths of Walter's heart, there was something about the sin he was involved in that had such a hold on him that he was not willing to surrender it to Jesus.

It was *unbelief* because the sin was so deeply rooted in his life, that he didn't think even Jesus could dig it up and make him a new man. I believe that is why he headed out the door. He could not believe that God could do what God had said He would.

Many of us, I believe, struggle with that same issue. I say that because there is something tantalizing and pleasurable about even the greatest of dysfunctions, because at least "it is predictable and I feel I have some measure of control. To give that up and believe God will take care of me when I let down all of my walls is like death itself."

That is why the book of Hebrews says in Chapter 3:12-14:

See to it, brothers, that none of you has a sinful, unbelieving heart that turns away from the living God. But encourage one another daily, as long as it is called Today, so that none of you may be hardened by sin's deceitfulness. We have come to share in Christ if we hold firmly till the end the confidence we had at first.

If you look at the broader context of these verses then you see that they were addressed to recent Jewish converts. They had heard the good news about Jesus and had come to believe in Him; they had tasted the presence and the power of the Holy Spirit and they were excited about living for Jesus. But then persecution came. Society gave them a hard time. They lost possessions, property, relationships and perhaps even their lives.

That scared them. Some of them began having second thoughts about following Jesus, because this was not what they had in mind when they came to Christ. They probably thought they were going to sprout wings, sport haloes, strum harps and go straight to glory! Instead, they experienced intense pain and deprivation.

The letter to the Hebrews was written to these Christians to encourage them to go on with God. And it is in that context that the author says, *See to it... that none of you has a sinful, unbelieving heart that turns away from the living God* (Heb. 3:12).

The teaching of Scripture, from one end to the other, is that no matter how we are put together, or what struggles we experience, God wants us to learn to overcome through faith in Jesus Christ. He has overcome all the force of the enemy. He has made complete provision for us to run the race to the end. He will either give us the grace to overcome, or He will transform our lives in such a way that we can live for the praise of His glory. The key is stepping out in faith and denying whatever sinful tendencies that remain in us. As we do that, He will direct and empower us. He will take our fears and woundedness and will transform them.

Practically speaking, that means three things:

We Need to Walk in the Fear of God

That is to say, we must walk in the reverence of God. Pleasing Him and doing His will must be uppermost on our agenda. Hebrews 4:1 says, *Therefore, since the promise of entering His rest still stands, let us be careful that none of you be found to have fallen short of it.*

I discovered a long time ago that if my motive in following the Lord is merely to make me feel good, then I will not be very far down the road of discipleship before I discover that it no longer feels good to follow Jesus. I mean, the glory of His presence very quickly evaporates in the agony of being called to do something you have never done before, and having to believe that God will get you through it! If being happy or feeling good is my primary motive for serving Jesus, then the moment obedience costs me any of those, I'm out of there. I will say, "Who needs it? I was happier before I came to Jesus."

One of the most liberating discoveries I made in my own life relates to this issue. It happened in the early years of my Christian life. I had just prayed that radical prayer: "Lord, do anything You need to do to make me the kind of Christian You want me to be." Fortunately, I had no idea what was in store for me, or else I would never have prayed that prayer. Today I am much more careful about what I pray for!

Naively, I assumed that things would get better and better. I would grow closer and closer to the Lord and find more and more delight in doing His will. Imagine my dismay when quite the opposite happened. The bottom fell out of my Christian world. Any sense of God's presence I'd had up until that point disappeared. Any certainty of faith I had disappeared and instead, waves of doubt and despair rolled into my life. Christian activities like prayer, witnessing and Bible reading which had previously been such a delight seemed dry and lifeless. Life itself seemed pretty dreary and hopeless. I was about ready to turn my back on the Lord. This surely was not what I had bargained for.

Then it happened. I remember it as clearly as the day of yesterday. I was doing chores around the yard, feeling thoroughly miserable and useless in the Christian life, when suddenly the thought struck me with the force of a revelation: The object of my life was not to feel good; it was to serve Jesus. If serving Jesus was going to make me feel good, fine and dandy. If it didn't, He was still Lord and worthy of my love and loyalty, devotion and respect. Truth is truth, I discovered that day, regardless of how I feel about it or whether it gives me any conscious joy.

I must add, that discovery didn't immediately lift my burden and restore to me my joy. That took a long time in returning and is a story that will need to be told elsewhere. It did, however, forever settle in my heart the issue of feelings in the Christian life. I don't have to feel good to obey. I just need to obey. If and when the time is right, the Lord will let me experience whatever feelings I need to serve Him. It broke the stranglehold that feelings had over my life. Unbeknownst to myself, my real motive in serving the Lord was not the Lord's glory, but rather my own happiness. That had to be broken, painful as that was.

Please do not misunderstand me. I'm not saying God delights in clobbering us over the head. Scripture does say, however, that He disciplines those whom He loves (Heb 12:6). And when He sees things in our lives that hinder our walk and relationship with Him, then painful as that may be, He has to tear them out of our lives so that we live for Him alone.

Sooner or later, each of God's children has to come to this realization. The question is not, "Does this make me feel good, or bring me happiness?" Rather, the question needs to be, "Is this something that God wants for His glory?"

We need to realize that our sin both offends God and hurts all the people around us. The closer our relationship to them, the more hurt they will be by our failure and sin. That is why it is so crucial for us to deal with our failures. People so readily and easily say, "I don't want to change; I don't need to change; the cost is too high, the pay off too little." And they keep living the way they always have. What again they don't realize is that other people suffer on account of their sin, particularly the people closest to them: their spouse, kids and immediate friends.

If I love God, then I want God to be glorified in my life. Anything short of that won't be enough to make me willing to face the pain of having the Lord change me from the inside out. We need to walk in the fear of God.

We Need to Walk in the Grace of God

Hebrews 4:15-16 says, *For we do not have a high priest who is unable to sympathize with our weaknesses, but we have one who has been tempted in every way, just as we are — yet was without sin. Let us then approach the throne of grace with confidence, so that we may receive mercy and find grace to help us in our time of need.*

To live in the *fear of God* without the *grace of God* is a frighteningly awesome way to live. To know what God wants you to do without understanding His grace and forgiveness is scary because you'll be afraid of taking chances. That will close your heart for sure. However, God not only tells us what He wants us to be, He has made provision in Christ so we can be what we need to be.

The Lord Jesus, by His life, death, resurrection and ascension on high, and by the outpouring of His Holy Spirit, has overcome all the things you and I are confronted with on a daily basis. He has promised to be with us in the middle of the pain, fire and water. He says He will walk through the fire and bring us out on the other side, purified to live for His glory, transformed throughout the inner man. *No temptation*, said Paul, *has seized you except what is common to man. And God is faithful; He will not let you be tempted beyond what you can bear.*

But when you are tempted, He will also provide a way out so that you can stand up under it (1 Cor. 10:13).

Practically speaking, that means that the will of God will never lead us where the grace of God cannot keep us. If God calls us to step out in faith in a given area, He will also provide us with the strength and power needed to be successful. Indeed, the less naturally capable we are, the more obvious it is to everyone else that this is indeed the work of the Lord.

We Need to Understand the Process is a Walk

This process of transformation has failures as well as successes. And this is where I believe a lot of God's people have their biggest struggle, once they come face to face with the fact that God is serious about transforming them. A lot of us start off very ambitiously and say, "Alright, I am going to walk on water because the Lord has commanded me to step out in faith." We look at Peter and say, "My, oh my, Peter, you don't have much faith." However, like Peter, we take two steps, begin to look at the waves of the water, see how big they are and down we go. I think it is a marvellous thing that Peter got out of the boat and walked on the water at all. How many of us would have gotten out of the boat and walked on the water?

A child doesn't learn how to walk without falling down. A child who has fallen down needs encouragement, support and help. With that, he can get back on his feet and, with exercise, eventually become stronger since his faculties have been trained by practice.

We understand that in the natural, but we have much more trouble understanding this process in the spiritual. One of the reasons the spiritual aspect is hard to grasp is that in a lot of evangelical theology there is the ideal that God will just snap His fingers and change your life in an instant. Often you hear testimonies to that effect. I believe in the miraculous. I believe there are times when God, in His sovereign wisdom, barges into someone's life and causes sudden transformation that produces a profound and lasting difference.

On the other hand, I also know that for every instantaneous transformation and change, there are scores of individuals who have to walk it out, line by line, step by step, arduous discipline by arduous discipline.

Do you know why that is? Character is built through step-by-step transformation. When Jesus calls us to follow Him and pick up our cross, He doesn't just mean for us to pick up our cross one time and that is all there is to it; from there on in it will be easy sailing. Not at all! He says you take up your cross *daily* and follow Me.

Do you know the difference between a person whose life really changes and a person who just sort of plays the game? The person whose life really changes is a person who has learned, step-by-step, to try to walk in faith and in obedience. He is a person who has learned that when he fails, he is to get on his knees, repent of his sin and plead the blood of Jesus. He receives forgiveness, gets back up and continues walking in the confidence that, as he walks in faith, our Lord will give him the strength and help he needs.

Please take a look at *Figure 14.1.*[1] The two circles are a diagrammatic presentation of this choice-making process. Notice that the core issue is "Loss – Real or Threatened." This represents a pain or woundedness we have experienced in life.

For example, a person says, "As a little kid, I was laughed at when I tried to talk because I couldn't talk correctly. I made a vow way back then that the ensuing hurt was more than I could bear, and now, no one is going to make fun of me again. I have learned to shut down my feelings." He now becomes very wounded by that, and woundedness will be followed by some measure of anger.

The Victim/Martyr Cycle

At this point, he can choose to go one of two ways, as demonstrated in *Figure 14.1.* He can continue to live in

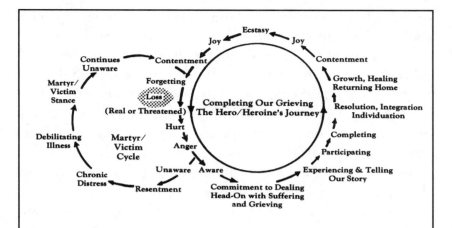

Martyr/Victim Cycle	Hero/Heroine's Journey
False self	True Self
Self-contraction	Self-expansion
There and then	Here and now
Unfinished business	Finished and finishing business
Few personal rights	Many personal rights
Stagnation, regression	Growth
Sharing little	Sharing as appropriate
Same story	Growing story
Repetition compulsion	Telling our story
Impulsive and compulsive	Spontaneous and flowing
Most is unconscious	Much is conscious
Unaware stuckness	Progressively aware becoming and being
Unfocused	Focused
Not working a recovery program	Working a recovery program
Less open to input from others	Open to input from safe others
Varying degrees of "dry drunk"	Working through pain and appreciating joy
Doing it "on my own"	Co-creatorship
Often grandiose	Humble yet confident
Fewer possibilities and choices	More possibilities and choices
Excludes God	Includes God
Illness	Health
Curse	Gift

Figure 14.1
Completing our Grieving

denial. He can continue walking in what a Christian would call unbelief and say, "No one is going to get at the core of what lives inside me. I am going to shut down the door and no one is going to get inside." As a result of this choice, he begins moving in the victim/martyr cycle (left circle).

He remains unaware of his anger and it turns into resentment which becomes a chronic distress which leads to debilitating illness. That in turn produces what is called the martyr or victim stance. You will see in the diagram how one leads to the other.

For example, if I want to speak my opinion, but am afraid to do so because you are going to jump on me, then I don't practice my ability to speak up. If I don't practice my ability to speak up, then I don't learn how to express myself very well. As a result, chances are good that when I grow up I will have difficulty expressing myself because I never learned to do so in a safe environment. It has been too risky.

In the list accompanying the diagram, you will see some of the things that can result. Your self contracts. You live in the past, you go over and over the things that happened years ago. You learn to share very little of your own person and you become impulsive and compulsive. Most of these thoughts are subconscious; you don't know they are there. What makes it even worse is that you don't know you are stuck in this rut. You have no focus to your life.

It can appear in the attitude of, "I can do it on my own; no one is ever going to help me out." Or it may surface in grandiose ideas that are way beyond one's capability, that can never be pursued and that are unrealistic goals. Unrealistic goals unfulfilled end up filling one with further feelings of defeat and discouragement, and with fewer possibilities and choices. They exclude God and bring on illness or curses. This is the person whose life shrivels up in those areas of woundedness. Those are choices of unbelief in a Christian. They say, "I don't want to face the pain. I don't believe God will be with me in the middle of this; I will just settle for what I have." I suspect there are degrees of that in all of us.

The Hero/Heroine's Journey

We do have another option, however. That option is called faith. We can choose to face our fear, hurt and woundedness head on in the confidence that in Christ we can overcome and become stronger, better people on account of the pain we have experienced. The circle on the right in *Figure 14.1* – the Hero/Heroine's Journey – shows exactly what this involves.

You begin to discover who you really are. You no longer have to bury your own feelings or thoughts because you no longer fear being socially unacceptable if you live them out. You can start living in the present. You finish the business of the past and are then able to live in today. You learn to share when appropriate, and to give of yourself as much as you think is safe. Life becomes spontaneous, it bubbles forth from within you. The giftedness God has given you in Christ is released to flow as a blessing to others. You don't have to sit down all the time, try to figure it all out, and be frightened that you are going to do it wrong. Life just happens intuitively according to your gifting. You become more focused; humble, yet confident – that curious paradox we find so clearly in Jesus. He was the most humble of all people who ever lived and yet, He was not wishy-washy in terms of self-identity. Your life starts to bear fruit as you become more and more who you have been made to be in Christ.

You will find, for example, that you go through a season where God tells you He wants you to learn to open up to some significant person in your life. When God comes to you with that idea, everything inside you will try to shut it out, because it is too close to home. The Holy Spirit will keep hounding you everywhere you go, and every sermon you hear, every book you read has your name all through it. You know

God is talking to you. At last, you become so miserable you finally let go and surrender to God. When you do, you discover He's been there all along and that He catches you. The mountain you feared the most turns out to be nothing more than a molehill. Ever notice that? What looks like a tremendous obstacle long before you ever get to it and fills you with fear and trepidation, dissolves before your very eyes when God gives you the faith and courage to face it head on.

Hannah Hurnard

Hannah Hurnard, author of the best-selling *Hind's Feet on High Places*, in her autobiography *Hearing Heart*, tells the story of her call to be an evangelist. Already early in life, she had a desperate longing to know God in an intimate way. Unfortunately, try as she might, God would not reveal Himself to her. The reason for that, she would eventually discover was a deep-seated fear of what surrender to God would mean. Intuitively, she realized that would mean yielding her handicaps to Him.

All through her life she had been plagued by two debilitating problems: 1) a serious speech impediment that made her stammer severely, particularly when she was tense; 2) fears of all kinds, particularly the fear of crowds. Surrendering these to the Lord and trusting Him with them seemed an insurmountable task to her. And so for years, she sought the Lord, but nothing happened until, in desperation, she faced her own personal Calvary. Here is how she tells her story:

> *Here it was. The place of terror and dread. The place of sacrifice. The place where I must yield myself utterly to One who would, somehow, in some agonizing way, put me to the horror of crucifixion. And the thought came to me vividly and clearly, in a dreadful flash of mental enlightenment, "What this unknown God is going to demand before he makes himself real, is that I yield to him my stammering tongue, and agree to be his witness and messenger."*

I can only say that that was the thought that came to me with terrible torturing clarity. All the time then this was why he had never made himself real. He was waiting until I would agree to give him my stammering tongue and tell him that he could use it in any way that he chose.

In imagination I saw myself opening and shutting my mouth in a crowded hall with a sea of embarrassed faces before me, unable to utter a single word. And I cried out in almost frenzied dismay, "No, I can't do that. I would rather go straight to hell. If I can't know God any other way, I won't know him at all." And then the dreadful realization swept over me, "But it's as though I am in hell already. Oh, I need him. I need him. No one else can help me."

It looked utterly impossible. I did not believe that I could yield. It was dreadful to say that deliverance was free and all of grace, and then to demand such a price as this. He was still so utterly unreal. I could feel nothing but agony and despair.

How he managed it I still cannot understand, but at last there came a moment when I cried out again, "O God, if there is a God, if you will make yourself real to me, I will yield my stammering mouth."

...And at that moment I became as sure that he stood there beside me as if I had seen him with my eyes. I felt nothing. I saw nothing. But into my lonely, dark, tormented heart, there flooded like a burst of sunlight the realization which has never left me all these twenty-six years. Jesus is real. He is here. He loves me, even me. After all, he loves me, and has come to tell me that he wants me, that he will use me, even with my stammering....

Life was utterly different and radiant from that hour. I do not mean that my whole nature was changed and self-absorption went. The new spiritual life of Christ develops slowly and only gradually changes the old temperament and character. Outwardly everything was exactly the same....

I was still the old Hannah, but in some miraculous and mysterious way I had been lifted into a completely new mental and spiritual environment, out of the border land of outer darkness, into the light and glory of heaven. It was as

*though a miserable, stunted plant had suddenly been trans-
planted from a tiny flowerpot, into a sunny, richly fertilized
flowerbed. I was lifted out of the dreadful isolation of self-
imprisonment and set down in the love of God.* [2]

As Hannah faced her fears and stepped out in faith and
obedience, God met her in a marvellous way, helped her con-
quer her disabilities and she went on to become an extremely
fruitful evangelist whose speaking and writing ministry has
touched thousands of lives for God. But it didn't happen until
she stepped out in faith.

There lies the key for all of us. As we step out in obedience, confident that God is there and will equip us, we discover that far from losing our life, we gain it. Skills and abilities we didn't know we had are released to bear fruit for God.

NOTES

1. Charles I. Whitfield, *Healing the Child Within* (Deerfield Beach,
FL: Health Communications, Inc., 1987. Used by permission) pp. 98,
111-112.

2. From *Hearing Heart* by Hannah Hurnard, © 1978 by The Church's
Ministry Among the Jews (Used by permission of Tyndale House
Publishers, Inc., Wheaton, IL. All rights reserved) pp. 24-27.

15 | Core Issue 4: Shame-Based Addiction

God is faithful; He will not let you be
tempted beyond what you can bear.
1 Corinthians 10:13

S cott was your classic addict. Born into a family where both parents were alcoholics, he himself started drinking at the age of 13. As time went on, he graduated to drugs, including cocaine, until at last his whole life revolved around his addiction.

Curiously enough, somewhere along the line he gave his life to Christ. For a while, it seemed he had turned a corner and that his life was getting on track. Each time, however, he fell back until at last his addiction threatened to destroy both his own life and that of his family.

For those of us who worked with Scott during those years, there often rose the question: "If Jesus has really come to deliver those who call on Him, why is it so hard for Scott to permanently break with his addiction? Why is it so hard for him to really change? Why do our prayers for him so often seem to go unanswered?" In this chapter, these are some of the questions I want to try to answer.

As we worked with Scott and other addicts, we soon found that any kind of addictive or compulsive behaviour is part of a very complex system or cycle of behaviour patterns. All of these need to be addressed in proper sequence if our compulsive behaviour is to be broken. Otherwise, we are only cutting off the limbs of the tree, leaving the root system intact. As a result, the addiction will continue to spring up and bear bad fruit.

THE CYCLE OF ADDICTION

Figure 15.1 describes the cycle of addiction.[1]

Note, first of all, that the compulsion of addictive behaviour is customarily rooted in *shame*, which is the *central issue*.

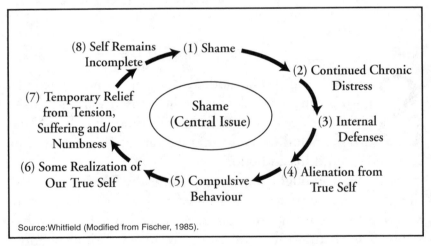

Source:Whitfield (Modified from Fischer, 1985).

Figure 15.1
The Cycle of Addiction

Understanding Shame

I used to think that *guilt* and *shame* were the same thing. I still think there is some overlap between the two. But I have come to understand that there is a substantial difference between guilt and shame. *Guilt* is feeling bad because of what you have *done*. You steal your mother's cookie, your conscience convicts you and you feel bad because you have done something against your moral standards.

Shame, on the other hand, is feeling bad because *you* are wrong. It is much deeper than guilt and much more controlling in our lives. Shame, as a rule, is characterized by the following elements:

I feel fundamentally defective

I not only feel bad because of what I have done, but I feel bad about who I am. I have a conviction that somehow or another, I am a misfit, a bad person, a dirty person. There is something about who I am fundamentally, at the core of my being, that is not acceptable to other people. What makes this so devastating is that there is absolutely nothing I can do to change who I am. So a person who is filled with shame ends up hiding from the pain of the shame. He can't afford to look at himself any more than Adam and Eve could. Their urgent need was to cover themselves with fig leaves.

I feel that people see right through me

Ever have that? You feel insecure, you think there is something wrong with you, and when you meet people, it is very hard to look them in the eye. When you do, you feel they can see right through you and know that you are a bad person. They are not going to want you. They are going to judge and ridicule you. They are going to give you a hard time. So you feel naked, just like Adam and Eve when they first sinned. What was their very first reaction after they ate the forbidden fruit? They discovered they were naked. That's how it is with us. We feel naked. We feel that everyone can see all our faults and that fills us with unspeakable shame.

I cannot talk about my shame

Shame binds. That is to say, it overwhelms me, overtakes me and shuts me up. Here's how it works: I am deeply ashamed of who I am; I feel dumb, I feel stupid, I feel bad, I feel wrong; I see things in me I don't like; I don't want anybody else to discover these things and therefore I can't afford to start talking about them, because that will expose them. I can't even begin to think about them because, when I do, I am just overwhelmed with a sense of shame and condemnation. The irony is that somebody else might not think it is a big deal at all. But it is so close to my heart and it is so painful that I cannot put it into words and so I am going to stuff it down inside me as deeply as I can.

Good Shame versus Bad Shame

It is important to understand that there is good shame as well as bad shame. *Good shame* is an honest recognition that we live in a fallen world and share a fallen human nature. That is to say, we are all sinners in need of God's forgiveness and healing. Good shame, therefore, helps us to realistically face our shortcomings and it drives us to God.

Bad shame, on the other hand, is a false shame. It is feeling bad about who I am when there is nothing wrong with who I am. It commonly occurs in dysfunctional families when authority figures shame some aspect of their children's character which, from God's point of view, is perfectly natural.

Let me illustrate: Let's suppose that as a child, you are emotionally sensitive. You get hurt or find yourself in a situation where you cannot cope and you want to cry. That is a perfectly natural reaction. But now, let's suppose your parents can't handle your crying. They make fun of you. "Big boys don't cry. If you don't quit crying, I'll give you something to cry about." What happens is they *shame* your crying. They condemn something in you that is perfectly natural and normal. In so doing, they are not allowing you to be your real self. As a result, you are likely to clam up and start pretending things are alright, when in fact they are not. That is false shame and it is much more prevalent than we sometimes

Negative Rules	Negative Messages
Don't express your feelings	Shame on you
Don't get angry	You're not good enough
Don't get upset	I wish I'd never had you
Don't cry	Your needs are not all right with me
Do as I say, not as I do	Hurry up and grow up
Be good, "nice," perfect	Be dependent
Avoid conflict (or avoid dealing with conflict)	Be a man
	Big boys don't cry
Don't think or talk; just follow directions	Act like a nice girl (or a lady)
	You don't feel that way
Do well in school	Don't be like that
Don't ask questions	You're so stupid (or bad, etc.)
Don't betray the family	You caused it
Don't discuss the family with outsiders; keep the family secret	You owe it to us
	Of course we love you!
Be seen and not heard!	I'm sacrificing myself for you
No back talk	How can you do this to me?
Don't contradict me	We won't love you if you...
Always look good	You're driving me crazy!
I'm always right; You're always wrong	You'll never accomplish anything
	It didn't really hurt
Always be in control	You're so selfish
Focus on the alcoholic's drinking (or troubled person's behaviour)	You'll be the death of me yet
	That's not true
Drinking (or other troubled behaviour) is not the cause of our problems	I promise (though breaks it)
	You make me sick!
	You're so stupid
Always maintain the status quo	We wanted a boy/girl
Everyone in the family must be an enabler	You _____

Source: Whitfield. Used with permission.

Figure 15.2
Conditions Encouraging Shame

think. (See *Figure 15.2* for a list of common conditions that encourage shame). [3]

That's what happened to Scott. He was born with a tender heart and sensitive emotions. Because his parents couldn't handle their own emotions, they couldn't handle his either. As a result, his emotions were constantly being shamed. "Real men don't cry. Real men never admit to being weak. Quit snivelling and grow up." These were some of the watchwords from his early youth. As a result, he felt terribly inadequate and totally deficient.

What happens when you feel that way? What happens when you feel that you are not as smart, clever or pretty as anybody else? That you are bad to the core and always wrong? It produces *continued chronic distress (Step 2, Figure 15.1)*.

Chronic distress means feeling bad all the time. Nobody can live very long in a world that tells him constantly that, fundamentally, he is wrong or has no right to exist. Every way he turns, he is confronted by his clumsiness, ineptness and stupidity. All the way through life he wonders, "What in the world is the matter with me? Nobody wants to play with me in the school yard, nobody wants to have me over for coffee. I want to be friends with everybody, but nobody wants to be friends with me."

This produces an incredible sense of distress within our lives, and we become tense, unhappy and incomplete. Everywhere we go, there is this message that we are inadequate, no good and don't measure up. We feel alone with no place to go with this distorted message. "No one will listen to me, no one will understand me. I am just stupid."

What do you do when you feel that way about yourself? We all feel that way occasionally, but an addict feels that way all the time. They just don't feel they have the capacity or the freedom to be themselves. So, they build up *internal defense mechanisms (Step 3)*. Nobody can live in a world of pain all the time and go through life being ripped apart with the feeling, "I am no good and I don't belong anywhere." So, we build walls around our hearts to protect and defend our own inner selves. As we saw in Chapter 6, these are called *coping mechanisms*. Their function is to keep us from looking at the shame of who we really are and what, fundamentally, we really don't like about ourselves.

For Scott, this took the form of becoming a hyperactive daredevil. The more he hurt on the inside, the more he tried to cover that hurt with outrageous behaviour.

Walking Alongside Yourself

The problem with living that way is that we become something other than what we really are. We take on an acquired personality. We become *alienated from our true self* (*Step 4*). Leanne Payne calls it "walking alongside yourself." [3]

Let me illustrate:

Suppose you are a very gifted and artistic child. You are creative, you love to draw and perhaps even write music. You live, however, in a family where the arts are viewed as unproductive and a waste of time, where being artistic is not a quality that is honoured, but rather one that is scorned. If you are a boy, you are "too much like a girl." Perish the thought!

So, because you want to be loved by your family and don't want to be shamed, you now hide behind your internal defense mechanisms and suppress your artistic ability. You become what your mother or father is calling you to be. If you do that from an early age and continue long enough into life, you build up a completely false personality that is far removed from who you really are. You begin living up to other people's expectations and try to be someone you are not.

Or, let's suppose you are born a boy and your parents were really looking for a girl. They can't really change your sex, of course, but they can pretend you are a girl. And so they dress you like a girl. They treat you like a girl. They encourage feminine qualities in you. Sometimes this is done in very subtle ways.

I have a good friend who was born into a very dysfunctional family where, as he grew up, his mother repeatedly told him not to be dirty-minded like his father. What had happened was that shortly after she got married to her husband, she discovered that he was seriously dysfunctional sexually. This filled her with disgust and she wanted to make sure her son didn't grow up to be like him. So, quite unconsciously I'm sure, she shamed his masculinity. "Don't be like your father."

Now put yourself in that boy's shoes. Here you are, a boy. Someone ought to be affirming you in your manhood, telling you what a wonderful gift your masculinity is. Instead you are constantly receiving ambivalent messages. "Yes, you are a boy but you better make sure you don't act like one!" Is it any wonder that when this boy grew up, he went through a major identity crisis, wondering by times whether or not he was homosexual. This is alienation from one's true self.

Instead of becoming who you are really intended to be, you start playing a role, so you will be accepted by other people. Some people are so good at role-playing that it becomes more than second nature. It becomes who they are, who people think they are, because the mask is in place so completely.

What happens when you get alienated from who you really are? You live an artificial life. And this leads to *compulsive behaviour (Step 5)*.

If you are free to be yourself, then life should flow naturally. Your gifts and abilities will grow and develop until you become all that you are meant to be. It is not that life will be without difficulties, but there will be a natural fruit bearing. You may not have all the talents everybody else has, but you will be good at some things. This will give you a sense of affirmation and usefulness.

However, when you are "walking alongside yourself" and you develop an artificial identity, your fountain stops flowing. Life becomes very difficult and laborious. This is true for two reasons:

1) It takes a lot of energy to suppress your true self. Deep down, under all these layers, you are who you are, and the real you wants to bubble up. In the example above where the young man grew up hating his manhood and acquiring feminine characteristics, it took a lot of energy to repress his masculinity that really wanted to come forth. He had to keep pushing his real self down all the time.

2) It takes a lot of energy to sustain the mask. You are always afraid of being found out. You are afraid people will find out that you are not really what you pretend to be. I often say that the problem with wearing fig leaves is that they keep withering! You constantly have to keep replacing them. You always live in fear that somebody is going to peek behind your leaves and discover how naked you really are.

This takes a lot of energy. And so, eventually, people get exhausted. Their energy level is no longer strong enough to fight these inner battles. They start to crash. This, in turn, opens the door for addictive or *compulsive behaviour*.

Addictive behaviour takes hold when your true self wants to come up for a breath of fresh air to feel alive, to be real, to be recognized. A classic case is the weekend alcoholic. He works hard all week, is an asset to the company and a good provider for his family. But on Friday night, he comes home with a couple cases of beer and he spends the weekend vegetating and guzzling down the beer, much to the pain of the rest of his family.

Why does he do that? He may do it for a variety of reasons, but I can guarantee that one of the reasons he does it is to unwind. Why does he want to unwind? Very likely, because there is a big sense of inadequacy in his life which he has never faced. When he is at work all week long, he has to pour energy into producing for his employer and covering up his inadequacies. By Friday night, he has just about had it and feels he can go no further. He says, "Over the weekend I am going to be who I really want to be. Nobody is going to boss me around and tell me what to do; I am just going to feed the needs of my life." And he gets drunk as a skunk. That is addiction.

What happens when you try to cover your inadequacy with some form of compulsive behaviour? You get *some realization of your true self (Step 6)*. That is to say, for the moment you feel alive. Your true self is able to assert itself. Witness for example the alcoholic who is normally very shy and insecure.

He starts to drink and suddenly isn't afraid to say anything. What is happening? He is merely expressing what otherwise he was afraid to say.

That is why Scott turned to alcohol. He has told me that the first time he drank at age 13, he knew this was going to be a way of life for him. Why? Because for the first time in his life he wasn't afraid to be himself. He felt like a man who wasn't afraid to speak his mind. He didn't have to be afraid of anybody.

That is why so many people engage in compulsive and addictive behaviours. For the moment, they feel alive. They feel like they are the person they are meant to be.

I might add, this is also why some people have extra-marital affairs, particularly as they age and become increasingly concerned about their inadequacies. It makes them feel good again. It makes them feel alive – they are in love.

The problem is these feelings don't last. The relief produced by an addiction never lasts and there are two reasons for that:

First, it doesn't deal with the root cause – shame. If inadequacy is the reason I drink, then when I am sobered up again, I am still going to feel inadequate. Drinking has not increased my ability one iota. It may help me forget my inadequacies for a while and *give me some temporary relief* (*Step 7*), but it does not change who I really am. In other words, my *self remains incomplete* (*Step 8*).

As somebody has said, "You start drinking and get drunk because you are two weeks behind on the rent. You stay on a drunken binge for two weeks, then you sober up. Now you are four weeks behind on the rent and nothing has changed except that now you are worse off."

Second, and it is important to understand this, our addictive and compulsive behaviours are almost always destructive. Sometimes they are destructive only to ourselves, even if we don't realize this immediately. Almost certainly our addictions are destructive to other people. The person who spends the weekend drunk does incredible damage to his family and his family relationships. The person who has an affair hurts his relationships, as well as his own body and soul. And that is true for every other kind of addiction.

For example, Scott's addictions did incalculable damage to both himself and his family. He lost his health. He almost killed himself twice. He tyrannized his wife and kids. He ran up bills into the tens of thousands of dollars. Only the grace of God pulled him through.

Each time he sobered up, he would, of course, be overwhelmed by grief and shame. That is typical of all of us. We know intuitively that we have been made to have dominion over the earth and control over our own bodies. When we are swept along by the tide of addiction and we hurt people all around us, it just makes us feel more stupid and more inadequate, particularly if we get found out and somebody rubs our noses in it. So now the addict feels even worse than before. His shame is bigger than when he first started. And the cycle repeats itself all over again, and keeps on repeating, faster and faster, until, apart from God's grace, something blows. And something will blow, because that is the nature of addiction.

What is important to understand is that you can pray all you want in the middle of that addiction, but if you aren't brought face to face with the shame that underlies the addiction and made to deal with it, the chances of being delivered from your addiction are next to nothing.

That is why Scott's initial religious experience didn't "take." He wasn't desperate enough yet to tackle the underlying issue of shame that coloured his life. He thought if only Christ came into his life, he would be set free, without having to deal with the deep wounds that were part of his life. And so, he would sober up for a little while, but inevitably, he would be drawn back to his addictive behaviour because the underlying issues that led to the addictive behaviour had not been dealt with. Not until he started looking at those did he find significant and lasting freedom from his addictions.

BREAKING OUT OF THE CYCLE

How then does one break out of this cycle of addiction? Here are some suggestions:

Join a Recovery Group

Very few people are able to break out of the addictive cycle by themselves. The habits are simply too deeply ingrained, the shame too deep. It was that realization that led a well-known surgeon and a New York broker, both severe alcoholics, to establish the first Alcoholics Anonymous chapter in Akron, Ohio in l935. By 1939, the 12 Steps as we know them today were codified in the book *Alcoholics Anonymous,* and the movement was off and running. Since that time, literally hundreds of thousands of people have received the necessary help to gain and maintain sobriety. Scores of alternative 12 Step Programs have been devised in the meantime to help people recover from virtually any addiction or compulsion. Though many are secular in orientation, there are many Christian 12 Step Programs as well. [4]

It wasn't until Scott finally entered a Christian Rehabilitation Program that he was able to come to grips with his addictive behaviour and the roots that fed it.

Deal With the Shame

Remember, there are two kinds of shame – real shame (who we truly are before the face of God) and false shame (that which others have placed on us). In either case, the shame has to be resolved. For shame to be resolved, we have to look at it and stare our biggest fear directly in the face.

This is very difficult because everything in us would rather deny our pain than face it. We don't want to admit what we are really like. We don't want to admit how we really feel. As a matter of fact, chances are we don't even know how we really feel. This is particularly true if we have been raised in a very repressive, legalistic environment where we were not allowed to be our true self. You think, "Real people don't have these kinds of feelings; therefore, if I have these kinds of feelings, I have to deny them, because if I don't, then I am a really bad person and have no chance at all of going to heaven. God will never love me; the church will never accept me."

That is why many people can't afford to look at themselves and why they run when the Holy Spirit begins to tug at their fig leaves. They don't want to be found naked. But the answer to not wanting to be found naked does not lie in denying our true condition. Rather, we need to face it squarely and then give it to Jesus. Jesus, when He hung on the cross, bore all our shame. When, by faith, we turn to Him and admit our true condition, He takes our shame and our paltry attempts at covering up and He clothes us with His righteousness. He changes us from the inside out and makes us the people we are intended to be. Then we don't need to resort to addictive or compulsive behaviours because we are living out of our true self instead of a false self.

For Scott, this was extremely painful. To discover and admit how badly hurt he had been as a child, how he really felt about some of the things his parents and other relatives had said and done, was almost more than he could take. And for the first several weeks of his recovery, he wept many a bitter tear, wondering by times whether he could survive the emotional pain. Even now, he has a difficult time talking about some of it. But he has made a significant start.

Identify the Addiction Trigger Points

Every addictive and compulsive habit starts under a certain set of conditions and circumstances. Even the sickest drunk in the world isn't drunk all the time. He sobers up at least long enough to get more alcohol to get completely drunk again. And this is true for most of our addictions. They go through a cycle. We say it is never going to happen again, but it does happen again.

Part of growing in Christ is understanding, with the help of the Holy Spirit, why it is we do what we do, and learning how to break out of the cycle in which we live. My experience is that one of the first ways in which that help manifests itself is by the gift of grace that enables us to get up after we have fallen.

For instance, we have just resolved to never do what we have been doing again, and what do we do? We do it! Remember the feeling? "Oh, God, I have done it again. I am no good, I am rotten, useless. It is never going to change!" We just bury our heads in shame and pain, and are down and out for a long period of time.

Finally, someone comes along and preaches the grace of God to us, and we receive forgiveness. We get back on our feet and are walking again. Then, before we know it, we get walloped again and are down once more. But now, instead of four weeks we are only down three weeks. And the next time it is two weeks. And then one week, until it is only a day. And, pretty soon, we pick ourselves up, dust ourselves off and say, "Well, God, here I am again. I thank You that You are big enough to handle this." We don't make excuses for our sin. Rather, we start catching the cycle quicker and quicker and, at the same time, God is teaching us what is at the root of the problem.

Now, instead of just walking into the problem and falling flat on our faces each time, we begin to understand that if we go out into that kind of situation, we are going to get into trouble. Because we don't want to get into trouble, we want to stay away from that kind of situation. If our drinking friends get us into trouble, then we will not go out with our drinking friends any more. Instead of thinking we are strong enough to sit there and drink pop while they sit there and drink beer, we discover that if we are pestered a little bit, along we go with the crowd and down we go for the fall. So, we become wiser.

I think that is what Paul is talking about. *No temptation has seized you except what is common to man. And God is faithful; He will not let you be tempted beyond what you can bear. But when you are tempted, He will also provide a way out so that you can stand up under it* (1 Cor. 10:13).

Sometimes when we are confronted with temptation, it is the better part of wisdom to turn tail and run. There is nothing spiritual about standing firm and thinking we can fight if we are going to be overtaken. *Flee from all this, and pursue righteousness, godliness, faith, love, endurance and gentleness* (1 Tim. 6:11).

Rebuild a True Sense of Identity

If one has been a false person all of his life and then comes to the Lord in repentance and faith, his true self will begin to emerge. Gifts and abilities that have been repressed and not allowed to be exercised all of a sudden start to surface. People who didn't think they could express themselves are now able to express themselves very well with little exercise or practice. People who never thought they had feelings begin to feel a whole host of emotions that they never knew existed.

All this can scare them witless for a time. But soon, they start experiencing not only the bad feelings, but the good feelings, as well. Now when you meet them, you meet real people, not plastic saints. You can connect emotionally with them.

As we step out in obedience and faith to what the Holy Spirit is calling us to be, we discover the irony of the gospel that, as we lay down our life for Jesus, we will find it. We become stronger, our gifts and abilities emerge and develop, we no longer need other people to give us artificial affirmation, but rather, we begin to receive true affirmation from God and others. There is something inside that says, "I am a real person because God really loves me, and God's grace is at work in my life. I am a useful individual, increasingly able to do the kind of things that God is calling me to do." This is the hope and message of the gospel.

Autobiography in Five Short Chapters

1) *I walk, down the street.*
   There is a deep hole in the sidewalk.
   I fall in.
   I am lost... I am hopeless.
   It isn't my fault.
   It takes forever to find a way out.

2) *I walk down the same street.*
   There is a deep hole in the sidewalk.
   I pretend I don't see it.
   I fall in again.
   I can't believe I am in the same place.
   But it isn't my fault.
   It still takes a long time to get out.

3) *I walk down the same street.*
   There is a deep hole in the sidewalk.
   I see it is there.
   I still fall in... it's a habit.
   My eyes are open
   I know where I am.
   *It is **my** fault.*
   I get out immediately.

4) *I walk down the same street.*
   There is a deep hole in the sidewalk.
   I walk around it.

5) *I walk down another street.* [5]

NOTES

1. B. Fischer, "Cycle of Shame and Compulsive Behaviour," Workshop on Shame (Baltimore, MD: The Resource Group, 1995). [Taken from Charles I. Whitfield, *Healing the Child Within* (Deerfield Beach, FL: Health Communications, Inc., 1987) p. 50]

2. Whitfield, p. 47. (Used by permission).

3. Leanne Payne, *The Healing Presence* (Wheaton, IL: Crossway Books, 1989) p. 62.

4. Following are two programs we recommend:

a) *The Twelve Steps – A Spiritual Journey: A Working Guide for Adult Children from Addictive and Other Dysfunctional Families* (San Diego, CA: Recovery Publications, 1988). (Based on Biblical teachings and available from Recovery Publications, 1201 Knoxville Street, San Diego, CA 92110).

b) John Baker, *Celebrate Recovery: How to Start a Christ-Centered 12 Step Recovery Ministry and Keep it Growing* (Lake Forest, CA: Celebrate Recovery Books, 1996). (Available from Celebrate Recovery Books, 25422 Trabuco Rd. #105-151, Lake Forest, CA 92630-2797).

5. Portia Nelson, *Autobiography in Five Short Chapters*, in Nelson, P.: *There's a Hole in My Sidewalk*, Popular Library, New York, 1977. (As quoted in Charles I. Whitfield, *Healing the Child Within*, p. 125).

16 | Getting It All Together

I have come that they may have life,
and have it to the full.
John 10:10

God is in the business of taking broken and wound-ed people and putting them back together again. He wants to present us before all the nations as His workmanship so everyone can marvel at His wisdom and love. With that in mind, let's look a little more closely in this chapter at what we can reasonably expect to happen as we come into wholeness.

We Are Set Free to Experience the Presence of God

In John 14:21, Jesus said, *"Whoever has my commands and obeys them, he is the one who loves me. He who loves me will be loved by my Father, and I too will love him and show myself to him."* When Judas asked Jesus, *"Why do You intend to show Yourself to us and not to the world?"* Jesus replied, *"If anyone loves me, he will obey my teaching. My Father will love him, and we will come to him and make our home with him"* (John 14:22-23).

All through the Scriptures, God expresses His desire to make His home with His people. You see it in the story of Adam and Eve in the Garden when they walk in fellowship with God, much as we do with one another. You see it in the life of Jesus when He walks so in tune with God the Father that His very thoughts, words and actions are the expression of His Father.

It is that fellowship, that sense of closeness to which the Lord wants to restore us through faith in the Lord Jesus Christ. When we repent of our sin and allow the Lord to search out the rebellious areas of our hearts, we are restored to fellowship with God the Father. We become His children. John 1:12 says, *Yet to all who received Him, to those who believed in His name, He gave the right to become children of God.* When we become His children, He gives us His Holy Spirit; and through the Holy Spirit, He makes Himself real to us and starts to work out the healing that is needed in our lives.

I believe that to be the key to understanding some of the manifestations that accompany revivals historically. All over the world and throughout history, when the Spirit of God is being poured out, very unusual things happen. People fall down on the ground, their bodies jerk, they make strange noises or utter ecstatic cries. The human intellect looks at some of those things and says, "I wonder what the purpose of all this is?" And the tendency is to write them off as weird, maybe even demonic.

That, of course, is always a possibility. Scripture commands us to test the spirits to see if they are from God. But there are many things in the spiritual realm that we don't understand. One reason for at least some of these strange manifestations is that God is working out His purposes in that person's life in an accelerated fashion.

Just recently, I heard the story of a man who went down under the power of God at a meeting like this and for the next couple of hours he was banging his head up and down on the floor in a forward and backward motion. Asked about it later, he didn't remember doing that. What he did remember was that in the time he was down on the floor, the Holy Spirit in rapid succession took him through his whole life, pointing out all the people he needed to forgive. Every time the Lord showed him something new, he remembers nodding his head emphatically and saying, "Yes." And so, what looked strange on the outside was God working healing on the inside in a deep and lasting way.

I don't profess to understand all the dynamics that take place when people are overcome by the power of the Holy Spirit and demonstrate strange manifestations. What I do know is this: When a person goes down under the power of the Spirit, and does what is euphemistically called "carpet time," there is an acceleration of healing deep in the inner core of that person's life.

Sometimes repressed emotions and memories are literally being shaken loose. Other times, proud obstacles and arguments against the knowledge of God are being destroyed. Still other times, there is a deep healing and cleansing of the heart and mind.

Everybody is different and God meets everyone in his or her own unique way. Some people show very little manifestation of the presence of God. Others fall over completely and can hardly get up. The purpose of it all, however, is to heal and restore us to useful service in the Kingdom of God. That becomes the litmus test. Does it produce greater love for God and greater love for other people? If it doesn't accomplish that, it is but a *noisy gong or a clanging cymbal* (1 Cor. 13:1, RSV).

It is important to understand this because when it comes to manifestations of God's presence in our lives, there is always a two-fold danger. One, we think other people need to have experiences like ours; if they don't, then they probably are not as spiritual as we are. Two, if we don't have the experiences that other people have, then there must be something wrong with us and we had better start seeking the same spiritual experience.

Both of these are nonsense. Scripture says, *There are different kinds of gifts, but the same Spirit. There are different kinds of service, but the same Lord. There are different kinds of work-ing, but the same God works all of them in all men* (1 Cor. 12:4). Everyone is not going to have the same experience. God is going to manifest Himself in our lives in ways that are unique and different for each individual. In this way, the myriad vari-ety of His character and nature can be demonstrated. What we have to do is make sure that He is free to flow through us in any way that He should choose for the glory of His name.

Personally, I seldom experience the presence of God in spectacular ways. I just quietly know when He is present. Yet I see Him work in me and through me in ways that are just as remarkable as in other people whose experiences are much more dramatic than mine. I wouldn't rule out that more heal-ing is needed in my own life, but I do know that what really counts is a relationship with the Father through faith in Jesus Christ. Once we have that relationship, God will make His presence known to us in His own way and in His own time.

We Are Set Free to be Ourselves

Part of the problem of living in a dysfunctional world which groans under the travail of sin is that often we are *not* free to be ourselves. We feel we have to be what others expect us to be, particularly the important people in our lives.

We are afraid to express our own opinion, because when we do, we lay ourselves open to criticism and rejection and we'd like to avoid that. So we learn to keep quiet and keep our thoughts to ourselves. After all, it is better to be thought of as a fool, than open our mouths and remove all doubt!

We'd love to talk about the deepest fears and secrets of our hearts, but we are afraid to do that. Someone might betray our secret and use it against us. And so we suffer in silence, won-dering if anybody really cares, wondering why, in the midst of the crowd, we feel so lonely. We put our masks firmly in place lest anyone should see what we are really like. Outwardly, we are successful and happy. Inwardly, we are miserable and broken.

We'd love to pursue our dreams and ideals but we are afraid. We are afraid of the risks that might be involved. We are afraid of alienating the people around us because they have already figured out what is good for us, and thus for them. And so, we have settled for what is, rather than what could be. We live out the role that other people unwittingly have come to expect of us, all the while knowing there has to be something more. Some of us become so good at it, it becomes a way of life.

A good friend of mine in college was like that. I suppose in the model of the dysfunctional family, his role was that of the clown. He tells the story of flying back and forth between his home town and the city where we went to college. He was quite a ladies' man and loved flirting with the stewardesses. On one flight, he was carrying his guitar with him. A stewardess asked him who he was, and he spun a marvellous tale about being some famous folk singer. She bought it, hook, line and sinker, and awe was written all over her face.

The next time he flew the same route, he had a different stewardess. This time he happened to be dressed in a suit and was carrying a brief case. So he passed himself off as an advertising executive with a college radio station organization. She was suitably impressed. (He was *very* good!)

Well, as he tells the story, to his great misfortune, the third time he stepped on the plane, both of these stewardesses were on duty together! His masquerading was exposed and he was forced to go back to being just Joe Blow, the college student.

Many of us can identify with that, can't we? We are not free to be our own selves most of the time. We put on the face that we expect people want from us, particularly if we crave their love and affection. The problem is, different people want different things from us. When we try to please them all, we have a hard time figuring out who we are supposed to be. That is particularly true when we meet them all at the same time!

All that changes when we come to know Jesus in a real way. When God becomes our Father in Christ, He accepts us unconditionally the way we are. Imagine – He knows us better than we know ourselves. He knows our sins, our weaknesses and our failures; yet, in Christ, He still loves us. That means we are set free to be who we really are. There is no need to pretend. We don't have to try to be better than we really are, nor do we have to hide our deep, dark secrets from Him. He already knows them all.

Because He loves us perfectly, He has no hidden agenda for our lives. His only plan is to make us everything that, in His love, He has destined us to be. He wants to deliver us from all the distortions and limitations brought on by sin and thus help us truly find ourselves. *For whoever wants to save his life,* said Jesus, *will lose it, but whoever loses his life for me will find it* (Matt. 16:25).

We Are Set Free to Discover Our Gifts

Ephesians 2:8,10 says, *For it is by grace you have been saved, through faith.... For we are God's workmanship, created in Christ Jesus to do good works, which God prepared in advance for us to do.*

One of the drawbacks of living in a broken world, particularly if you were raised in a dysfunctional family, is that your unique gifting is not allowed to come to full expression.

Alexandra's Story

Martha Horton, in her excellent book *Growing up in Adulthood,* tells the story of Alexandra, a stunningly beautiful 32-year-old artist who, in the middle of a highly successful art show, panicked, grabbed her coat and ran home to hide under her comforter with her cat. Though the newspaper review the following day raved about her art, she never went back to that gallery and never again exhibited her art. Instead, she continued her work as a receptionist in an advertising agency, remained in her very small apartment and continued creating good art that she was too afraid to show or sell.

Why the fear? Due to early childhood pain, Alexandra was encased in a shell. Outwardly, she looked mature and competent. Inwardly, she was an emotional mess. She couldn't bear the thought of other people looking at her art and perhaps criticizing it. Nor could she accept her own talents and the attention and possible responsibility that came along with it. So, instead, she chose to hide her true self from the rest of the world. Only within the confines of her own very private world could she afford to be real.[1]

The world is full of people like that. They are stunted in their growth, afraid to move, burying their treasure, unwilling, unable to ever risk taking chances because they might lose even the very little bit of talent that they have.

People like that live by the letter of the law, not its spirit. They are people who are often afraid to try new things. They are frozen deep down on the inside. They feel they have to work twice as hard as everyone else in life to get only half as far.

If they do manage to get anywhere in life, they get there by sheer force and discipline, but it always seems like their fountain doesn't flow, their river isn't moving. Everything they do is such hard work because all their behaviour is learned behaviour. Life doesn't spontaneously well up from deep inside.

When God fills us with His Spirit, He changes all that. He removes what I like to call the stones from the fountain. When He does that, the fountain begins to flow. The gifts and abilities that have been locked up in people's lives are released for the praise of His glory!

I am constantly impressed and amazed at what happens when people truly surrender themselves fully to the Lord Jesus. Gifts and abilities which they never thought they possessed begin to emerge. When they lose the fear and self-consciousness that has held them captive and the Holy Spirit is free to flow, creativity finds a whole new outlet.

Laura is a good example of that. Raised in a very dysfunctional home, she closed off her heart early in life. As a result, her gifts were never able to blossom. Then she met Jesus, who healed her broken heart. As she grew in her relationship with the Lord, one of the first things that started to happen was that her gifts were being released. In our conversations, she soon demonstrated an unusual grasp of biblical truth and a remarkable ability to articulate her faith. I'd get off the phone with her and say to my wife, "Where did she get that insight from? We didn't tell her about that!" And we didn't. It was definitely a gift set free by the Holy Spirit.

We Discover Our Niche in Life

I am convinced, biblically, that there is a particular niche in life for which God has created and redeemed us. I believe that is what Paul means in Ephesians 2:10 when he says that we are *God's workmanship, created in Christ Jesus to do good works, which God prepared in advance for us to do.* I take that to mean that there is a particular slice of life for which God has prepared us. The circumstances of our birth, the family we grow up in, the characteristics we inherit and the events that shape us are all sovereignly arranged by our heavenly Father to equip us for the task we have been destined for in life. Success, in biblical language, is fulfilling the unique destiny for which we were created and redeemed.

Contrary to what many would have us believe, success and fulfillment do not flow from having the biggest company in town or the largest bank account, the best looking spouse or the loveliest children; fulfillment comes from knowing you are fulfilling the destiny for which God has made you. When you do that, the will of God won't lead you where the grace of God won't sustain you. Though the journey might be difficult and there will surely be times of trial and pruning, there is the satisfaction of knowing you have accomplished the purpose for which you have been created and redeemed. To hear God say in that final day, *"Well done, good and faithful servant! You have been faithful with a few things; I will put you in charge of many things"* (Matt. 25:21), will be the most marvellous commendation that any person will ever be able to receive.

As we grow in our walk and relationship with the Lord, then, and our gifts become more clearly defined, so does our niche in life. Knowing what we are or are not good at, and knowing that is God's design for our lives, we don't have to fret about all the things we are not. We can bless God for who we are by His grace, and concentrate on those areas where we feel He places a call on our lives. That makes our lives both more fruitful and more pleasurable. More fruitful, because we can now concentrate on our area of expertise. More pleasurable, because we are doing what we have been called to do, and are thus also equipped to do.

So many people go through life as a round peg trying to fit into a square hole. Out of duty rather than calling, they are trying to be this, that and the other thing. It leaves them frustrated, bored and often overwhelmed. There are few things in life more annoying than being in a job that you're not suited for or engaging in ministry that is beyond your training. Christ redeems all that. In Christ, God brings us into the place in life that He has designed for us.

Now, I don't mean to imply that this is always easy or automatic. Not at all. Quite often it is difficult and fraught with many dangers and challenges. At the same time, as we grow in our relationship with the Lord and learn to step out in obedience and faith, we will discover God has His own providential ways of making His will clear. And in the process of embracing that will, we'll have that sense of God's approval that makes it all so very worthwhile.

Eric Liddell, in the book *Chariots of Fire,* expressed it this way when his sister tried to discourage him from running and persuade him to enter the ministry instead: "When I run I feel [God's] pleasure." [2]

We Leave Behind a Trail of Good Fruit

Jesus put it this way in John 15:8: *"By this my Father is glorified, that you bear much fruit, and so prove to be my disciples"* (RSV). The Book of Proverbs puts it this way, *Misfortune pursues the sinner, but prosperity is the reward of the righteous. A good man leaves an inheritance for his children's children, but a sinner's wealth is stored up for the righteous* (Prov. 13:21-22).

As we have been seeing throughout this book, our actions have consequences, particularly for our children. When we blow it, that impacts our children negatively to the third and fourth generation. Whether we do it on purpose or not makes little difference in terms of final outcome. Whether I fall out of a ten storey window accidentally or jump out on purpose, the net result is likely to be the same. Barring a miracle, I'll go splat on the pavement. That is why Paul says in Galatians 6:7-8, *Do not be deceived: God cannot be mocked. A man reaps what he sows. The one who sows to please his sinful nature, will reap destruction.*

But, there is another side to the story. Paul goes on to say in Galatians 6:8-9, *...the one who sows to please the Spirit, from the Spirit will reap eternal life. Let us not become weary in doing good, for at the proper time we will reap a harvest if we do not give up.* In other words, our actions have consequences, not only negatively, but also positively! That is why it is so critical to not only deal with areas of sin and woundedness in our lives, but to start bearing fruit for God. It is not only ourselves we are concerned with, but also our children and their children after them.

Who of us haven't been blessed by the spiritual inheritance left by a godly parent or even a grandparent? I was deeply moved some time ago as I read the story of how Bill and Gloria Gaither came to own the land on which they now live. As Bill tells the story, when their eye first fell on the land they now own, it belonged to a grouchy old man who had stubbornly refused all previous offers to sell. Bill decided to approach him anyway and sure enough, the answer was the same as always: "No!" Nothing Bill said or did caused the old man to budge even the slightest.

Nothing, that is, until the old man discovered that Bill's grandfather had been an acquaintance of his years earlier. That immediately changed the picture because, apparently, Bill's grandfather had done the old man a good turn years before which he had never forgotten. As a result, the old man relented and eventually sold the property to Bill and Gloria. When he did, here is what he said: "I want you to know I'm not doing this for you. And I'm not doing this for your father. I'm doing it for your grandfather!"

As Bill observes, "I reaped the harvest of seed sown in the ground by my grandfather!"

What a blessing it is to reap a harvest like that. Many of us who read these words have perhaps little or no understanding of the pain that many people live in day after day. We can read all about the dysfunctional family, and intellectually perhaps, we can understand it. Emotionally, it is miles removed from our experience. It seems like another world.

Do you know why that is? Because God in His grace has given us a godly heritage. He's given us parents or grandparents – and sometimes it goes a long way back – who have feared Him and loved Him. Though they weren't perfect by any stretch of the imagination, they walked with God, confessed their sins and received His grace. And we have been the beneficiaries of His mercy. We have been spared many of the pains and ills inflicted on so much of humanity.

That, in turn, ought to make us more determined than ever, to leave a godly inheritance for our children. That will only happen as we learn to come to the cross and receive healing in our own lives and learn to walk in obedience. I believe that is what God is wanting to do in the world today. He wants to break the cycle of dysfunction and replace it with a never-ending cycle of blessing.

NOTES

1. Martha Horton, *Growing Up In Adulthood*, (Tarrytown, NY: Triumph Books, 1992) pp. 1,2.

2. W.J. Weatherby, *Chariots of Fire* (New York: Quicksilver Books/Dell Publishing Co., 1982) p. 87.

PART THREE:

Raising Functional Kids

17 | Dealing With Blind Spots

Take the log out of your own eye, and
then you will see clearly... the speck...
in your brother's eye.
Matthew 7:5

Some years ago, my family and I were driving along Highway 401 in Toronto when we had one of the closest calls we have ever had in an automobile. It was one of the few occasions in recent years when all of our children were in the car with us. We were headed, as I recall, to St. Catharines to celebrate my wife's parents' 50th wedding anniversary.

I was driving, but wasn't really paying as close attention to the traffic as I should have been. All of a sudden, one of the kids from the back yelled, "Dad, watch out!"

I looked up just in time to see a big transport truck cutting rapidly into our lane, without any warning. By the time I saw him, his front wheel was inches from our front fender. I never knew truck wheels were that big! At any moment, I expected to hear the crunch of metal on metal and to lose control.

What do you do in such an instance? Well, you instinctively try to move out of the way and that is what I did.

Unfortunately, when you do that you run the risk of skidding out of control and for a moment it seemed that indeed was going to happen. Providentially, it didn't. I managed to get the car under control and, heaving a sigh of relief and a prayer of thanksgiving, we continued on our journey. The truck driver, in the meantime, appeared totally oblivious to our plight. He plowed straight ahead on his course. Later, as we gave pursuit to report him to his company (which is what we did), we observed him veering from lane to lane trying to pass still more vehicles. Obviously, he was in a desperate hurry to get somewhere.

Afterwards, you reflect on these things, of course. You wonder what all happened, what could have happened and what should have happened differently. As best as I can figure, the driver either was not watching his mirrors to see who was beside him, or else his mirrors were set up in such a way that I was driving in his blind spot.

In this chapter, I want to take a look at blind spots, particularly as it relates to parenting.

PARENTAL BLIND SPOTS

In the preceding chapters, we have examined closely the dysfunctional patterns that God wants to break in our families. Now I want to take this a step further, and in subsequent chapters, we are going to look at some positive steps we can undertake as parents so that, by God's grace, our children can avoid some of the mistakes that we have made and live in families that are increasingly functional.

I want to begin by dealing with blind spots in our own lives as parents.

Jesus talks about blind spots in Matthew 7:3-5 where He says,

"Why do you see the speck that is in your brother's eye, but do not notice the log that is in your own eye? Or how can you say to your brother, 'Let me take the speck out of your eye,' when there is the log in your own eye? You hypocrite,

first take the log out of your own eye, and then you will see clearly to take the speck out of your brother's eye" (RSV).

My experience is that many of God's people misread and misinterpret this passage. A lot of people pick up on the fact that Jesus talks about being a hypocrite, and deduce from this passage that Christians ought never to exercise judgment relative to another person's behaviour. *"Judge not, that you be not judged"* (Matt. 7:1, RSV) is probably one of the best known verses in the Bible. Every pagan in North America seems to know it because when you see them sin and try to correct them, they ask, "Doesn't the Bible say, *'Judge not?'"* From that they conclude it is presumptuous to ever exercise criticism relative to someone's behaviour or lifestyle.

That, of course, is absolute nonsense. If that is what Jesus meant, then He contradicts Himself elsewhere in Scripture because He says in John 7:24, *Do not judge by appearances, but judge with right judgment* (RSV). Jesus never says we shouldn't exercise judgment over against other people. What He says is we had better make sure that the standard of judgment we apply to someone else's life is the same standard of judgment we are also willing to apply to ourselves. That is why He says, *For in the same way you judge others, you will be judged, and with the measure you use, it will be measured to you* (Matt. 7:2).

So what Jesus is addressing in these verses is our common tendency to see the wrong in someone else's life, while overlooking the wrong in our own life. When He says, *"Take the log out of your own eye, and then you will see clearly to take the speck out of your brother's eye,"* (Matt. 7:5) the point He is making is that unless you deal with the unresolved issues of your own life, you are blind to see what is happening in the other person's life; your biases either cause you to underreact or overreact. In other words, a log in your own eye keeps you from seeing the speck in the eye of the other person. It is the unresolved garbage in your own life which keeps you from having a proper perspective about someone else's life, and which prevents you from having the ability to bring about correction in another's life.

For example, suppose I cheat on my taxes, and now I see that you cheat too. How is my cheating at taxes going to affect my behaviour towards you and your behaviour? Well, either I will make excuses for your sin because I am not dealing with my sin; or, if I am under conviction about my sin and don't feel good about it, I will overreact and try to correct you in a harsh and improper fashion because I am speaking out of my own woundedness. That is why, often, the actions we most criticize in other people's lives are a clear indication of what lives in our own life. I must take the log out of my own eye so I can see the speck in my brother's eye.

Now, if that is true about life in general, it is true about raising children in particular. Why do so many parents have so much difficulty raising their children?

Well, there are many reasons, of course, but certainly one of the major reasons is that parents have blind spots in their own lives. Not having removed the logs out of their own eyes, they are incapable of seeing the specks in the eyes of their children. Consequently, as they deal with their children, they are not dealing with what the child's real needs are. Rather, they are dealing out of their own unresolved woundedness. That, in turn, causes woundedness in the children and the dysfunctional pattern continues unabated.

Let me illustrate.

Tug of War

A woman came to see me because of the many problems she was facing in her family. She had a constant tug of war with her adolescent daughter about what the daughter should wear to school. This mother wanted her daughter to dress nicely, so she took her to stores and bought nice clothes for her. The mother thought her daughter would like that. However, the daughter wanted to dress like her friends and so, when mother and daughter got home, the daughter took her nice, new clothes, laid them on the shelf and continued to wear the grubby clothes that were in keeping with what everybody else was wearing. There was this constant tug of war between mother and daughter, to the extent that it really disturbed the peace and tranquillity of the household.

Why the battle? Well, in part because the mother had a log in her eye. She had some unresolved issues from her past that she was bringing into the present. When she was growing up, she hardly ever got new clothes and had to wear the hand-me-downs from her older siblings. She made a vow, saying, "When I grow up and have kids of my own, I am not going to do that to them. I want my kids to look nice and dress well."

The problem was that her daughter was not raised in the same kind of environment as she was. The daughter just wanted to be liked by her friends, so she dressed down to match them. I recall saying to the mother, "Set some minimum standards as to what you and your daughter think is appropriate dress for her on various occasions, and don't sweat the little stuff. Pick your battles carefully. Allow your daughter to be herself." A log keeps you from seeing the speck in the eye of someone else.

Family Chaos

Another example: A man and a woman came to see me a number of years ago. Their family was in chaos, and one of the reasons for the chaos centered around their second youngest girl, who was adopted and of another race.

As she was nearing her teens, this girl was struggling with a lot of the rejection that had been a part of her life. She would not behave and would not listen to her mother or her father. What made matters worse was that the mother was the disciplinarian, and the father would not support the mother in trying to bring about any correction in that girl's life. So, she moved in a swirl and her whole family swirled with her, because she was not subject to any control or discipline. In desperation, they sought counsel and told me their story.

It really didn't take very long to understand that what was happening here was caused by a log in the man's eye. An unresolved issue kept him from seeing truth. He had fought in the war between the Netherlands and Indonesia in the early 1950s. That war, for a lot of people who fought in it, was in some ways far more traumatic than fighting in World War II. World War II was bad and ugly, but at least the Allied forces felt they were on moral high ground. They felt they were fighting against an unjust oppressor for a worthy cause. People who fought in Indonesia have told me time and time again that when they went to fight that war, they thought they were going to fight a just war. But in the end, it turned out to be very much the Netherlands' equivalent of the Vietnam War, because the world's opinion turned against the war and viewed it as a colonization exercise. So the soldiers were left hanging with a war that did not get fuelled by the righteousness of a cause. Add to that the fact that the war was fought on Asiatic soil, and thus included a whole other level of cruelty and heartache, and you get the picture. The psychological pain experienced by many young soldiers caught up in the ugliness of this bush and guerrilla warfare is beyond words to describe.

This father had been one of those soldiers. He remembered one incident when as soldiers they had been badly frightened and just randomly fired their rifles at everything that moved. In so doing, they not only killed enemy soldiers, but many civilians as well. Can you imagine living with that guilt in later years and not knowing where to go with it?

So, he decided one of the ways to relieve his guilt was to adopt a child of another race, and that is how this girl had come to be in this family. But because the girl was an expression of his guilt, he was not able to exercise his responsibility as her father, because that would involve dealing with the stuff in his own life that was still unresolved. So, the log in his own eyes coloured his whole behaviour towards this child and she could do no wrong, to the great dismay of the other children in the family. I told him that unless he dealt with that log and came to grips with unresolved issues in his own life, he would never have peace and tranquillity in his family. He would never know how to treat his adopted daughter in a just and fair manner.

REMOVING THE LOG

I believe that one of the reasons we have so many unmanageable kids in today's culture is because parents have not dealt with the log in their own eyes. Rather, they have read their own hang-ups into the lives of their children. As a result, their children are left without a good, firm sense of guidance, and are confused, bitter and angry. Understand me well. I am not at all trying to pin the blame for all the rebellious children in the world on their fathers and mothers. Kids themselves are responsible for the choices they make. At the same time, we cannot ignore our responsibilities as parents. We need to begin looking closely at ourselves and that is not easily done.

If you have ever tried correcting a parent about the behaviour of his or her child, then you know how difficult it can be. People who are perfectly normal and rational at all other times can become amazingly irritable and resistant when it comes to having their children's faults exposed! That is because our children are an extension of ourselves. All the things in our own lives that we haven't taken to the cross, all the ideals we admire, we also tend to admire in the lives of our children. Or we swing the other way and can't stand them!

For example, people who haven't dealt with immorality from their past, either turn a blind eye to what they see in their children, or overreact and accuse their children of actions they haven't even begun to consider. People who haven't dealt with rebellion in their own lives, when dealing with their child's rebellion, will either underreact or overreact. And you can go on and on, drawing the scenario of how those sins are passed from one generation to another, because parents haven't taken seriously God's instruction to take the log out of their own eye so that they can see clearly to take the speck out of their children's eye.

How can we go about removing the log out of our own eye? Introspection, looking inwardly, does not work. All that does is fill you with doubt and uncertainty, and the Lord knows we don't need more parents in this day and age who are filled with doubt and uncertainty about their parenting skills. How do we then remove this log?

I believe the remedy to removing this log is to abide in close union with the Lord Jesus Christ. The Bible says in Colossians 2:3,10: *In... [Christ]* are hid all the treasures of wisdom and knowledge... you have come to fullness of life in Him *(RSV). Jesus Christ knows all truth and has keen insight into the deepest needs of the human heart and the human experience. When by faith we are joined to Jesus and the power of His Spirit flows through us, He will give us wisdom, insight and the skills we need to be parents who are vehicles of grace in the lives of our children. This allows His love to flow through us and our children, with all our faults and shortcomings, and it allows us to know that biblical balance between justice and mercy.

Abiding in Christ

How do we work out the union we have in Christ? Again, there are many ways to do this. One method I have come to favour is Neil Anderson's *Personal Steps To Freedom in Christ*.[1]

Neil Anderson says the Bible calls us to make the following choices in our lives:

Counterfeit versus Real Spirituality

All of us are inherently spiritual beings. Many times we fail to get through to God because we are not prepared to meet

Him on His terms. Instead, we often turn to pseudo or false spiritual forces, false religions, demon worship, Ouija boards, or even fortune tellers. If you had told me years ago that psychic fairs and hotlines would be big business in the 1990s, I would have said you were out of your mind! But their present popularity reflects the spiritual vacuum in the lives of many people today.

All counterfeit religion needs to be renounced and our allegiance pledged instead to Jesus Christ and to Him alone. We need to say, "Lord Jesus, I have sought to experience life and power through sources outside of Yourself. In so doing, I have sinned. Please forgive me. I renounce all involvement in false religions and occult practices. I want to serve You and You alone. You alone are Lord of my life and to You alone does my heart belong."

Deception versus Truth

Scripture says Satan is a liar and the father of all lies (John 8:44). One of his primary tools for holding people in bondage is making them believe lies about God, about themselves and about their relationship with God. He does that in such a clever fashion that often we don't recognize the lie for what it is. For example, he will whisper in our ear, "Nothing good of lasting significance is ever going to come your way. You're just not worth it. Your mother and father didn't want you. Why should anyone else ever want you?" And then he'll go on and illustrate the truth of that lie from our experience. He'll remind us of all the times it didn't work out in the past. And then he'll say again, "See, what did I tell you? It'll never be any better. God doesn't really care about you and neither does anyone else."

Those lies can be pretty powerful and very convincing, and they need to be renounced. We need to say, "Lord, in Christ, I have become Your child. Your Word says that You love me, and that You make all things work together for my good (Rom. 8:28). I renounce the lie and choose to believe the truth." As we continue to practice that and stand in faith on the Word, the lie loses its power and the truth will set us free. But it is a choice we must make.

We see many times in counselling that one of the most pervasive lies Satan imposes upon people is, "God does not love me. He is not there for me. He is not going to take care of me, so I have to build defenses around my own heart to make sure I don't get hurt." As a result, we resort to denial, fantasy, trusting ourselves instead of trusting Christ, emotional insulation, regression, displacement, projection, rationalization and many other coping mechanisms we have discussed in earlier chapters. All of these things need to be renounced and surrendered to Jesus.

Bitterness versus Forgiveness

Bitterness comes from being wrongly treated and then being unable to let go of the injustice you have experienced. It is the wall you build around yourself to make sure you don't get hurt again. When it comes to bitterness, you have choices to make. As we will see in more detail in Chapter 25, you can hold on to the bitterness and pain and seek to protect yourself, or you can acknowledge it, hand it over to God and ask Him to cleanse your life, remove your sin and give you a heart and attitude that enables you to really live from the core of your being.

That is certainly not easy to do if you have been deeply wounded. I don't at all suggest that you lightly forgive if you have not relived and worked through the pain. But Scripture teaches that, sooner or later, we must forgive. If we do not, Satan retains a foothold in our lives through the judgment we hold against those who hurt us. We all live by the mercy and grace of God, and if God were to impart to any one of us our iniquity and our sin, we would be in major trouble. So, forgiveness becomes a very practical expression of our understanding that God has also forgiven us.

Rebellion versus Submission

Most of us, I'm sure, do not think of ourselves as being rebellious! It is not until our will is crossed that we discover human nature by definition is rebellious. Every one of us wants to be king or queen of his or her own castle. We come by this honestly. It is part of original sin.

When God starts dealing with us, we have to make choices. We need to repent of our rebellion, which means saying, "Lord, I confess my rebellion as sin. Please forgive me. I don't need to be rebellious. I don't need to live out of reaction against authority or the fear I have of being hurt by authority. In Christ, I am Your child. You love me and have promised to protect me. You will give me the skills to know whom I can or cannot trust, how much I can give of myself to whom, and when and how to do it.

"So, Lord, in Jesus Christ I renounce rebellion. I choose to submit to Your authority, and then to the authority You have placed over my life for my protection. I do that, even though I know that authority is not without sin and, left to themselves, might very well lead me astray or cause me pain. I choose to trust You and I give myself into Your hands." This is hard to do, but it is very important that it be worked out.

Pride versus Humility

Pride is known as the deadliest of the proverbial seven deadly sins. Pride is an attitude of heart which says, "I don't need anyone. I don't need God. I can do it myself." Pride surfaces not only in the proverbial snooty nose up in the air, but it also surfaces in much more subtle fashions, such as in the desire to be noticed, to have things our way, to look good or to give a better appearance than what is really true. Pride even surfaces, oddly enough, in the person who has a low self-image, and goes around saying, "I am no good."

Low self-esteem is the reverse side of pride. We only feel badly about ourselves because we are not living up to certain expectations we have for ourselves. That is a form of pride. If you don't believe that, then watch what happens when you agree with someone who tells you they are no good! They usually get offended, because what they really want you to do is put your arm around them and say, "You are not bad at all. Look at all the skills and abilities you have."

Humility comes from the Latin word *humus*, which means "ground." The literal definition of humility, then, is "to lie face down on the ground." It means that apart from God, we have no life of our own and that we are therefore constantly beholden to Him for everything that we are and have.

Humility is an offensive concept to much of our culture. Many people think being humble means being a worm, having no identity, being a doormat and allowing everyone to walk all over you. That's not the biblical concept at all. No one was more humble than Jesus. No one had more of a sense of identity than Jesus. Humility is not weakness. It is strength which says, "I choose to trust in God and to submit to Him; I choose to believe in God and in His Word because I know He loves me and will vindicate me, and He will take me to where He wants me to go." We need to renounce pride and embrace the humility of the cross.

Bondage versus Freedom

The bondage Anderson refers to here is the bondage of habitual sin. I believe that many of God's people fall into the trap of sinning and confessing, sinning and confessing, and it is a continuous cycle. God is gracious and forgives all our sins as often as we repent of them. But you know as well as I do that part of repentance is leaving our sins behind us and looking to Jesus for deliverance and freedom. This is really a lot like the AA program where you do a fearless moral inventory and try to deal with the specific sins in your life that hold you in bondage. If need be, you also confess the sin to others, so that you can receive God's mercy and grace and His power to heal, forgive and restore. And so, by faith in Jesus, we can grow stronger and stronger and live for His Glory.

One of the things we often find very helpful in ministry situations, is encouraging people to take various parts of their being, often parts that have been enslaved to habitual sin, and present them to God as living sacrifices. There is tremendous power in saying, "Lord, I used these hands to sin. I repent of that. Please cleanse them by the blood of Jesus. I dedicate them to You. Please make them holy hands and use them in Your service and for Your glory.

"And, Lord, with my mind I have served evil. I have entertained thoughts that I should not have entertained, and I have made decisions that have been wrong and ungodly. I renounce those thoughts and decisions and give them over to You. I give my mind to You to be renewed by the power of Your Holy Spirit so I can learn to think as You think. I ask You to take all the force of evil and drive it out of my being. Fill me instead with the strength and power of Your Holy Spirit.

"Lord, I have placed these parts of my being on the altar. I dedicate them to You, and ask You to live in this whole part of my life." And when you see the results of those prayers, you appreciate what a tremendous power God has made available to us in Jesus Christ.

Acquiescence versus Renunciation

Anderson is really talking about renouncing ancestral sins. This is not a concept most of us think about very often, but it is certainly biblical. The Bible talks about confessing, not only our own sins, but also the sins of our ancestors. For example, Jeremiah says, *O Lord, we acknowledge our wickedness and the guilt of our fathers; we have indeed sinned against You* (Jer. 14:20). In many situations, when you cannot break free even though you have prayed and sought the Lord, you are dealing with a pattern of generational sin.

When that is the case, we need to repent before God not only of our own sins, but also those of our ancestors. A good case in point is the story in 2 Samuel 21 where a famine devastates the land of Israel during the reign of David. As David seeks the Lord, it becomes clear that the famine is caused by a curse that rests on the land. Saul, the previous king, had violated a treaty with the Gibeonites. He had put many of them to death when they were supposed to be spared. As a result, God judged the whole land with a severe famine. Only when Saul's sins were appropriately atoned for did God lift the famine. This is called "Identificational Repentance" and is the subject of John Dawson's excellent book, *Healing America's Wounds*. [2]

The Outcome

What happens when we deal with the log in our own eye? Jesus says we can then see clearly the speck in the eye of others. That includes our children! Instead of reacting out of unresolved fears and sins in our own lives, we can now see clearly what our children need and act accordingly. As a result, they won't be bent by our woundedness. Rather, they will be free to grow up in the way the Lord intends.

NOTES

1. Neil T. Anderson and Charles Mylander, "Personal Steps to Freedom in Christ," *Setting Your Church Free* (Ventura, CA: Regal Books, 1994) pp. 327-352.

2. John Dawson, *Healing America's Wounds* (Ventura, CA: Regal Books, 1994).

18 | Acquiring Basic Trust

*From my mother's womb You
have been my God.*
Psalm 22:10

I remember very clearly when years ago, as a young pastor, I did my first series of messages on raising children. Our own kids were still pretty young then. Older and wiser people would look at me with that knowledgeable look in their eyes and you could almost hear them think: "Just you wait until your kids are grown up. Then you will talk differently!" Some of the braver ones even said it out loud. I remember responding, "All that may be true, but one thing will never change, and that is God and His Word." When His Word says, *Train a child in the way he should go, and when he is old he will not turn from it* (Prov. 22:6), that's what God means, regardless of how my kids may turn out or whether I see that promise fulfilled in my experience.

It is now many years later and I believe that more than ever before. God's Word is truth and what God promises, He will fulfill. If I don't find that truth to work in my experience, then the problem doesn't lie with God. It lies elsewhere. Sometimes it lies with me. For most of us as parents, that is a bitter pill to swallow.

I sometimes hear people say, "I did the best I could for my children. Some turned out well. Others did not turn out so well. I don't want to take responsibility, particularly for those that didn't turn out well."

I can appreciate that. None of us would want to put the onus of how our children turn out on the parents alone. Life is way too complicated for that. Our kids have lives of their own. They make significant choices and decisions for which they alone must learn to accept responsibility. At the same time, and it is important to understand this, in God's wisdom, parents are still the primary source of grace flowing into a child's life. And Christian parents, particularly, ought to do all they can to become the best possible parents they can be in order to raise their children in the fear of God.

With that in mind, in this and the next few chapters, we are going to look at the stages of personality development as formulated by the famous psychologist Erik Erikson (See *Figure 18.1*).[1] Though to the best of my knowledge he was not a Christian, Erikson's stages of personality development provide us with a convenient framework to help us understand that very complex process we call growing up.

According to Erikson's theory, growing up is much like building a house. You lay the foundation, you pour the basement concrete, you put in the sub-flooring, you erect the walls and you put up the roof. Each subsequent action is built on what was done previously. So it is with personality development. Who we become depends very much on the successful completion of all the preceding phases. Skip one, or learn it incompletely, and there is a price to pay later in life. For example, a person who has not learned to stand on his own two feet as a child is likely to encounter problems in standing against the crowd later in life and so on.[2]

Stages	Ages	Description
1. Basic Trust	0 - 18 mo	The child must form a first loving, trusting relationship with a caregiver.
2. Autonomy	18 mo - 3 yrs	The child learns he is a person in his own right and starts exploring.
3. Initiative	3 - 6 yrs	The child becomes more assertive and learns to take more initiative.
4. Industry	6 - 12 yrs	The child must deal with demands to learn new skills.
5. Identity	Adolescence	The teenager must achieve a sense of identity in all areas of life.
6. Intimacy	Young Adult	The young adult must learn to develop intimate relationships with his peers.

Figure 18.1
Stages of Personality Development

As with all theories, this is no magical formula that explains all the mysteries of life. We are all individuals and as such we are all exceptions to the rule at some point or another. Nevertheless, in my own counselling experience, I have found this to be a very helpful framework in helping people come to wholeness of life through faith in the Lord Jesus Christ.

In this chapter, then, let's look at the first stage of personality development: Acquiring Basic Trust.

BASIC TRUST

John and Paula Sandford, who use a modified version of Erikson's theory, define Basic Trust as follows: "The ability to open your heart to others even when they disappoint you and even if you can't believe they mean to do you good all the time."[3] In other words, Basic Trust is opening your heart and learning that the world is a reasonably safe place in which you can relax, grow and develop. This is the first and most basic of all lessons we must learn, and we need to learn it by the time we are 18 months to 2 years old. Children who do not successfully learn Basic Trust will have a very difficult time growing up normally.

We don't often think about it, but the number of things a child has to learn in the first few years of his life is phenomenal! Several years ago, a best-selling book was entitled, *All I Really Need to Know I Learned in Kindergarten*. The author's premise was that all the basic things in life like honesty, fairness, cooperation, how to give and receive love and so on need to be learned by the time you are 3 or 4 years old – in other words, by the time you finish kindergarten! [4]

And that is true. Psychologists tell us that a child's basic personality is formed by the time he is 4 years old. It is further true that the bulk of that learning takes place before the child is even 2 years old!

Consider for a moment some of the things a child learns by the time he is 2. He needs to learn to see, hear and smell. He needs to learn to chew, control his bladder and his bowels. He needs to learn how to roll over, crawl and walk. He needs to recognize his parents and distinguish them from strangers. And the list goes on and on.

Most of the time these things happen so normally that no one stops to consider what a marvel this is. Only when something goes wrong, like when Junior doesn't learn how to talk or cannot hear, do we become concerned.

One of the most important lessons each of us needs to learn then, in the first 18 months or so of life, is Basic Trust. This involves learning at least two fundamental lessons:

Lesson One

First, it means *letting people into my life*. That is to say, I am willing to receive input – love, affection, nourishment, care – from other people. I trust that they have my best interests at heart and I am willing to let them help me in the areas where I need help.

From a child's point of view, this is of fundamental importance because he is virtually helpless at this stage of infancy. He
is literally at the mercy of his mother, father or other significant caretakers in his life. In a normal family situation, we
cuddle our children and love them, and they learn that the
world is a safe place. Their needs are legitimate and when they
cry out for help, we are there for them.

Unfortunately, that is not always the case. There are homes
where the child's legitimate needs are not taken care of; where,
instead of finding safety and protection at the hands of key care
givers, the child instead receives pain, rejection and even abuse.

One young man I know was born into a home where the
mother had minimal mothering skills and the father was a
"bad" drunk who would beat up both mother and child. His
mother would frequently leave him home alone for the day
while she went about her business. Not surprisingly, one day
he suffered serious burns to one third of his body when he fell
into a tub of boiling water that someone had thoughtlessly left
on the floor. When at age 3 he was placed in a foster home, his
front teeth were missing, he had scars on his eyeball, a hole in
his eardrum and had 70% of his stomach removed due to
ulcers! He was not in good shape!

What happens when a child experiences such pain? He
concludes, quite correctly, that the world is not a safe place.
Adults are not to be trusted. If you open up your heart and
expect good things from them, they will only turn around and
break your trust, disappoint you and cause you hurt. So, the
child closes off his heart. Intuitively, if not rationally, he concludes that if you want to avoid pain, you must not let yourself be at the mercy of grown-ups. The tragedy of that, of
course, is that if he is to grow up properly, he must learn from
grown-ups. He doesn't have the maturity to manage on his
own. As a result, his emotions remain frozen at a very primi-
tive level. Because he hasn't learned how to receive love, he also
cannot give it.

The young man to whom I referred earlier has grown up to be what psychologists call a borderline personality. He has been tested as being below average in intelligence and having virtually no conscience. Barring a miracle, he has little hope of having an independent life and will always need some form of supervision. He has no sense of personal identity, no sense of loving without conditions and no sense of responsibility for wrong actions. Obviously, whole areas of his personality have shut down so thoroughly that only a miracle of resurrection can truly restore all his emotional and intellectual capacities.

Other friends of ours tell a similar story. They adopted a little boy when he was only months old. He had also come from a painful, abusive background. They tell me when that little boy came into their house, for the first couple of months he would just go rigid every time they tried to hold him. He lived in that household for months and months before they could even begin to discern on his face the slightest evidence of a smile. Already at that age he had shut down and said, "The world is not a safe place for me to be. I am not going to trust anyone or allow anyone into my life."

It makes me cringe when I think of what must be happening in places where war rages and children see their parents slaughtered. What an anger and psychological time bomb is being generated in places like that!

Lesson Two

Second, acquiring Basic Trust involves *accepting myself for who I am*. How we view ourselves depends a great deal on the input of the significant people in our life. If the people around me cherish and value who I am and what my gifts are, then chances are pretty good I will like these things about myself. Conversely, if the important people in my life do not like me, if they consistently shame me, then chances are good I will end up disliking these qualities in myself as well.

A mature adult who experiences rejection at the hands of another can normally reason his or her way through this and figure out whether the problem is his own or someone else's. Part of growing up and establishing boundaries is that you don't want to make someone else's problems your problems. A child does not yet have this ability. A child who experiences rejection tends almost always to personalize it. "There must be something wrong with me. Mommy likes my sister more than she likes me because my sister is prettier, or smarter, or nicer than I am. Father likes my brother more than me because it is better to be a boy than a girl." These things, of course, are never thought through logically or even discussed. They are just the fleeting conclusions of a childish mind. They may or may not have any bearing to reality whatsoever. But that is irrelevant. What matters is that this is how the child perceives it.

This creates a deep-seated sense of shame. "If only I was somebody else, then I would be worthy of being loved." A child hungry for love and approval will do almost anything to try to earn that love and approval. For many that means a deep striving for acceptance. The child sees what she thinks the parent wants her to be and tries ever so hard to succeed. The problem is it is never enough. Even when she succeeds, it is never noticed or, if it is, suddenly the rules change and it is still not acceptable.

One of the women in our church recently shared her deep-seated sense of rejection at the hands of her parents. She and her sister had always carried on an intense rivalry because each felt the parents liked the other better. One day, when they were already adults and the whole family was vacationing together, they decided as a lark to enter a beauty contest. The one woman won first prize, which gave her a curious satisfaction since her parents had always favoured her sister as being the more beautiful. As they were talking about this unexpected turn of events, the mother piped up and observed in all seriousness that she really thought the other sister should have won! The devastation was complete. She told us later that was the moment when she closed off for good and started really hating herself.

Self-hatred is the typical consequence of not being able to measure up to other people's expectations. We think, "The problem must lie with me. If I could only be as cute and nice and intelligent as someone else, maybe then my parents would really love me." The problem is, I'm not. If anything, because I'm craving love and affection, chances are I become an especially difficult child. That presents me with more rejection and more self-hatred.

People who hate themselves start living in a fantasy world. Unable to face the ugliness of their own person, they deny that this is who they are and start pretending they are someone else. I know many people who have gone through life effectively masking their true identity, presenting a false face, or even faces, to the people around them. This, of course, takes a tremendous amount of energy because they have to act all the time. Life doesn't naturally flow out of them. They constantly have to work hard at keeping up appearances. Eventually, the strain becomes too much. Their health deteriorates, their coping ability diminishes and they have a crisis on their hands that forces them to seek help.

Leanne Payne, in her book *Restoring the Christian Soul Through Healing Prayer*, tells one such story of a woman named Linda. All through her adult Christian life, Linda had this incredible longing to be loved through a relationship with another woman. Before her conversion more than three years earlier, Linda had been a lesbian because of that drive within her. Then she came to Christ and invited Him into her life. Things really began to change, but deep inside there was still this incredible longing to be held by a woman and to feel secure. This plunged Linda into an agony of soul, trying to understand why she felt the way she did.

As the story goes on, it becomes very evident that one of the reasons she felt this way was because, very early in her life,

she had not bonded with her mother. Something very significant, from her point of view, had happened which broke a
basic trust in her relationship with her mother. When she was
just 3 days old, she developed a staph infection and was put in
isolation for a week before her mom took her home. Even
there, she had to be kept in isolation. Breast feeding, of course,
also had to be suspended. This had left a gaping hole in her
soul, a hole she desperately tried to fill with a lesbian relationship. Crying out for help, Linda wrote to Leanne:

> "...just knowing of it has not healed me.... If my problem is
> not something that can get really, miraculously handled in
> prayer, then I am lost. Write me, please. God only knows what
> continent you're on; you are probably deluged with mail, but
> please write me fast.... Please help. God, please help."[5]

Such is the story of people who haven't learned Basic Trust.
They have a deep hole in their psyche. They have a hard time
believing anyone can really love them because they have a hard
time loving themselves. Much of their life is spent looking for
something or someone to fill that hole. They are constantly
looking for affirmation and you can pour untold amounts of
love into them, but it is never enough. Their wounded hearts
are a bottomless pit.

That is why adopting wounded children so often becomes
a journey of pain for parents. Many parents think if they give
the child all the love they can give, it will somehow fill him up
to overflowing and they will get a return on their love invest-
ment. Normally speaking, that should be the case. But when a
child has been wounded, no amount of love can fill up the
heart. What is needed is a deep inner healing that only the
Lord Jesus can provide.

An ounce of prevention is worth a pound of cure. That is
why it is very important for us as parents, particularly if our
children are still young, to understand and practice these
things. We must avail ourselves of God's grace to build Basic
Trust into the lives of our children.

BUILDING BASIC TRUST

How do we do that? Here are some practical guidelines:

Create a Safe Spiritual Environment

I am firmly convinced that the devil not only hates humanity in general, but he hates children in particular. He knows that if he can get at a child's life early, he can cause untold damage that will affect that person's life for years to come. One of our jobs as parents is to try to protect our children from that.

There are several ways in which we can do that. One is to pray for our children, starting at conception. In our own marriage, as soon as we knew we were expecting a child, we started praying. I would lay my hand on my wife's tummy and ask the Lord to bless and protect the unborn child. This is a vulnerable period of time when the child's whole being is being shaped. The enemy would love to get in there and wreak havoc.

The same thing is true for delivery. Scripture says, *You brought me out of the womb; You made me trust in You even at my mother's breast. From birth I was cast upon You; from my mother's womb You have been my God* (Ps. 22:9-10). Safe child birth is not anything to take for granted. The transition from the mother's womb to the outside world can be pretty traumatic for a child.

When our youngest was born, his delivery was a particularly difficult one. His head was fairly large and for a while we wondered if he would be born safely. Eventually he was, thank God! But for years afterward, we noticed that he would resist anything that encumbered his head. He wouldn't want to be held tightly or even have a blanket around his head. Not until we prayed for healing in this area did we see a significant improvement in this behaviour. Today this is no longer a problem.

That's another advantage believers have. We can pray for the Lord to heal our children of any trauma that would in any way have injured Basic Trust. The results are often astounding, as the following story illustrates.

A young mother came to see me some years ago with serious concerns about her own sanity. One of the reasons she was so close to the edge was that her oldest son, Philip, was an extremely difficult child. For the first eleven months of his life he cried almost constantly. He would sleep maybe two hours at a stretch, was colicky and drove his parents to absolute distraction; so much so, that his mother was close to a nervous breakdown. They visited doctors and specialists, none of whom could find anything wrong with the child, nor could they promise any relief.

At her wits' end she came to see me for advice. As we talked and prayed about this problem rather extensively, it became apparent to us that there was a root of generational sin at work here. In personality and behaviour, the young child bore a great deal of resemblance to other family members, who came across as having very strong personalities. Furthermore, the pregnancy had been exceptionally difficult. The mother had to stay in bed for a good deal of it and, understandably, this didn't endear the unborn baby to her. Hard as she tried and wanted to love this child in her womb, it was just very difficult.

With a double whammy like that, is it any wonder the child proved to be exceptionally difficult? As noted in Chapter 9, research indicates that unborn children are sensitive to what is going on with the mother. And if the mother goes through a lengthy period of stress, this is known to significantly affect the unborn child.[5]

So we talked about that and took it to the Lord in prayer. We asked Him to cut off any roots of generational sin. We asked Him to forgive the mother for the bitterness and anger she had demonstrated towards her unborn son. We claimed the riches of God in Christ for healing in both the child and the mother and to bond the two of them together in a healthy way. And God heard our prayer. In one of those dramatic ways that God delights in when we are truly brought to the end of ourselves, He acted. It is no exaggeration to say that within the space of one week's time, the situation dramatically altered for the better. The child's crying spells lessened, his sleep patterns improved, his mother was able to get more rest and the whole family situation improved immeasurably. Never again have those problems come back with the same degree of severity and pain!

The prayer of faith is a powerful tool God gives to us as believing parents. When our children were growing up, I made it a practice to stop for a moment each night before I went to bed, to put my hand on their heads and pray for the Lord to bless each of them.

I also advise people to pray for their house that it will be a spiritually safe place for their children. Sometimes children have a lot of nightmares and bad spiritual experiences, particularly when they are asleep at night. One possible cause for that is that the house has been defiled spiritually. Sometimes a house will have had a lot of evil associated with it in the past that has left a tense atmosphere. Most of us have been to places that gave us the creeps. Other places just feel really good and peaceful. That is a spiritual function and kids are often more sensitive to that than adults. When our children experience such disturbances and we sense a bad atmosphere in our home, then we need to do some spiritual house cleaning. We need to ask the Lord to cleanse and take away any spiritual defilement that abides in the house for any reason and to fill it with His presence and power. Done with understanding and faith, the differences can often be remarkable.

Nurture Our Children

We need to provide for all their needs – emotionally as well as physically. We need to hold them a lot. We need to pour our love, protection and security into their lives. Both fathers and mothers play an important role in that. Mothers tend to be the primary nurturers of very young children, but fathers are needed to impart their own peculiar brand of masculine strength to the child. In this way, the child learns that the world is a safe place. There is someone who loves him unconditionally and will try to protect him at all costs.

What happens when we do that? The child grows and matures and will soon be ready for phase two: Autonomy and Independence.

NOTES

1. Laura Lefton and Lester Valvante, Modified from "Erikson's Eight Stages of Psychosocial Development," *Mastering Psychology*, 4th ed. (Needham Heights, MA: Simon & Schuster, Inc., 1991) p. 321.

2. Lefton and Valvante, "Development," *Mastering Psychology*, pp. 320-322.

3. John and Paula Sandford, *Restoring the Christian Family* (Plainfield, NJ: Logos International, 1979) p. 6.

4. Robert Fulghum, *All I Really Need to Know I Learned in Kindergarten* (New York: Villard Books, 1986, 1988).

5. Leanne Payne, *Restoring the Christian Soul Through Healing Prayer* (Wheaton, IL: Crossway Books, 1991) pp. 104-107.

19 | Finding Your Own Way

Train a child in the way he should go, and
when he is old he will not turn from it.
Proverbs 22:6

The following scenario is often typical for a new mother: Her baby is born; baby and mother bond; after the initial shock of getting to know each other, they develop a close relationship. The baby is very helpless and dependent on the mother, and the mother feels really needed and useful in the life of the child. Both of them develop a very true sense of having bonded and belonging to each other.

When the baby is about 3 or 4 months old, the relationship gradually begins to change. Baby grows more wiggly and independent and starts exploring things. Eventually, he starts preferring toys to his mother. For some moms, this can be very difficult, particularly for moms who need to be needed by their children. As one mother put it rather despairingly, "He needed me for four months. Now motherhood is spending the next seventeen and [a] half years letting him leave me!"[1]

There is a lot of truth and wisdom in that statement because the whole process of raising children is for one purpose only: *helping them to leave you, the parent!*

We have seen in the previous chapter that this whole process of growing up is a very complex process that consists of several clearly defined stages. So far we have looked at stage one: the need to learn Basic Trust. In this chapter, let's look at stage two: discovering Autonomy or Independence.

DISCOVERING AUTONOMY

The word *autonomy* means, literally, "to be a law to one's self." The word *auto* in Greek means "self." *Nomy* comes from the Greek word *nomus* which means "law." When a child begins to learn independence or autonomy, he starts to move out into the world to try to make his own way. He can only do so if he has learned security in the early stages of his life. A child who knows he is loved unconditionally and has the freedom to try things can now step out and do new things. In that process, he will learn the difference between right and wrong, and between his own will and the will of other significant people in his life.

This stage of Autonomy, or Independence, is addressed by Dr. Henry Cloud and Dr. John Townsend in their excellent book, *Boundaries*. They subdivide this stage of personality development into three distinct stages. [2]

Hatching

The first, they call *hatching* or *differentiation*. Hatching takes place in a child's life normally between the ages of 4 and 10 months. This is the stage in which the mother mentioned above was finding herself with her child. The child had learned basic security, acquired the physical and emotional well-being needed for growing up and now is ready to explore the broader world. He no longer sees himself as the placid, passive individual who is merely an extension of his mother.

He discovers that he is an individual with a mind and feelings of his own, so he begins to move away from his mom. In this crawling stage, he sets out to explore the world around him. He no longer needs his mama in quite the same way as he did for the first weeks and months of his life. This is hatching, or differentiation. Baby discovers that he and his mother are not the same person. Rather, they are two different people, and so he begins a movement away from her.

Practicing

Stage two is called *practicing*. This stage typically occurs between the ages of 10 months and 18 months, and corresponds with the time the child is learning to walk, and perhaps talk. Walking, for a child, opens up, as you can imagine, a whole new vista of exploring and discovery. Townsend and Cloud make the observation that a lot of classic pictures of baby's first step, show mom and dad standing with their arms outstretched and the baby walking towards them. In actual fact, they note, it's the other way around. Baby's first step is more commonly away from mom and dad, who are often in hot pursuit trying to keep the baby out of mischief!

This is the stage where the baby should learn that initiative and aggressiveness in proper measure are a good thing. In a normal and a healthy family, he is encouraged to start exploring different things. It can be an irritating time for mom and dad because he gets into everything. This is the time when he gets into the cupboards and tries Drano to see what it tastes like. This is the time he'll try driving his walker down the basement stairs just to see what gravity is like. Our youngest child actually did that. And he did it not once, not twice, but three times!

You say, "What kind of parents are you anyway?" The answer is, pretty conscientious, I think, but all it takes is a moment's lack of attention. The door to the stairs was left open and before we knew it, down he went. The amazing thing was that though the stairs were long and steep, not once did he get hurt. I rather think there must have been a big angel catching him each time. Not that I recommend you try this at home!

All of us, I'm sure can relate many stories such as this. When our two oldest boys, David and Michael, were young, they slept in the same room. David wanted to get something that was lying out of his reach on top of a chest of drawers, so rather ingeniously, he pulled out the drawers and proceeded to climb his way to the top. Well, you can imagine what happened. The whole chest of drawers tipped over. David managed to jump clear but not so his younger brother, Michael, who was about to bear the full brunt of this heavy piece of furniture. Providentially, this chest of drawers had drawers in the lower half only and doors in the top half. As it came crashing down, the doors swung open and stopped the dresser from crushing Michael. To this day, I shudder to think of what would have happened if the doors had not swung open. Michael could easily have been badly hurt, perhaps even killed. I think that is why the Bible talks about children having angels who protect them!

In this stage, the child discovers new abilities and horizons, and he thinks he is omnipotent. There is nothing he cannot do. He doesn't see any danger and plows ahead trying to make his way in life, learning all these exciting things God has put there for him to learn.

Rapprochement

Stage three is *rapprochement*. That is a French word which means "restoration of harmonious relationships." This stage generally covers the ages of 18 months to about 3 years, and is the time the child discovers he is not omnipotent after all. There are limitations to what he can do, and he needs his parents to protect him and keep him safe. As he goes about exploring the world, he discovers that the world, in fact, is not always a safe place. You can get hurt out there. Dogs bite; hot water burns; cars can run you over; the neighbourhood bully can beat you up and so on. And so, having ventured away from mom and dad to explore life, he now goes scurrying back to them whenever he gets hurt and feels threatened. He still needs mom and dad, but it's in a new way because as soon as he feels better he launches out on his own again. It's a little bit like when your teenager goes off to college and then comes home for Christmas. He is still glad to come home and you're glad to see him. But things are different now. He is starting to grow up and is rapidly forming an identity of his own.

That is what starts to happen with a toddler at this age. He tries all these new things, gets burned in the process, goes back to mom and dad and needs them. But things are different now. He has tasted the world out there and it is only a matter of time before he goes out and explores it further. He is well on his way to having a mind and identity of his own.

Learning to Say "NO!"

How does that surface? It surfaces in the most famous word in a 2 or 3-year-old's vocabulary: NO! "No, I don't want to eat those peas." "No, I don't want to go to bed." "No, I don't want to do this and I don't want to do that either."

For many parents, this is a tremendously frustrating time, because all of a sudden their cuddly little teddy bear has now changed into a little monster with a mind of his own! A lot of parents don't know how to deal with this and so a battle of the wills prevails. Guess who wins in many families today? Unfortunately, it is not always the parents. Rather, it is the child, and that, I might add, leaves children as well as parents frustrated.

Nevertheless, learning to say "No" is a fundamental step in becoming your own person and important preparation for growing up. A child who has not learned to say "No" will not be able to say "No" to his friends when he hits the teenage years. The teenager, then, will not have the ability or courage to fend off peer pressure. Instead, he will be very much at the mercy of what his friends want him to do. That is why so many agreeable children who never gave their parents one ounce of resistance can nevertheless get into so much trouble later in life! They have no will of their own. They've never had the opportunity to practice saying "No" in an environment where it was safe to do that. Saying "No" is something that has to be learned. And it has to be learned in an environment where you won't be penalized for saying it, where your primary care-givers will not withdraw love just because you have a mind of your own.

Now, that doesn't mean the child needs to run the household, or have his own way all the time, as many parents today seem to assume. Not at all! It simply means the child needs to be able to practice his ability to say "No" without being made to feel guilty for it. Parents are still responsible for making the final decision.

Me! My! Mine!

The same applies to the words, *"Me," "My"* and *"Mine,"* which are also a very important part of the vocabulary of a child at this age. Christian parents sometimes get bent out of shape because little Johnny is not very anxious to share his toys with a little buddy. He says, "This is my truck." Often Johnny is playing with something else and may not want to play with the truck until the other child plays with it, and then, all of a sudden, Johnny wants to play with it, too. And moms and dads, especially Christian parents, often say, "You are supposed to share," and we admire compliant children who share.

We should recognize, though, that if a child is too ready to share, there is good likelihood that he has a boundary problem. He hasn't learned that it is safe for him to have a mind of his own and that there are legitimate things which he is allowed to own and exercise control over. The choice to share must be his.

It is important to understand this. You cannot share that which you are not allowed to own. You cannot give of yourself until you have developed a sufficient sense of self so that you can choose to give it away. (I might add, this explains the paradox of the Christian life. How do you lay down your life for others and avoid being a doormat with no life of your own? The answer lies in having a keen sense of self-identity and then making the choice to give your life away. No one is taking it from you. You are freely giving it away. Jesus, of course, is the prime example of that. He freely sacrificed His life. Yet, no one took it away from Him. The choice was His to make.)

So, part of growing up for a child in this stage of life is learning what is his domain, what are his toys and what he can legitimately claim as his own. Only then can he learn to share with others without giving away a portion of his own sense of identity.

THREE FUNDAMENTAL LESSONS

Normally, a child should learn these concepts by the time he reaches the age of three. By this time, he should have learned the following three fundamental lessons of life: [3]

Lesson One

You can be emotionally attached to another person without giving up a sense of self. In other words, he has learned, "I can have a relationship with you. I can love you and you can love me in return, but I can continue to be a person in my own right. I am allowed my opinions and thoughts, and I can be me even while we are together in this relationship." The opposite of that, of course, is that in order for me to be loved, I have to surrender my own thoughts, feelings and opinions for yours. I have to think what you think, feel what you feel, like what you like and so on. If I don't, you won't like me anymore. That leads to serious boundary confusion because my own thoughts and feelings are not legitimized. I have to deny who I really am.

Lesson Two

You can say "No" and still be loved. Think this one through with me for a moment. The world is full of people who are afraid that if they say "No," they won't be loved any longer. What a child needs to learn very early in life is that he can have a mind of his own, he can say "No," and even on occasion be very naughty, and he will still be loved by his parents. Just because they disagree with his decisions or his behaviour doesn't mean they are going to withdraw their love from him.

Unfortunately, that is often what happens. The child does something really bad, or expresses an inappropriate or outrageous opinion. Mom and dad get really bent out of shape and communicate by their actions if not their words, "If you behave that way, then you are not my child." When this happens, the parents put a tremendous emotional burden on the child. Now that child has to choose between being true to his own wishes and desires and being loved by his parents. If he wants his parents' love, then he cannot be his own person. He must deny his own thoughts and feelings. As a result, he cannot afford to say "No," because if he does, he will not be loved. This child will likely grow up to be too compliant.

Lesson Three

You learn to accept being told "No" without withdrawing emotionally. Many people have never learned that lesson. Say "No" to them and they turn inward, sulk, become angry and walk away from the relationship. They cannot handle being denied their wishes because they equate such denial with rejection. But that is not necessarily true. We cannot all have it our way all the time. Just because we are told "No" does not mean we are not loved. It simply means, "No, you may not do that." It may, in fact, be the most loving thing anyone can do for us, depending on the nature of the situation.

• • • • • • • •

A child who has not learned these three lessons by age 3, will likely grow up emotionally handicapped. He will not have acquired a sufficiently strong sense of personal identity to be able to form healthy and meaningful relationships in life. Typically speaking, he will tend to become one of two extremes when he grows up. He will either become *compliant* or he will become a *controller.*

The Compliant Person

A *compliant* person has no opinion on any subject. If he is with friends whose hair is all green, then he dyes his hair green and thinks it is wonderful. Or, if he is with someone else who walks with his hands up in the air, then he thinks that is the normal way of life. And when you try to pin him down for an opinion, you can never get one out of him, because he learned very early in life, "When I state my opinion, people don't like it. They won't love me anymore and they are going to reject me. So if I want to be loved, I had better not state my opinion."

That, by the way, is why so many grown-ups have such a hard time expressing themselves and stating what is in their hearts – they have not had the practice they need to express their opinion. Rather, they have felt rejected in this process and so have shut down and become compliant.

Compliant people are usually filled with a deep anger because they feel constantly violated. If Karla Homolka's testimony at her former husband Paul's murder trial for the grisly sex-slaying of two Ontario teenage girls is to be believed, this is the category into which she fell. She went along with her husband's fantasy and wishes, joining him in both the abduction and murders of the girls, because she was dominated by him. For the sake of being loved and having his approval, she was prepared to sacrifice every value and standard to which she had ever subscribed.

Now, it may be that her testimony was self-serving.

Perhaps it was. The fact remains that there are many people who live this way. They have such a love deficit in their hearts that they'll do almost anything to be loved and wanted by someone who can give them what they think they need.

The Controller

A *controller,* on the other hand, is a person who has learned it is not safe to go through life allowing himself to be at the mercy of the approval or disapproval of significant people in his life. So he makes up his mind, often very early in life, that he is not going to give anyone that power. He moves out into the world and says, "I will hold the power myself and I will decide who I am going to dominate in my relationship."

If it is true that Karla Homolka was compliant in her relationship with Paul, then Paul can be said to be a very controlling individual. Controlling is a way of ensuring a false sense of emotional security. "If I can dominate this relationship, then I don't have to worry about somebody else taking advantage of me and hurting me." As we have seen before, it is one of the core issues that flows out of dysfunctional families.

How does a child learn this healthy ability to say "No," to be his own person and to do it in a way that doesn't make him a little tyrant who thinks he rules the world? Two conditions must be clearly established: 1) Firm Boundaries; and 2) Consistent Discipline.

Firm Boundaries

A boundary is a line of demarcation. It marks off my property from my neighbour's property, my area of responsibility from other people's responsibility. Boundaries can be physical, emotional and/or spiritual.

A fence is a good practical example of a physical boundary. The distance we keep from other people physically is another example of a physical boundary. Protecting our children emotionally is an example of an emotional boundary. Not allowing my heart to be unduly engaged in a relationship is an emotional boundary. An example of a spiritual boundary is being able to follow the Lord's call on my life and not allowing other people to impinge upon my destiny and calling.

Children in their growing-up years need firm boundaries. They need a line of demarcation around them big enough for them to explore their gifts and abilities, but not so big that they can be harmed in the process. They need those boundaries physically, emotionally and spiritually.

A playpen is a good practical example. When our kids were little, we put them all in the playpen. I know many parents today do not think that is fashionable. They think baby ought to be free to roam all over the house to develop his wonderful little personality. Be that as it may, we found as we were rearing our children that up to a certain age, a playpen provided a very clear line of demarcation. It provided a place where they were safe and yet had limited freedom to explore and play. We would do it again and recommend it highly because it helped us preserve our sanity as well.

The challenge for parents in establishing boundaries for their children is that they need to be age-appropriate. As the child gets older, the boundaries ought to become broader and the freedom greater. The whole object of giving them boundaries is to keep them safe until they are mature enough to decide for themselves that this is how they want to live. That means they need enough freedom to try things on their own, but not so much freedom that they destroy themselves in the process.

My experience has been that many parents do it backwards. They give too much liberty to their children when they are little. Then as they get older and it becomes obvious that they have not learned to make wise and godly decisions, parents try to take that freedom back. And that never works, of course.

Take the case of Eric. When he was little, his parents admired all his antics. If he didn't get his way and threw a temper tantrum, they just shrugged it off and said, "He'll grow out of it." Well, he didn't. By the time he was thirteen, he was a terror to both his classmates and his teacher. Alarmed, his parents tried to rein him in. By then it was too late and nothing they said or did made any difference. Unfortunately, that is all too typical for many parents today.

If we love our kids, we provide consistent boundaries for them. We give them enough space to be themselves, to practice their skills and even to get into a measure of trouble if need be. But we're there to limit the damage, lest they get irreparably hurt in the process.

Consistent Discipline

We'll deal more extensively with disciplining children later in Chapter 24, but let me say a few things about it here.

The word *discipline* is related to the word *disciple*. A disciple is a learner, one who is seeking to acquire a certain way of life. Discipline flows out of establishing proper boundaries. If I have marked off a line beyond which my child is not allowed to go, his natural curiosity coupled with his rebellious, sinful nature will cause him to try to cross that line again and again. You tell him to stay in bed after you put him to bed, but what does he do? He gets back up, and comes up with the most ingenious reasons for getting out of bed: "I gotta go pee; I gotta have another drink; I think there is a monster under my bed; Johnny won't stop squeaking the bunk bed." When that happens, the battle is on. And the question is, are you going to maintain the boundary and exercise consistent discipline, or are you going to give in and let the child run the household?

I am not being critical when I say this, but it has been my observation that in much of our culture today, the children run the world. And children who run the world are not very happy children. Many of them are crying out for a parent who will be firm enough in love to say to them, "Don't do it. If you do, there are going to be consequences for your behaviour."

When our kids were growing up, other than placing very valuable things out of reach, we didn't do much to baby-proof the living room. We tried to make it a point to teach the kids not to touch everything. Sometimes that was a fascinating study in psychology, because every so often as one of the children would try to reach out for something they weren't supposed to touch, you could see the wheels of their minds turning. "Is the pleasure of touching this thing worth the pain of disobedience?" I remember instances when one of our kids would be ready to grab something they knew they weren't supposed to have, stop half way with their hand still extended and steal a look at us to see if this was worth taking a risk. It's pretty funny when you see it happen. It is not funny if you don't discipline consistently because then all you are doing is teaching them to be smarter about their disobedience. Children need parents who are consistent in their discipline.

Discipline teaches a child one of the most fundamental lessons of life: "You reap what you sow. There are consequences to your actions." I am convinced that if Satan wants to lead someone astray, he will try to blind him to the consequences of his actions.

Three weeks after Kristen French was killed, Paul Bernardo was visited by two policemen who interviewed him, presumably about the Kristen French case. Bernardo turned on his charm and pretended perfect innocence. The police left and never gave him another thought because he just didn't seem the type who would commit such a dastardly crime. Later, Bernardo crowed about that and how he thought he would never get caught. It gave him a false sense of security that he could go on living this way indefinitely. Thank God, he eventually got caught.

Have you ever noticed that people who love God tend to get caught all the time? Everyone else can sin and get away with it. You decide you're going to try it too, figuring if they can get away with it, why shouldn't you? So you do it and the first thing that happens is what? You get caught red-handed! That is not a very pleasant experience, but it's a sure sign of God's favour, because Scripture says, *The Lord disciplines those He loves* (Heb. 12:6).

When our oldest son, David, was 15 or 16, he worked for a while at McDonald's. Though he had been warned not to take food for his personal use that he had not paid for, he saw other people doing it regularly and getting away with it. Thus emboldened, he decided one day to throw a few extra pieces of chicken in his order. Wouldn't you know it? The manager caught him red-handed and fired him on the spot! Thus ended his promising career at McDonald's! All kinds of other people got away with it, but not him.

It was small consolation to him when I told him the Lord loved him enough to let him get caught. But it taught him a valuable lesson. You are free to make your own choices, but you are not free to avoid the consequences of your choices. Parents who protect their kids from experiencing the consequences of their choices are not thereby demonstrating love for their children. Rather, they are teaching them irresponsibility. Come the Judgment Day, if not before, these parents will see that what they have done was not helping, but rather hindering their kids.

As parents, we need to let our children experience the consequences of their actions, always, as I said earlier, in the context of God's forgiving grace. This will establish within them the necessary groundwork for moving into the next phase of life – taking initiative.

NOTES

1. Dr. Henry Cloud and Dr. John Townsend, "How Boundaries are Developed," *Boundaries* (Grand Rapids, MI: Zondervan Publishing House, 1992) p. 67.

2. *Ibid*, pp. 61-82.

3. *Ibid*, pp. 72-73.

20 | Testing Your Wings

*In all your ways acknowledge
Him, and He will make
your paths straight.*
Proverbs 3:6

Having learned Basic Trust and Autonomy (Independence) in his first three years, the child is now ready to launch into the next phases of life, which are Initiative followed by Industry.

Initiative runs typically from ages 3 to 5 years. *Industry* runs from about age 6 to age 11.

Because Initiative and Industry have so much in common, I am going to lump them together in this chapter.

During this period of time, there are at least three fundamental lessons our children need to learn: 1) Sexual Identification; 2) Relating to Peers; and 3) Task Completion. Let's look at each of these.

Sexual Identification

Sexual identification is learning the difference between being a boy or a girl. To most of us that may seem fairly self-evident, but in a world where the confusion surrounding sexual identity is growing in leaps and bounds, it is a vital lesson to learn.

When a child is first born, he or she, of course, has no awareness of gender or sexual identity. The child hardly knows he's alive, let alone what it is to be a boy or a girl. But in the normal course of events, as that child grows, he becomes aware that people come in two different versions: male and female. Tests have shown that already at a very early age, children have a remarkably clear idea of what toys or clothing they think is appropriate for a boy or girl. Particularly between the ages of 3 and 5, children have a keen interest in and awareness of the differences between boys and girls, not only physiologically, but also emotionally. Sexuality is not merely a physical issue. It is very much an issue of the whole person. A man and a woman are not only different biologically, they are also different emotionally as well as many other ways.[1]

Modelling

One of the ways in which children learn this sexual differentiation is by identifying with the parent of the same sex. A little girl will, for example, be drawn to her mother, and her mother models for her what it means to be a woman. Likewise, a little boy will be drawn to his father and see modelled there what it means to be a man. Sometimes they will play one parent off against another. Shades of Freud! The little boy may say he wants to marry his mother or may want to compete with his father for his mother's affections. Sometimes a little girl will do the same thing; she'll want to marry her dad. All of that is relatively harmless; it's part of sexual identification – finding out what it means to be a boy or a girl.

Understandably, it is a very critical stage in a child's life, and again, most of the time it happens quite automatically. We don't think much about it nor make too much of a point of it. Not until something goes wrong do we stop to think how critical an issue this is or how complex. Witness the rise of the gay rights movement in our time and you understand what a pro-foundly complex issue this is.

Affirmation

It is particularly important, then, for parents to not only model proper biblical roles of masculinity and femininity for their children, but to also affirm them in the legitimacy of their gender. If you want to mess up a child and cause him to undergo serious sexual role problems later in life, then confuse him concerning his sexual identity. Dress your little girl as a boy or vice versa. Share your emotional baggage with your child, instead of with your spouse or therapist. Soon you'll see one very confused child whose lack of clear identity may well spread chaos everywhere.

Paul Bernardo

At the time of this writing, the Paul Bernardo murder trial in Toronto has concluded. The jury has found him guilty and he's been sentenced to life in prison with eligibility of parole after 25 years. With the trial over, the media are now making public more of his background information. The *Toronto Star* published a whole section entitled, *Bernardo: Portrait of Evil.* They dug into a childhood of deep, dark secrets.

Here, in part, is what they said:

> *Paul Kenneth* [Bernardo] *was the last of three children to be born to this particular family. He was the darling of both sides of the family. But their youngest child had some early difficulties with his speech. By the age of 5, he had barely uttered a word. He was tongue-tied. It took a minor operation to relieve the problem. Then he developed another speech problem – a stammer – which his public school class-mates often teased him about.*
>
> *Later, he got tagged with the moniker "Barnyard," a play on his surname. Other children always found it fun to pick on the stammering young boy with the baby face.*
>
> *Paul was just five when his father's trouble started. In*

later court transcripts, it would be revealed that Kenneth, Paul's father then, was sexually assaulting a female, who cannot be identified.

The attacks went on for five years, but they wouldn't come to the attention of the authorities for another seventeen years, when the woman finally complained to the police. Kenneth Bernardo was charged with indecent assault, and found guilty in February, 1993 – just days before his son's arrest. He was sentenced to nine months in jail.

His father's sexual deviations during those years had a devastating impact on the family. Marilyn Bernardo stopped sleeping with her husband, moving to a room in the basement of their home.

Paul didn't realize what his father was up to until he was 10. It remained a deep secret, and he never talked about it with any of his friends. Personal problems stayed in the family, was the Bernardo credo.

When Paul was 16, his mother chose to reveal to him that the man he had grown up with and believed to be his father, wasn't really his father. She said Paul had been conceived by another man and born out of wedlock. The effect was devastating. Paul ran out of the house crying, later confiding the awful secret to a friend. [2]

Of course, this in no way excuses his actions, but it shows you how important it is to learn proper sexual identification early in life and what happens when you don't. It is absolutely imperative that a boy learns what it means to be a boy and a girl what it means to be a girl and to become comfortable with the fact that is how God has made them. Certainly, the burgeoning growth of the gay movement ought to show us what happens when these issues are not properly addressed.

Relating To Their Peers

We don't often think about it, but getting along with other people involves considerable skill. You have to develop some sense of personal identity and learn what your likes and dislikes are. You have to be able to communicate that to someone else in such a way that they understand you and are willing to go along with you. When conflict arises, you have to be able to identify what is happening and why and acquire the skills to work it out.

For most of our kids, these things come pretty naturally. They grow up, they acquire friends and they get along reasonably well most of the time. When they have a falling out, they learn how to work things out and, by trial and error, they learn to form meaningful relationships.

Every so often, though, you'll find a child who hasn't learned these skills. These children grow up to be loners. They have difficulty establishing intimate relationships, and when they do form friendships, they tend to latch on so tightly that other people push them away. That discourages them from establishing other friendships. So, they have a hard time making friends, and they have an almost impossible time holding onto them.

Each of us can think of youngsters who are misfits in the school-yard. They just don't fit in and kids pick on them. They aren't liked, and they in turn won't like other kids. And what an incredible anguish it is for a parent to see that their child does not get along with his peers.

Why does this happen? One possible reason is that the child has not learned the necessary skills for forming personal relationships which he normally should acquire, usually between the ages of 6 and 11.

How can we help our children to acquire the necessary skills for healthy interpersonal relationships?

Here are some suggestions:

Lay a Solid Foundation

What I mean by this is that the first two stages of personality development – Basic Trust and Autonomy – need to be clearly established in the lives of our children. Unless a child has learned that the world is a secure place and it is safe for him to be his own person and establish personal boundaries, he will not be able to interact with other children in a meaningful way. In the words of John and Paula Sandford, he will play "alongside" rather than "with" other children. [3]

Think that one through with me for a moment. What happens when you play "with" someone? You interact. There's give and take. You learn to respond to each other's cues and needs, and hopefully, by God's grace, you will grow up with some sensitivity to other people's needs and desires. You are thus able to interact with other people without losing your own identity.

A child who does not have his own sense of identity cannot risk entanglement with another person without risking his life. So he plays "alongside." These children will sell their souls to belong. They desperately want to be included in what other people are doing, and will deny their own feelings, likes and dislikes in order to be part of the gang. Because they so desperately want to belong and to be loved, they will do whatever they need to do in order to be part of the gang. Other children, of course, sense that. They sense, "Here is a person who has no core, no identity in his soul." And so they take advantage of that. They start picking on that person and, in many cases, become very cruel and mean to that child because they sense intuitively that there's a weakness in him or her.

That's a tragic thing to witness. Children like that need protection from the significant adults in their lives. More than that, they need help to become whole so they can erect appropriate personal boundaries to keep themselves out of harm's way. Many victims are repeat victims for precisely that reason. They lack the personal wholeness that can help them see danger coming and keep out of its way. Whether that lack of personal wholeness precedes the original abuse or is caused by it is relatively irrelevant. We need to be whole to know where to draw the boundaries.

Pray For Your Kids to Find the Right Playmates

It's a fact of life that by the time a child reaches the teenage years, his relationships with his peers outweigh his relationship with his parents. What his friends tell him, demand of him or think of him, will often be far more important than what his parents think or want him to do. That's a normal part of growing up, because you can't leave home unless you have developed other social relationships that take the place of parental relationships.

Finding the right friends, therefore, is really important. That is easier for some than for others. I often hear people idealizing small churches, and while these have their advantages, they also have their disadvantages. One of them is that it is often very hard for children to have friends their own age in church. My experience is that if kids don't have friends their own age in church, they will very often make friends elsewhere. These friends, in many instances, will have significantly different values. That can readily become a bone of contention between parent and child, not to mention a considerable danger, particularly for a child who is a follower.

A wise parent will encourage his or her children to make Christian friends even if that takes considerable effort and expense. That may mean making sure they get involved in church youth programs, or attend schools where there are Christian kids their own age. That may mean moving to another city or church where there is a healthier environment for the kids. Of course, that is no guarantee that the kids may not still get into trouble, but the chances are considerably less than if they run around with an unbelieving crowd.

Teach Them Healthy Interpersonal Relationship Skills

That means, first of all, that we help them learn to *fight fairly*.

People sometimes idealize the perfect child as one who never gets into a fight with other kids. Sometimes they will say,

"Oh, Susie is just a wonderful child, or little Johnny is such a great kid. They always play so nicely with other kids and always share their toys. They never fight."

Well, I've not met too many of them! But assuming they exist, I'm not at all sure that is always such a healthy thing. I am more than a little suspicious of children who are too perfect. I suspect that in many cases they are afraid to be themselves and assert their own desires and wishes. As we noted earlier, if that is not addressed, they do not learn the skills they need to work things out. We should not be afraid to let our kids get into an occasional squabble. What we do need to do is teach them how to fight fairly, how to look at the situation from the other person's point of view and to take responsibility for their own actions.

Secondly, it means helping them *work through the conflict*. We need to help them understand what went wrong in the relationship. We need to hear out their sense of injustice or violation. We may need to stand up for them if it is obvious that they have been mistreated. (This, of course, should only happen if the facts have been carefully ascertained and both parties have had a fair hearing.) Then we need to help them work things out. They need to take responsibility for where they have been wrong. They need to learn to ask for forgiveness and to extend it with integrity.

Too often people walk away from conflict and leave it unresolved. The result is anger and bitterness that will crop up again years later to do irreparable harm. Many adult conflicts could be avoided, or at least seriously minimized, if parents would teach their kids healthy interpersonal relationship skills.

Task Completion

When I was a child, I grew up on a farm on Prince Edward Island. In those days, we had a dairy farm. I say "those days" because later, after my father had a stroke, we sold the cows and went more fully into potato farming. As is typical for most farm families, everybody had to pitch in and help with the chores. One of my chores was to milk the cows, as well as clean out the manure gutters and the calf pens.

I must honestly confess that I didn't particularly like farm work. The hours were long, the work hard, and I have always been grateful that was not my calling in life. So you can well imagine that as a teenager there were times when I would grumble about all that. I still remember my father saying to me on one such occasion, "I know you hate it now, but one day you will thank me for it." Sound familiar?

I, of course, thought that was ridiculous. Me be thankful for all this hard work? Never!

Guess what? I'm considerably older now, and probably a little wiser. And I can honestly say that I am truly appreciative of the hard work that I had to do because it taught me to stick out unpleasant jobs until the work was done. And that taught me the practical disciplines that we all need to know – how to identify a task and then stick with it until the job is done. That is task completion and a primary skill people need to learn during this time period in their lives.

Have you ever noticed how many people there are who are not focused? They flit about from one thing to another. They move from one job to another. They move from one friend to another, sometimes even from one spouse to another. They have never grown up. They have tremendous creativity, in many instances, and a great deal of ability, but by the time they come to the end of their life, it's been squandered. Like a shotgun blast, their energy has been scattered in many different directions. They have never learned to focus.

Stephen Covey, in his popular book *The Seven Habits of Highly Effective People*, says surveys show that the single most important factor that separates successful people from those who are not successful is not intelligence or hard work as we might be inclined to think. Rather, he says, it has everything to do with people's ability to set priorities and then stick to them.[4]

Again, these are disciplines that need to be learned, at least in a rudimentary fashion, between the ages of 6 and 11.

Let's look a little more closely now at what is involved in learning task completion. Task completion has three components:

The Child Needs to Learn to Accept Responsibility

One of the characteristics of a child is to automatically defer responsibility to parents. We have noticed, for example, that when we are away and the kids are left alone in the house, they are much more responsible than when we are around. Why is that? Because as long as the parents are around, the children revert back to being children who have learned to let their parents handle responsibility.

For some of us, that surfaces even when we have become adults. We go back home, and before you know it, in one way or another, we revert back to childish roles.

Let me illustrate.

My wife, Michelle, and I were married on a very hot September day just before my last year of school. When that year was done, and I was waiting to see what job opportunities there would be, we moved back in with my mother and older brother who were at that time still living on the family farm.

That summer was a very difficult one in some ways because I went through a pretty significant identity crisis. On the one hand, I was now a new husband and I had to learn to do all the right things in that regard. At the same time, I was back home, and my tendency was to simply slide back into the family role. (I was the fifth of seven children.) For a while that summer, I nearly drove my wife to distraction, because it was hard for her to know with whom she was dealing: a husband or a son of the family. Eventually, we got it sorted out, but not without some difficulty. Ironically, when we did finally get a call to a church, it was clear across the country in Alberta and with three children born close together, it was four years before we were able to get back home again. That was hard at times, but certainly provided an opportunity for us to become our own family unit.

So part of growing up is teaching our kids to accept responsibility that is appropriate to their age and skills. We need to help them to identify what their tasks are and then, as we will see a little later, help them learn how to do them properly.

I must say that doing this is a lot easier for some people than for others. This is a good case of needing to remove the log from your own eye before you can take the splinter out of the eye of others. Parents who themselves are not disciplined or organized will have a hard time imparting organization to their kids. And while there are all kinds of books around to tell you how the job ought to be done, these books only work when you have the ability to do the job in the first place! Have you ever noticed that?

Fortunately, God is a God of grace and His mercy covers a multitude of our shortcomings!

The Child Needs to Acquire the Necessary Skills

No matter how simple or complex a task may be, they don't get done automatically. Children have to learn to do them. Very often it is a lot easier for us as parents to jump into the fray and do the job ourselves rather than teach our children. But that robs our children of the opportunity to acquire the kinds of skills that will stand them in good stead as adults.

You have heard the story, perhaps, of the father who was working in his garden and had a number of his young children with him. They were supposed to be helping him, but even as he was busy planting they were trampling all over the plants right behind him. The neighbour, who was watching this from across the fence, was shaking his head in consternation at the obvious foolishness of this. Quite clearly, these kids were ruining what their father was doing. When the father finally caught a glimpse of what the neighbour was shaking his head over, he looked up and said, "I know what you are thinking, sir, but you are dead wrong. It's not a garden I'm planting. It's kids I'm growing."

I find that an important distinction to keep in mind when delegating things to your children. It is not just a matter of getting the work done. It is also a matter of training our kids to do it and to do it right. The best way to do that is by modelling the skills and taking our kids through them until they have learned to do it right.

The Child Needs to Learn the Discipline of Seeing Something Through to Completion

We live in an age of instant gratification. The greatest insult that children today can express is what? "It's boring!" Children, by definition, are easily bored. They easily give up and walk away from something long before it is finished, or certainly long before it's finished the way you think it ought to be finished!

Again, the tendency for parents is to jump into the fray and bail the child out. "Johnny isn't doing his job, so I better do it for him." We rationalize it by saying that we love him and don't want to see him get hurt. In fact, we're not doing him any favour because we are failing to teach him one of the most fundamental principles of life: choices have consequences. We are all free to make a variety of choices. We are not free to avoid the consequences of our choices. Parents who love their kids make sure their children learn that lesson early in life.

The book *Common Sense Discipline: What To Say and Do When Kids Need Help*, by Dr. Roger Allen and Ron Rose, is one of the best I've seen for parents with children in this age group. They talk in very practical terms about what to do with your child when he won't do his homework or when he or she refuses to get ready for the bus on time in the morning or when chores are not being done. They also give advice on what to do about nightmares or fears children often suffer from, and what to do when they are getting bullied by somebody else.

Throughout, they emphasize the importance of teaching kids to face the consequences of their own actions.

They include the following delightful little story about a girl named Suzy:

The mother of a fourth grader came to my office deeply troubled. It seems that sweet little Suzy refused to take a bath unless Mom ran the water for her. Then Suzy would complain until Mom scrubbed her back. Suzy wouldn't get dressed unless Mom laid out her clothes. Of course, Mom's selections were never the right ones... Mom was at the end of her frazzled rope. Our conversation went something like this: "What can I do? She refuses to take a bath unless I scrub her back, and then she won't go to school unless I take her in the car."

"How far is it to school?" I asked.

"Four blocks."

"How do the other kids in your neighbourhood get to school?"

"They walk or ride their bikes."

"What would happen if you let Suzy get to school on her own?"

"She'd probably be late, because she waits until the very last minute because she knows I'll have to take her."

"Have to take her?" I asked incredulously.

"Well, if I didn't, she'd be tardy because she waits so long."

"Uh huh. And then what would happen if she came to school tardy?"

"Well, I guess she'd get a detention and have to stay after school."

"Uh huh, and how long do you think Suzy would allow that to happen before she decided to get going on time to avoid being tardy again?"

"OK, I think I see what you mean. Well, I could let her be tardy, but still she'd wear the most outlandish clothes if I didn't select some for her."

"I know that's embarrassing, but if the clothes were really inappropriate, what would her teachers do?"

*"They'd probably send her home and make her serve a
detention for the classes she missed."*

*"OK, what do you think would happen if you quit co-
operating with her stalling routine and stopped running her
bath and scrubbing her back? They don't even give that kind
of service in expensive hotels, so why do you do it at home?"*

*"Well, if I didn't make her take a bath, she'd probably
go to school smelling bad."*

*"Uh huh, and how long do you think it would be before
the other kids or teachers said something to her about it?"*

*"Oh, OK. In other words, you think she's old enough to
learn to take care of this by herself, or suffer the consequences?"*

*"Right. If she's smart enough to figure out how to
manipulate you, the adult who's supposed to be in charge
here, then she's certainly smart enough to figure out how to
be responsible, resourceful and self-reliant."*[5]

Later on, they tell another story about a child who was
flunking out at school, refusing to do his homework, and his
mother was just in a complete panic because they had already
planned their whole family's vacation. They were going to take
a trip to Mexico in the summer, but if he failed his course, he
would have to go to summer school and that, she figured,
would ruin all their plans.

The remedy, of course, was quite simple – let him face the
consequences. So they did. They told him that if he didn't get
his act together in school, they would make arrangements for
him to stay with a neighbour and go to summer school while
they went on vacation. Guess what? Within one week, he
caught up on all his school work and was able to graduate with
his class. Nothing like having to learn to face the consequences
for one's own actions.[6]

Come the Day of Judgment, the Lord is not going to ask
us whether other people have done their share. He is going to
ask us, "Have you been faithful in what I have asked you to
do?" If we love our children, we will stick it out with them
until they have identified their tasks, acquired the skills to do

them and the discipline to stick it out until it is done properly. Only then can they go on and truly discover who they are.

NOTES

1. For further reading on this topic, refer to Gregg Johnson, *Recovering Biblical Manhood and Womanhood: A Response to Evangelical Feminism,* ed. John Piper and Wayne Grudem (Wheaton, IL: Crossway Books, 1991).

2. Nick Pron, John Duncanson and Jim Rankin, "Bernardo: Portrait of Evil," *Toronto Star*, 2 September 1995, pp. E1, E4-E7.

3. John and Paula Sandford, *Restoring the Christian Family* (Plainfield, NJ: Logos International, 1979) p. 17.

4. Stephen R. Covey, *The Seven Habits of Highly Effective People: Restoring the Character Ethic* (New York: Simon and Schuster, 1989) p. 148.

5. Dr. Roger Allen and Ron Rose, "Helping Kids Learn Self-Control: 6-11 Years," *Common Sense Discipline: What to Say and Do When Kids Need Help* (Ft. Worth, TX: Worthy Publishing, 1986) pp. 123-125.

6. *Ibid*, pp. 144-145.

21 | Knowing Who You Are

Whoever tries to keep his life
will lose it, and whoever loses
his life will preserve it.
Luke 17:33

A curious thing about people in general, and teenagers in particular, is that the degree of self-confidence they possess very often has little or no relationship to their gifts, abilities or looks.

For example, a person who is only of average intelligence or ability and whose looks range from average to maybe even below average may not seem to have much going for him or her in worldly terms. Yet, when you get to know them and work with them, it soon becomes apparent that they have it more or less together. They are pretty comfortable with who they are and fairly secure in their relationships with the people around them.

Conversely, you can have a person who by the world's standards really measures up to things that "really matter." They have looks, ability and talent that would make any lesser mortal absolutely jealous. And you say to yourself, "Now here is a person who has it all together. He should really feel good about himself." Yet, when you get to know him, he is a bundle of insecurity. Perhaps you have met people like that.

In actual fact, a person's self-perception has very little to do with reality. It has everything to do with a person's *perception* of reality. Let me try to explain what I mean by that.

Psychologists tell us that a healthy sense of self-esteem involves three factors: 1) A sense of belonging – *I have a sense of security*; 2) a sense of worth – *I have value as a person, apart from what I accomplish*; and 3) a sense of competence – *what I do matters to people*. When these three converge, the result is a healthy sense of self-esteem (See *Figure 21.1*).[1]

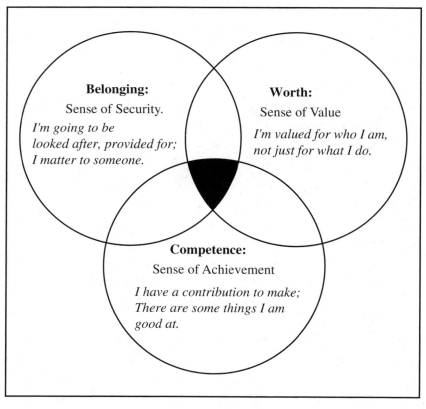

Belonging:

Sense of Security.

I'm going to be looked after, provided for; I matter to someone.

Worth:

Sense of Value

I'm valued for who I am, not just for what I do.

Competence:

Sense of Achievement

I have a contribution to make; There are some things I am good at.

Figure 21.1
Elements of Self-Esteem

It ought to be immediately clear, then, that how I see myself has more to do with how I have been brought up than with what I really am. If I grow up in a home where I have a keen sense of belonging, where I am valued as a person just for who I am and not for what I do and where my gifts and abilities are affirmed and appreciated, then chances are pretty good I will be comfortable with myself, even if in some things I may be below average. Conversely, if I am brought up in a family where I feel like I am not wanted, where I feel nobody notices me for who I am, and where I feel I can never do anything right, then chances are I will have self-esteem problems later on in life, no matter how gifted, talented or beautiful I, in fact, may be.

PERSONAL IDENTITY

That brings us in this chapter to the fifth stage of personality development – the shaping of a sense of personal identity. Having learned Basic Trust, Autonomy, Initiative and Industry, the child now starts to emerge with a sense of personal identity. Identity means, "I know who I am, I know what my gifts and abilities are and I have made peace with who I am."

Typically, this issue comes to the fore between the ages of 11 to 14. This, of course, is the age of puberty. It is the time when significant changes take place, emotionally as well as physically. It is also the time when children start breaking away from parental control and start trying to find out who they really are. For that reason, this is often a difficult and confusing time, both for the parents and for the child. The child wants to be treated like an adult while maintaining the privileges of childhood. Parents are sometimes hard pressed to know how to handle the emerging teenager's inconsistencies.

Historically, of course, there was no such thing as a teenager in the sense that we know it today. You were either a child or an adult. Once you came of age, you left the world of the child and took your place among the adults. Many societies had an appropriate rite of passage to mark this significant milestone. Identity crises, in the way we know them today, were virtually unheard of because along with adulthood came adult responsibilities. Children lived and worked alongside their parents in the shop or on the farm. Their responsibilities grew with their own physical and mental abilities to handle tasks.

Today that is all changed. Long after they have matured physically, many kids today have no place in the adult world. There is nobody to give them a sense of belonging, a sense of worth and a sense of competence. The result is the proverbial identity crisis: "Who am I? What am I here for? Does my life matter? How can I make a mark?" The result for many is to excel in crime or some other form of deviant social behaviour that will make people take notice of them. "If I can't be good at good things, I can at least be good at bad things!"

When I was in high school, I had two classmates in grade ten who fell into that category. They didn't have great academic minds and consistently flunked the courses they were taking. I don't remember which of the two thought of it first, but eventually they made a lark out of their academic achievements and started competing for the lowest grade in the class! Understandably, their grades kept on dropping from 50 to 40 to 30%, until one of them figured out that if he handed his test paper in blank with only his name on it, he would win hands down. And that is what he did. Needless to say, neither of them stayed in school long after that!

So this process of identity formation, discovering who I am, is an important part of growing up and needs to happen in a significant way during the early teen years. That is not to imply it will be finished then, of course. Finding out who you are, in some ways, is a life-time learning experience. We constantly change and re-define who we are. Witness the many mid-life crises that occur! It is true, though, that the foundations of this must be laid during these early teen years. As we'll see in the next chapter, people who do not learn this lesson will have difficulty later in life forming healthy intimate relationships. They draw their life from other people. Inevitably, that makes people tired of them and strains any relationships they might have established.

Let's look now at four issues I believe the pre-adolescent teenager needs to navigate successfully if he or she is to grow up and have a firm sense of personal identity.

Physical Appearance

The very first issue that needs to be settled in the young adolescent's life is that of physical appearance. Hands down, surveys indicate this to be the most pressing issue teenagers face. "Am I attractive? Do other people like me? Do I fit in with the crowd?" – these are some of the critical issues for teens.

The reason for this, of course, is that early adolescence is the time when hormones kick in. Major bodily changes are taking place. It is also the time when the child is trying to grow up enough to get away from his parents and live in the world on his own. If he is to succeed in that, he has to be able to form significant relationships with other people. To form significant relationships with other people, he needs to be liked and accepted by them. Hence, the emphasis on appearance and conformity.

Our culture places a premium on physical appearance. We are constantly bombarded with unrealistic images and standards of beauty and fashion that many young people try to emulate. The result is disappointment in their own looks and appearance.

Recent surveys taken among kids in this age group indicate that 80 % of young people are dissatisfied with some fundamental aspect of their body or their appearance! Fad diets are now common even among pre-teen children as young as 9 or 10 because they already feel they are "too fat."

Understandably, for many kids this is a time of considerable anxiety. "Will I be pretty or will I be ugly? Are my ears too big? Is my nose too long? Will I look like my mother or will I look like my father? Will I be too tall or will I be too short?" And the list goes on.

Other people, particularly adults, can look at that and say, "Ah, just let it be. It'll all come out in the wash." And most of the time it will and we make peace with our limitations. But getting there is not always easy. When you are in the middle of it, it can be pretty scary stuff. Peer pressure can be incredible.

Dr. James Dobson, in his book *Preparing for Adolescence*, tells the hilarious story of studies done with teenagers in order to test their level of conformity. In one test, a series of lines of different lengths was drawn on a card and flashed in front of a test subject who was asked to identify the longest line. The test group consisted of ten people, nine of whom had been prompted to identify the second longest line as the longest! Only the test subject was left in the dark. Quite naturally, he would be the only one pointing to the longest line. All the others pointed to the second longest line. Almost invariably, the test subject looked around, saw the apparent sincerity of the other nine, and reversed his decision. Common sense might dictate which line is the longest, but when it runs against the opinion of the majority, the majority must be right. That is conformity. [2]

So, for many kids, this is a difficult time. Most of us, though, get through it relatively unscathed. As long as we have someone we can talk to about our changing bodies and are not too different in dress and appearance from everyone else, we fare alright. Sooner or later we come to grips with our looks and appearance. We know we are not the most beautiful or handsome people in the world and that is alright. We're not the ugliest either. Besides, there is a lot more to life than looks.

Every so often, though, there will be somebody in whose life this process of identity-shaping is damaged almost beyond repair. That happens particularly if you have a child who is out of the norm physically. For example, sometimes a child may mature much earlier or later than his or her peers. I have known people whose whole life was derailed because they didn't mature at the same rate as their friends. They wondered, "What's wrong with me? I'm not developing like everyone else." As long as they can talk about that with someone else and get the help they need, they are usually OK. But often the shame and embarrassment runs so deep that they suffer in silence the jeers of their peers. This is especially true for people who have physical deformities. They are often teased mercilessly.

We say sometimes, "Sticks and stones may break my bones, but names will never hurt me," but that's a lot of nonsense. How many kids haven't come running home because they were ridiculed and made fun of on the school playground or by their so-called friends? Many a person has gone through life with a complex because of some cruel and uncalled for remark.

An attractive young woman in our church told me recently of an incident that occurred when she was in grade six. Some of her classmates didn't like her and on one occasion got all the kids to taunt her that they hated her! That's pretty devastating stuff and set her on a course that caused her and others considerable heartache. Emotional damage is sometimes far more severe than mere physical damage.

This is especially true for people who undergo some form of sexual abuse, particularly in the early phases of life. Forming your sexual identity and being comfortable with that is of critical importance in terms of defining what it means to be a man or a woman. When you are sexually abused, it messes up your sense of what is normal and fills you with confusion and shame. It's not safe to be a boy or a girl. And so, instead of taking delight in your maturing and developing sexuality, it becomes something to be avoided. You think, "It's not safe for me to grow up. Growing up gets me into trouble. I can't handle that trouble, so just let me stay a kid." I believe that is one reason we have so many eating disorders, such as anorexia nervosa and bulimia, in our culture. They are subtle attempts at self-rejection. The person is saying, "I don't like who I am. I don't want to live any more. I don't really want to grow up." The problem is epidemic in our culture.

Statistics indicate that approximately one out of twenty girls in North America today is anorexic. One in five is said to be suffering from bulimia. An anorexic has difficulty eating because she always thinks she is too fat, even if she is undernourished to the point of dying. It is truly a modern disease and frightening for those caught up in its clutches. A bulimic, on the other hand, is a binge eater. She will gorge food to dull a deep inner pain and then induce vomiting because it doesn't feel good. Bulimia is much more subtle than anorexia because it is much more difficult to spot. It doesn't usually lead to as drastic a weight loss as anorexia. Princess Diana, recently went on record as having struggled with bulimia during the turbulent years of her separation from Prince Charles. Both eating disorders are a cry for help and represent an unwillingness to grow up and face the painful realities of life. Some kind of professional intervention will usually be required if the root causes are to be addressed and the problem overcome.

It's very important, then, for parents not only to provide protection for their children from the cruelties and abuses of life, but also to help them be comfortable with themselves and their bodies. We need to teach our children that their bodies are a gift from God and that even their looks are ordained of God as part of the calling He has on their life. Instead of being endlessly occupied trying to be something other than what they are, they need to learn to accept with gratitude the person God has made them to be. As Psalm 139:14 says, we are *fearfully and wonderfully made.*

Emotions

The second area in which we have to help our children grow is the area of emotions. When all these hormones kick in, they not only affect our kids physically, they also affect them emotionally. Powerful emotions that were unheard of before now come into play. A person who never even noticed the opposite sex existed, suddenly discovers they not only exist, but are fairly intriguing as well! Surprise, surprise! A person who has always been very even-tempered and nice to have around suddenly becomes an emotional roller-coaster. One moment he or she is ecstatically on top of the world, life is great and going just wonderfully. The next moment, they are holed up in their room, crying their eyes out, tearfully proclaiming that their world has just come to an end and, no, they aren't interested in living any more! One minute they are grown up; the next they are still only a child.

Dr. James Dobson tells the story of the time when he was in Junior High and he began goofing off to the extent that his grades were suffering noticeably. He says:

> *"One day* [my mother] *sat me down for a little chat. She said, 'I know what you're doing in school. Not only could you be making better grades, but I'm sure you're being disruptive in the classroom, too. I've been thinking about what I should do in response. I could punish you or take away your privileges, or I could visit your principal. But I've decided to do none of those things. In fact, I'm not going to do anything about your behaviour. However, if your teacher or principal ever calls me to complain about the way you're acting, then the very next day, I plan to go to school with you and sit by you in all your classes. I'll hold your hand as you walk down the hall and I'll be two feet behind you as you stand with your friends. I'll have my arm draped around your neck through the entire day at school. You won't be able to get away from me for a minute.'*
>
> *"Believe me, that threat scared me to death! I would much rather have had my mother beat me than go to school with me. Just the thought of that awful possibility straightened me out in a hurry. I couldn't run the risk of having my mama following me around at school! That would have been social suicide. My friends would have laughed at me for the rest of the year. I'm sure my teachers wondered why I suddenly became so cooperative during the latter half of ninth grade! Think about it. This tragedy could happen to you, too!"* [3]

How can we help our kids when their emotions are dragging them all over the map? Here are some suggestions:

Give Them Space to be Themselves

At this age, everything is new and emotions are intensified. The crush they have on that cute boy, or the attraction they have for their teacher is their first true love. Our tendency as adults is often to minimize their feelings. We say, "Ah, smarten up, you'll grow out of it." And surely, (hopefully!) they will. But we need to give them the space to discover the full range of their emotions. They need to be able to practice their moods, feelings and expressions on their parents and other significant people in their lives. Otherwise, they will never come to grips with what they are feeling and experiencing and they won't know what to do with their mood swings as their lives are changing.

Give Them Firm Guidelines

Parents, I find, tend to lean to one of two extremes. Either kids are allowed to get away with murder in the interests of not stifling their personality, or else they aren't allowed to get away with anything, usually in the name of good upbringing. Neither extreme embodies biblical truth. The truth of the matter is that we need to give our children the freedom to learn to be their own persons, but we need to do it in the context of firm guidelines as to what is appropriate emotional behaviour. It's one thing to learn to express your feelings. It is quite another to learn to do that in a way that is socially acceptable. Very often, that is a fine line.

For example, in our own home when our kids were growing up, we always encouraged our kids to be real about their feelings and to speak their minds. That is a necessary part of growing up and learning how to deal with your emotions in a constructive fashion. At the same time, we have always made it very plain that there are limits to what we will accept. We do not allow them to be disrespectful towards their parents or any other grown-ups. We do not allow them to be mean towards one another. And we do not allow them to use foul language. We don't always succeed a full one hundred percent, mind you! But we do hold them accountable and make them take responsibility for what they do with their emotions. A lot of damage is done to other people when we just let it all hang out. That is inexcusable before the face of God. Scripture says:

> *Do not let any unwholesome talk come out of your mouths, but only what is helpful for building others up according to their needs, that it may benefit those who listen... Get rid of all bitterness, rage and anger, brawling and slander, along with every form of malice. Be kind and compassionate to one another, forgiving each other, just as in Christ God forgave you* (Eph. 4:29,31-32).

Help Them Realize that Life is More than Emotion

We live in a world where decisions are often made, not on the basis of the will, but rather on the basis of emotion. "If it feels good, do it," is a popular adage of our times.

That is, of course, a dangerous course to pursue. It is guaranteed to lead our kids into a lot of trouble. When you think with your hormones rather than your brain, you are going to get caught up in the emotion of the moment and make some very stupid decisions that may seem pleasurable at the time, but that afterwards leave a legacy of pain and misery. Deferred gratification is one of the most important principles we can teach our children. Often in life we have to suffer short-term pain for long-term gain. People who haven't learned that lesson often suffer long-term pain for short-term gain. We need to help our kids understand and practice that.

Talents and Abilities

A third area where we need to help our kids accept themselves is in the area of their gifts and abilities. A sense of competence, as we saw earlier, is an important part of self-esteem. Everybody needs to have some sense that what they are able to do is valued in a significant way by the people around them. The problem is, we live in a very competitive world. There will always be some people around us who are better at something than we are. There will also likely be people around us who are worse at things than we are. The result is that very often we swing between two extremes: We are either proud (thinking we are better than others), or unduly modest (thinking we have nothing to offer). We either over-estimate or under-estimate our abilities.

Discovering Your Gifts

Part of growing up is discovering what your real gifts and abilities are and learning to be at peace with that.

Scripture says in Romans 12:3,

I say to everyone of you: Do not think of yourself more high-ly than you ought, but rather think of yourself with sober judgment, in accordance with the measure of faith God has given you.

God wants each of us to have an increasingly clear sense of where our talents and abilities lie and concentrate on those. That includes our kids. Kids who do not come to grips with this will often turn to antisocial behaviour. If they feel they cannot be good at something that is good, they will attempt to excel at something bad.

If you understand that, you understand the appeal of teenage gangs. It is a place where they can be accepted for who they are and where they can excel among their peers. If our kids are going to stand against that pressure, they need to be pretty clear on who they are and what their gifts and abilities are.

How can we help them in that? Two suggestions:

First of all, we need to *love them unconditionally*. That is to say, we need to love them for who they are, not for what they do. We will deal with this in more detail in Chapter 24 but let me illustrate what I mean. When I attended high school, I did very well academically. I was usually at the head of the class and received a significant number of prizes and awards for my academic work. So much so, as I recall, that they had to change the rules by which the prizes were awarded so that other kids could get something too. I don't say that to boast. It is just the way it was.

My parents got a good deal of affirmation from this as well. People would meet them and comment on a prize I had won in this area or in that, and that was kind of flattering, particularly for an immigrant family.

Yet, there was never a question in my mind during those years, that if my grades would have been at the bottom of the class instead of at the top, that they would have loved me any less. Their love for me would not have changed one iota. Love at our house wasn't based on what you accomplished academically. As a matter of fact, it didn't always count for a whole lot. I remember my father lamenting one time, after I had done a particularly stupid thing, that he couldn't understand for the dear life of him how anybody who could get the kinds of grades I got in school could do such a stupid thing! Nothing like a lesson in humility!

We need to love our kids unconditionally for who they are, rather than just for what they do. That is not always easy because, on the one hand, you want your kids to do the best they can; on the other hand, you want to love them even when they fail, without encouraging or rewarding failure! The trick is to encourage them to do the very best they can and hold them accountable for that and then love them unconditionally. Kids who grow up with that will feel loved and secure enough to venture out and develop their gifts.

It saddens me when I see families or hear of stories where parents are pushing their children to perform competitively, long before they are really ready for it. I think kids ought to be kids. They grow up fast enough in a very complex world. They don't need to be exploited by power-hungry adults who want to experience success vicariously through their children.

It's one thing to want your child to do his or her best. It is quite another making your love and favour dependent on that success. They need to know that whether they succeed or whether they fail, they are your children, you are proud of them and you are going to love them no matter what.

Secondly, we need to *help them discover and develop areas of interest.* I believe Scripture teaches that God, in Christ, has a specific calling in life for all of His children. I think the circumstances of our birth, our family, our appearance, our giftedness or lack of giftedness is all part of God's grand design to mold us and equip us for the variety of gifts and tasks He wants to give us in life. Part of growing up for a child is to have the freedom to experiment and find out what the range of his gifts is.

Though I was pretty good in school academically, I was not great in sports. I played a little intramural stuff, but I did not excel. I didn't excel either, at least in public high school, on a social level. I did fine with my peers at church. I had a lot of friends there, but I didn't have very many close friends at school. One of the reasons for that was that we lived in different worlds – most of the kids at school were not Christians. Another reason was that I lived on a farm and that didn't leave much time for a lot of socializing. So, throughout much of high school, I was a bit of a loner. As a result, I poured my energy into my "shack." Let me tell you about my shack.

My shack was an old one-ton truck box. It stemmed from my brother-in-law's vegetable-growing days. He used to haul vegetables in it to the processing plant some twenty odd miles away. Once he quit that, the old truck box just sat around in our yard. So I inherited it. I put a floor, a window and a stove in it. I ran electricity to it and connected an intercom system from it to the house and the barn. During most of my high school years, that is where I spent my evenings, studying a bit here and there and carrying on a whole series of "mad scientist" experiments! (That's why the family made me move the whole shebang to the edge of the field, away from the fuel tanks!)

I made all kinds of interesting discoveries in my shack. I learned how to electrocute flies (one of the darker chapters of my life!). I learned how to synthesize a compound that would copper plate any metal object that came in contact with it. I also discovered that when the fire in my little tin wood stove died down, and I threw in some diesel fuel to get it going, it would occasionally blow up on me. I remember clearly the one time it nearly blew the door off its hinges. In retrospect, that was a rather dangerously foolish thing to do! But I had a great time doing it all the same.

I had a bit of a reputation during those years as a science experimenter because that was where my interest lay. I remember clearly the day we just about blew up the chemistry lab. We had received permission from our chemistry teacher to do some unsupervised work in the lab during lunch hour. Big mistake! We promptly proceeded to create and set off a huge smoke bomb, which filled the whole lab with smoke. Undaunted, we asked our teacher if we could demonstrate our new creation in chemistry class which met in a different room right after the lunch hour. Having secured his permission, we proceeded to fill that whole room with smoke, forcing the whole class to retreat to the chemistry lab, which was still filled with smoke from the lunch hour. The teacher was not amused. Neither was the principal!

But, you know, I look back on those years, and they were fun. They really were. As I look back on those years, I see that God used them for two very basic things in my life.

First, I learned about abstract thinking, which is to say, I did a lot of figuring out in my head, trying to build this project and that project, and it developed an ability to think abstractly, which has been really important in terms of my calling and ministry. But even more importantly, I learned perseverance. I don't know if I ever built anything that worked the first time around. Usually it was only after much trial and error that something eventually got going. That has stood me in good stead over the years because many things in life and ministry are that way. We need perseverance if we are to see things through to their completion.

No doubt you have your own stories to tell from your childhood years. Sometimes you look back and shake your head at all the crazy stunts you pulled and you hope quietly that your child won't do what you did. At the same time, we need to understand that experimentation in its varied forms is an important part of the process of discovering who we are. Our job as parents is to give our kids enough space to spread their wings and discover their gifts and abilities. At the same time, we need to give them tight enough guidelines so that they don't destroy themselves and others in the process.

Values and Beliefs

A child growing up at home tends to automatically buy into the value system of the parents, particularly during the early childhood years. "As the twig is bent, so grows the tree," goes the saying. Part of growing up is that sooner or later we have to start thinking for ourselves. We ask ourselves the question, "Do I believe all this stuff my parents have taught me about God, about what is right and wrong and how I should or should not live?"

This can be a time of tremendous conflict. Parents, understandably, want their children to share their value system, particularly if they are Christian parents who know Jesus is the only way. At the same time kids grow up and have a mind of their own. That is particularly true if they move away from home and eventually attend a secular university or if they hang around with friends who do not share the family's values. Besides, the mass media through television and music has an incredible influence in shaping all our lives in ways we don't even begin to fathom. How can we impart biblical values to the next generation? Here are some suggestions:

Model What You Believe

In our church, when parents present their newborn children to the Lord, one of the questions we ask them is this: "Do you promise to do all in your power to lead this child by your example into the life of Christian discipleship?" I love that question because it so clearly gets at one of the most basic ideas of child raising: children learn far more from what they see than what they hear.

Parents say to me sometimes when their children have gone astray, "I don't understand what went wrong. I took them to church, I taught them how to pray, even sent them to a Christian School, but when they grew up, they went their own way."

For parents that can be a very painful scenario. Surely there are many reasons a child might go astray. What I encourage parents to do, though, is ask the questions, "What did I model? What example did I show them in terms of living the Christian life? Did they see in my life a love and devotion for the Lord and for other people that was unmistakably the fruit of my relationship with the Lord? Or did they hear me say one thing and do another?" Nothing turns kids off faster than hypocrisy in its many varied forms.

Children, of course, have very sensitive antennae towards hypocrisy and if we tell them one thing while doing another, all we are teaching them is that there are two standards of behaviour – one for kids and another for grown-ups. When they get old enough, they don't have to do what God tells them to do. They can do what they've seen other significant adults in their lives do.

As I look back on my life, one of the things I am truly grateful for was my father's unquestioned commitment to the Lord Jesus Christ. He was a man who stood firm in his convictions, even when sometimes it proved costly. I recall an incident years ago when money was hard to come by and a truck driver wanted to load produce on Sunday. My father, who had strong convictions about sabbath observance didn't have to think twice. That load was simply not going to be loaded. That and many other incidents like it made an indelible imprint on my mind as a youngster.

Explain Your Convictions to Your Children

Time was when kids believed simply on the basis of parental authority. "Because I say so," may have been enough at one time. It surely is not enough today. Kids need to know what they believe and why. That means parents need to be able to talk them through the issues of the day and discuss them in the light of eternal and biblical truth.

There are many different ways we can do that.

One way is to make sure they know the grand themes and stories of Scripture. Dr. John Patrick, a Christian physician as well as a professor of biochemistry at the University of Ottawa, says one reason secularism has made such inroads in our culture is because many Christian parents fail to teach the Scriptures to their children. He believes we need to take Scripture seriously and teach our children biblical revelation at every available opportunity. He quotes Deuteronomy 6:7-9 where God says through Moses,

> *These commandments that I give you today are to be upon your hearts. Impress them on your children. Talk about them when you sit at home and walk along the road, when you lie down and when you get up. Tie them as symbols on your hands and bind them on your foreheads. Write them on the doorframes of your houses and on your gates.*

When I grew up, we read a chapter of Scripture at virtually every meal. I know that with today's hectic pace and variety of work schedules that is often no longer possible. However, I encourage people to make sure they have at least one meal together and use that time to read through Scripture as a family. At our house, we find it helpful to read through the

Scriptures sequentially, if not the whole Bible, then at least individual Bible books. I know many of us read daily devotionals with little snippets of Scripture here and there and that can be good and helpful. But it ought not to be a substitute for a broader exposure to the whole message of Scripture.

I know parents often think, "My kids are bored and aren't hearing a thing." But you know, it is a remarkable thing about kids. They really can do two or three things at once! Even when they are not actively listening, it is amazing what they can pick up! I am sure my mind wandered as much as anyone during my youth. Yet when I became an adult and started reading the Bible on my own, I found that there were very few stories in it with which I wasn't already familiar. Bible reading lays a solid biblical foundation in our lives that will stand us and our children in good stead when the philosophies of the world come along and try to seduce us.

Another way is by relating the mighty acts of God from our own lives to our children. My father was a consummate story teller and he would do this constantly. I remember him sitting around the table, telling us what God had done here and there. And I remember growing up with the very vivid sense that God wasn't some stuffy old man way out there somewhere, but that He was very much alive and could do the same miracles today as He did in Bible days!

That is the kind of familiarity with God that our children need today. We live in a time that is very experience-oriented. Theory about God alone is not going to move them to put their trust in Him. They need to see that He is very much alive and really cares about the practical, everyday concerns of their lives.

One of the men in our church told me of a recent motor vehicle accident in which he had been involved. Without warning, another motorist had cut in front of him and in the resulting crash, both vehicles had sustained extensive damage. Fortunately, neither of them was seriously hurt. When he came home and told his wife about it, she related that at almost that very precise moment she had this incredible and unusual burden to pray for his protection! There are many stories like that in all of our lives. We need to share these with our children so they can learn firsthand to put their trust in God.

It also means critiquing today's culture in light of biblical truth. Anybody that works with young people today will know that the media is extremely effective in shaping the minds and hearts of a whole generation. I wish I could say that only applies to the secular population. Unfortunately, that is not true. It also applies to those of us who call ourselves Christian because we are exposed to the same music, the same television shows and the same movies. And though we often think we are strong enough and clever enough to sort out the wheat from the chaff, the fact of the matter is, our minds are being shaped by a secular phi-losophy that is significantly at odds with biblical revelation. The problem is that it happens so gradually, little by little eating away at our Christian convictions. Let me illustrate.

Some years ago, my family watched the movie *Robin Hood, Prince of Thieves* on television. It is quite an entertain-ing film with lots of action. In the film, Robin Hood has a friend who is a black man, a Moor, whom he met during the crusades. Throughout the film, the Moor consistently comes across as the one who is the noble individual as opposed to the Christian clerics who are scoundrels and incompetent. It espe-cially surfaces in one scene where a woman is about to have a baby. She is having a difficult time and the cleric, who is sup-posed to be the nurse here, doesn't know what to do. He throws up his hands in despair and is about to let her die. Along comes the Moor, who is filled with compassion for the woman. He deftly performs a caesarean section, delivers the baby, saves the mother's life and emerges as the hero.

What's the message here? The message is that Christians are uncaring and incompetent while other cultures and religions are more compassionate and effective. And if you think that is pushing things too far, ask yourself these questions: When is the last time you saw a Christian preacher portrayed sympathetically on television or in the movies? Is it not true that normally speaking they are pictured as either scoundrels or ineffective do-gooders? And when is the last time you saw a really good father image portrayed in the media? More often than not, they are pictured as abusive and/or incompetent, and desperately in need of straightening out by their brilliant children and long-suffering spouse! [4]

Some time back a survey was done to try to find out which sitcom on television viewers felt was the most accurate reflection of real life. You know which one won? *Roseanne*! Hands down. That's held up as the model of the family with which our culture can most readily identify. God help us!

So, we need to talk with our kids about these issues. We need to help them understand what values are being taught and how they relate to biblical truth. Then, when people come along and espouse values that are at odds with biblical revelation, they will be able to stand up on an intellectual level and say, "That is a bunch of nonsense! That is not what Scripture teaches."

As I look back, I am so grateful for conversations around the dinner table where the events of the day could be discussed from a biblical perspective. I attended a public high school and was exposed to the usual mishmash of secular thought, particularly from certain teachers. I remember coming home from school spouting off about this or that thing I had learned. Every so often, my father would take me aside and say, "You know, that is not the way life really is." And he would go on to explain how it really is from a biblical point of view. And if one of us kids got carried away with other ideas that weren't biblical, such as Hollywood's version of romance or things of such nature, he would do the same thing. To be able to go home, talk about them freely and get a biblical perspective was invaluable beyond words.

Pray Lots

When all has been said and done, faith is a gift God has to give to your children. You can sow and you can water, but only God can make them grow. Pray that God will help them see Him for who He really is. Pray that God will help them see what the world is really like. Pray that God will give them the right friends. Pray that God will raise up someone in whose life they can see the love of the Lord Jesus. Pray to surrender them to the Lord. Remember, God is more interested in their eternal well-being than you are!

THE PAYOFF

The challenges are great, but so are the rewards. As God works in their lives, they will grow up to become the young men and women they were intended to be. They will know their strengths and weaknesses. They will come to terms with who they are and they will be comfortable with that. Then, when everybody else in the crowd says the second longest line is really the longest, they will be secure enough to say, "I don't care what the rest of you say, that other line appears longer to me." When all their friends want to drag them this way and that way, they will have the ability to stand firm in their own convictions. They will develop the skills to form true and intimate relationships because they are able to give as well as receive.

NOTES

1. I am indebted to Dr. David Sherbino of Ontario Theological Seminary, Toronto, Ontario for this figure.

2. Dr. James Dobson, *Preparing for Adolescence* (Ventura, CA: Gospel Light Publications, 1978) pp. 32-34.

3. *Ibid*, p. 103.

4. For a thorough analysis of the subtle bias of much of the mass media see Michael Medved's book *Hollywood vs. America: Popular Culture and the War on Traditional Values* (New York: HarperCollins Publishers, Inc., 1992).

22 | Making Friends

*There is a friend that sticks
closer than a brother.*
Proverbs 18:24

The capacity to form close and meaningful relationships with other people is one of the most crucial areas of growing up. People who succeed in this are able to form close and warm friendships that will see them through the toughest of times. People who fail at this are often loners who simultaneously long for and hate intimacy. They want it because they sense intuitively that is what we have been made for. They fear it because it exposes them to simply too much pain.

INTIMACY

Intimacy is the sixth stage of personality development. This phase runs approximately from age 13 or 14, through the teen years and perhaps even into the 20s, depending on the rate of maturation of the individual.

These are the years in which our young people increasingly declare their independence from their parents and become close friends with people outside the parental home. That may include same-sex friends, members of the opposite sex or even other significant adults with whom they can share their heart more easily than with their own parents.

For both parents and teenagers, this can be a very difficult time. For parents it can be a difficult time because they see their children growing away from them. This may be especially true if the parents have looked to the child to fill their unmet needs. As parents sometimes lament, "My son, my daughter, they used to tell me everything. Now they are 13 and 14, and they don't tell me anything anymore."

This can create a real sense of loss and be a very difficult time for parents because there is no guarantee that when their kids start launching out in relationships, they will make wise decisions. Many parents fear that once they let go of their kids, they will become friends with worldly teenagers and be dragged off to some place where they don't want to see their kids go. And that's not an unrealistic fear.

Statistics indicate that the denomination to which I belong loses 50% of the kids raised within the church. And we are a family-oriented denomination! Not all of these are lost to the faith, of course. Some go to other churches; some come back in later years. The fact remains, however, that many do not come back and are essentially lost to the faith.

Recently, I had the opportunity to conduct a worship service in another congregation. What I saw shocked me. I counted about two or three children younger than 12, maybe two teenagers and perhaps two people in their 20s or 30s. All of the rest, and no disrespect intended, were grey-haired folks, well along in years.

Friendships is one of the primary factors in that decline. I often tell our people to encourage their kids to be actively involved in the life of the church, if for no other reason than that is a good place to make good friends. Kids who do not have their primary friendships in a community of faith will likely be lost to that community.

These years are also a difficult time for the kids themselves, because they are trying to break loose from their parents and make their own way in life. That creates considerable anxiety. Many ask themselves, "Will people accept me the way I am? Will I be able to find friends? Will I manage to get in with the right groups of friends?" One of the big fears of many kids is that of not fitting in. "Nobody wants to be my friend. Nobody wants to hang around with me." An adult might just shrug his shoulders and say, "Who cares? That is their loss, not mine." But for kids in their early teen years, it is not so simple. To safely be able to leave home and make their own way in the world, they must be able to develop a network of friends who will support and sustain them. Without this, they are dead in the water. So, finding friends and keeping them is a major pre-occupation of kids in this age bracket.

Unless a person manages to develop solid relationships apart from his parents, he is never really free to leave home. He remains tied to his mother and father's apron strings. That is why there are so many people who have never really grown up. Physically, they may have moved away from home, but emotionally and in every other way, they are still tied to their parents. That, of course, plays havoc with new relationships. It always feels like there is a third party present. How many times haven't you heard one spouse say to another, "Sometimes I feel you are more married to your mother and/or father than you are to me"? For parents, particularly aging parents, it can be wonderful to have a son or daughter who is so loyal and devoted. For anyone else, it's a royal pain!

So, it's critical that in our growing-up years there be a healthy separation from our parents so we can truly be our own person and make wise and godly choices in forming and maintaining healthy relationships. Only children who have grown up can relate as adults to other adults.

Let's take a look then in this chapter at some practical things we as parents can do to help our kids form meaningful and lasting relationships that glorify God.

Lay the Right Foundation

As noted earlier, intimacy is stage six of personality formation. It is preceded by 1) Basic Trust; 2) Autonomy; 3) Initiative; 4) Industry; and 5) Identity. As we have seen, these are sequential. Each subsequent stage depends on the successful completion of the stage that precedes it. It stands to reason then, that the greatest favour we can do our children, if we want them to learn healthy relationships, is to lay in their lives the right foundation. A child who has successfully conquered stages 1 through 5 is likely to have the necessary skills and maturity to tackle stage 6. One who has not will likely have trouble.

Let me give an example. A very distraught father and mother came to see me some years ago. They came because they were at their wits' end as to what to do with their 15-year-old daughter. She had fallen in love with a young man of whom her parents did not approve. They tried everything they could think of to try to make her break off the relationship, to no avail. The more they tried, predictably, the more stubborn she became. So they came to me for advice. What should they do?

I don't remember whether I said it to them or not. But I do remember clearly saying to myself, "Sorry folks, it's too little, too late. If you were not able to make her mind you when she was 3 years of age (they had told me how stubborn and self-willed an individual she had been), there is no way you are going to make her mind you today."

There are many kids like that. They are raised in the faith, come from good spiritual homes and look like models of virtue. Then along comes a prince or princess charming, and presto, quick as a flash, everything they have grown up with is rejected. They latch onto a relationship you know is going to be harmful and destructive, but they refuse to listen to any reason.

Why is that? It's because the foundation in their lives is not solid. As I have observed earlier, many kids grow up with a love deficit. They have a hole in their heart. They don't know who they are. They have no self-confidence. They try to draw their life from other people. And when someone comes along and offers them love, it is such a powerful inducement, it readily carries the day. Many try to find in one night, the love that has evaded them all their lives. Of course, it doesn't work. But that doesn't keep people from trying. After all, everyone thinks they are the exception to the rule!

The antidote is not more lectures or desperate measures to keep them on the straight and narrow. The antidote is doing what we can to lay a strong and healthy foundation. Here again the old adage, "An ounce of prevention is worth a pound of cure," applies. It is far easier to build right the first time, than to try to tear down old structures and rebuild. If that is true in the world of construction it is certainly true in the process of character formation.

What that means, practically speaking, is that we need to help our kids acquire Basic Trust, learn healthy Autonomy, practice Initiative and Industry and discover a true sense of Identity. A person who discovers all of these through union with Christ will be able to stand firm in the midst of the most adverse circumstances.

Some years ago, a magazine did a survey on a secular university campus to find out which students demonstrated the healthiest and happiest out-look on life. Imagine their surprise when they discovered that the kids who were the healthiest emotionally were the kids hanging around the chapel, kids who not only had come from solid homes, but whose lives were rooted and grounded in God's love. I believe that is what Psalm 1:1-3 means when it says,

Blessed is the man who walks not in the counsel of the wicked, nor stands in the way of sinners, nor sits in the seat of scoffers; but his delight is in the law of the Lord, and on

His law he meditates day and night. He is like a tree plant-ed by streams of water, that yields its fruit in its season, and its leaf does not wither. In all that he does, he prospers.

The key to fruit-bearing is being rooted firmly in God's saving love in Jesus Christ.

That is why it is so important for us, particularly if we are parents of young children, to take seriously what Scripture has to say about parenting. We need to be a channel through which God's love and grace can flow into the lives of our children. In this way, by the time they are in their teens, they will have some idea of who they are, what they are capable of and the kind of life they can have in relationship with the Lord.

That is, of course, no absolute guarantee that they won't make wrong decisions when it comes to picking friends. They are, after all, still very human. But it will significantly diminish the likelihood of their bonding with the wrong kind of friends. Instead, it will help them cultivate meaningful relationships in the Body of Christ.

Somebody asks, "What do I do if that kind of foundation has not been established in the life of my child? What do I do if my child insists on hanging around with the wrong kinds of friends?"

Well, that's a tough one, because short of tying them down and making them mind, there isn't a whole lot you can do about it once they reach a certain age. About all you can do is surrender them to the Lord and pray for them. Pray that God will pour out His grace and mercy and heal them at the core of their being. That almost certainly won't be easy nor without pain. Often it means making wrong choices and living with the consequences of those wrong choices. But God is powerful as well as gracious, and the world is filled with young men and women who, like the prodigal of old, have traded in their inheritance for a shot at life in the fast lane. Once there, they discovered it wasn't what it was cracked up to be and they came to their senses and eventually returned home where they belonged.

Help Them Develop Necessary Social Skills

Developing meaningful intimate relationships requires many skills. Here are some of them:

Discernment

Discernment is the ability to look beyond the surface and discover a person's true character. One reason parents and kids often fight about the friends they hang around with is that parents often see things that the kids do not see. Because they have lived longer, parents often see character traits that they know will damage their own children. The reverse of that is true as well. Sometimes parents are so turned off by externals that they never bother to find out what the person is really like on the inside. Either way, what shows on the outside isn't always indicative of what lives on the inside.

I was reminded of that recently as I watched a television interview with Doug and Donna French and Dan and Deborah Mahaffy, the parents of the two school girls who were brutally raped and murdered by Paul Bernardo. This was their first public interview in the aftermath of the very sordid trial. One of the probing questions the interviewer asked was, "Were you offended by the police and their supposed mishandling of the case? If they had caught him earlier, your daughters might have been alive today." I found their responses fascinating. Not only did they indicate that they had no ill will towards the police, but they went on to make the following observation: "Had Paul Bernardo looked the type who would commit this type of crime, they would have taken him in a lot earlier. The problem was, he didn't look the type. He knew just how to conduct himself so as to cast all suspicion away from himself." And that is so true. People seldom are what superficially they appear to be.

Discernment is a skill we all need to develop, especially our teenage children. It will help us to stay away from relationships that in the long run will do us more harm than good and gravitate towards relationships that are good and healthy.

Communication Skills

This is the ability, first of all, to understand your own emotions, feelings and thoughts. Secondly, it is the ability to put these into words in such a way that another person can really understand what you are trying to communicate. Thirdly, it means having the ability to really listen to another person and hear what they are saying, no matter how poorly worded it may be or laden down with emotional content.

These are pretty significant skills and there are many adults who have never learned them to any significant degree. As a result, they have difficulty establishing close, intimate friendships. When trouble or misunderstanding arises, they don't have the skills to work it out. Anger and emotion take over and the relationship will often fall apart. New relationships often fare no better and so life becomes a merry-go-round of broken relationships. They want to be close to someone, but just don't know how to do it.

Boundaries

How close do I get to whom? Where do I draw the line in sexual intimacy? What is normal in friendships and what is not? Again, these are pretty significant questions and many people do not have the skills to establish appropriate boundaries. They either become too intimate too fast, or remain too distant too long. In either case, it usually leads to failure in establishing healthy relationships.

Establishing appropriate boundaries is a skill that needs to be learned. As always, the challenge for parents with growing children is to provide their kids with enough space so they can learn by trial and error, without giving them so much space that they destroy themselves in the process.

Parents often tend to go to extremes. There are parents who see their kids growing up, developing a mind of their own and making decisions which they, as parents, don't like or agree with, and they lower the boom. They try to clamp down, often with varying degrees of success, until the child either becomes mouthy or big enough to defy the parents or chooses to submit. "As long as you're under my roof you are going to do it my way," is a common reaction. "If you don't like that, you can leave home." That, of course, often puts a teenager in a terrible bind and can lead to long-lasting bitterness. It does nothing to teach them healthy boundaries.

Other parents, when it becomes obvious that their kids have a mind of their own, throw up their hands in despair and renege on their responsibilities. Their favourite line is, "Well, you know how it is. Kids will be kids. They have to sow their wild oats sometime. Look at what I was like at their age and how I turned out." These parents allow their kids to go through life with a minimum degree of supervision, forgetting that life in society today is considerably different than what it was even five or ten years ago, let alone twenty or thirty when the parents were teenagers. Things people didn't get into until their late teens or early twenties, like drinking, sex, drugs, etc., are now increasingly readily available for kids much, much younger.

As always, both extremes are detrimental to the child. My experience has been that kids who have been held too tightly for too long will tend to rebel. By the time they leave home and go to college, they are like a tightly-wound spring that has suddenly been relieved of the pressure. They go wild. Everything that has been forbidden now becomes pleasure and they sin with a vengeance. Eventually, many of them come to their senses and settle down. Hopefully, the damage will be minimal and they will have learned their lesson. Sometimes, though, their actions will haunt them for the rest of their lives. You cannot always undo the mistakes you have made.

Kids who have been raised too leniently, on the other hand, tend to be without focus and direction. They do not have the strength of character and discipline to see a given task through to completion, particularly when things get rough. As a result, they often wander aimlessly, eventually pouring themselves into whatever gives them some measure of pleasure and self-esteem.

Some practical areas now, where parents need to help their teenagers establish clear boundaries are:

• **Curfew.** I happen to believe that younger teenagers, particularly, should have some limits as to where they can go and how long they can be away from home. I know there are many parents today who are so broad-minded that they establish virtually no limits on where their kids go and when. I respect their decision, but believe it to be unwise and unbiblical for two reasons: 1) It is utterly irresponsible to give a child increasing freedom unless he has a proven track record that shows he can handle it. For that reason alone, kids in their early teens, particularly, need very clear limits as to where they can go, how long they can be there and when they are expected back home. This gives them an opportunity to demonstrate that they can be trusted to use good judgment. 2) Parents are people too, and they need their sleep! I suspect I am not the only parent who sleeps a lot better when the kids are home safely and asleep in their beds. I think kids have some responsibility on this score towards their parents. Coming home at all hours while their parents are at home wondering what has happened to them is pretty inconsiderate most of the time.

At our house, we set curfews for our kids, usually adjusting them as they got older (and their parents more practiced at parenthood!). If it was necessary to come home later than their curfew, they were expected to call and get permission or at least let us know. Apart from the occasional hassle ("All my friends get to stay out later. Don't you trust me?"), that worked pretty well.

Parents whose kids are friends with each other can save themselves considerable frustration, in my opinion, if they were to agree to a common set of rules for their kids. You will have found, as we have, that peer pressure is a tough thing to stand against. When all the other kids can stay out much later and do things you won't allow your kids to do, the push to give in becomes pretty strong. "His mother says it is OK to watch that video. Why can't I go to his place and see it with him?" Of course, the other kid is doing the same thing to his mother and father. The best way to nip that in the bud is to get some parents together and agree on what the rules are. They will never be entirely the same and certainly don't need to be, because each household is different; but a general consensus will save a lot of hassles.

• **Friendships.** As we noted earlier, many parents are concerned about the company their kids keep. Understandably so. Once kids hit their teenage years, what their peers think of them often far outweighs anything their parents might happen to think. Consequently, many homes are often in turmoil over which friend their child brings home. Part of helping our children establish healthy boundaries is to determine what latitude you are going to give them in picking friends. We need to sit down with them, explain biblical criteria for friendship, seek to win their agreement and cooperation and then stick to it. That will mean telling them by times, "I don't think so and so is a good friend for you and I want you to give up that friendship."

That is not an easy thing to do. Many parents are, in fact, afraid to do that because they fear it will just make their kids more stubborn and determined, particularly if it is a boy friend or a girl friend. So many kids marry out of spite that parents often feel the less said the better. And there certainly are times when saying little or nothing is the better part of wisdom. At the same time, though, as parents we do have the responsibility to help our kids establish meaningful boundaries and if we think that a certain friendship is not going to be helpful for our children, we have every right as parents to at least warn them about that and strongly discourage them to pursue it any further. If we have a healthy relationship with our kids, even in their teenage years, they will often respect our judgment. If they don't, the problem probably runs deeper and they may just have to learn the hard way.

• **Music and fashions.** The same principles apply to all other areas of contention between parents and teenagers, including music and fashions. I suppose there are few places where the differences between the generations show up more readily – or more contentiously – than in those two areas. Preferences in music and fashion are highly individualistic and shaped largely by the culture of the day. I frankly don't like a good deal of modern music and I'm still old-fashioned enough to think that if you have a hole in your pants, it ought to be patched, but, hey, that's strictly personal preference. Many of these things are not necessarily good or evil in themselves. They are often simply another way for a new generation to define their own existence.

What's important is that as parents we pick our battles carefully. Not everything is worth fighting for. Conversely, some things are definitely worth fighting for.

As parents, it is understandable that we want our children to grow up without making some of the mistakes we have made. The danger comes in sitting on them so tightly that everything becomes a battle. Many things they are going to have to learn on their own, by trial and error if need be. Our job is to see that they don't get destroyed in the process. So, pick your fights carefully. Sit down and discuss which are the non-negotiables in your household.

Music that is too loud, lyrics that are blasphemous or indecent, fashions that are too revealing or otherwise inappropriate should not be tolerated in a home that professes to be Christian. Here again, consensus in community can go a long way to forestalling the "anything goes" mentality that is so prevalent even in Christian circles.

Once these guidelines are established, stick to them and make sure there are appropriate consequences. Remember, kids long for some measure of structure and will, in the long run, respect you if you defend your values consistently and sincerely.

Be There For Our Kids

For all their bravado and determination not to need their parents, teenagers in so many ways are still just kids. They are going to face rejection sooner or later. Let's face it – the world is a scary place. I mean, they may think they have it rough at home, but at least at home, if the family is at all reasonably normal, there is love and a commitment to see it through together. Out in the world, you have no such guarantee. People can really hurt you, make fun of you, take advantage of you, use you and scar you for life. When that happens, we need to be there for them, even when sometimes it will be their own fault and they "had it coming."

Listening

That means, first of all, we need to *learn to listen*. I know that is very difficult for many parents. Parents tend to see themselves as God-given instruments for spouting off advice. And certainly there is a time for parents to do that. Long before we do that, however, we need to first earn the right to give advice. And that means listening – listening to the real concerns, questions and struggles that our kids are facing. If the values that we seek to impart to our kids are ever going to be truly internalized, then our kids need time to work these issues through. Just because they have been settled in our minds twenty or thirty years ago, doesn't mean they are settled in their minds. We need to give them space to vent their feelings and their frustrations and do it in such a way that it is safe for them to be real. That doesn't mean we let everything go, but it does mean that we cut them some slack.

That can be scary for parents because it means your own value system may be seriously challenged. It will also likely be inconvenient because you will find, as I have, you cannot always plan and schedule these sessions. They tend to arise serendipitously as the need comes up. Wise parents know how to take advantage of such moments, even if that means rearranging the schedule.

Giving Advice

Secondly, it means we *advise them* but we do it *sparingly*. The temptation, of course, for us as parents is to rush in and help them figure everything out. That not only robs them of the opportunity to learn to some degree by trial and error, it also robs them of the joy of having conquered something on their own. If we do give advice, it should be as much as possible in the form of encouragement. Sharing real life incidents from our own experience (in a non-lecture format!) can be a very effective way of doing that. At any rate, we need to give them space to decide whether or not to take our advice. As they mature and have less to prove, that will become easier and easier for them, assuming we have demonstrated love and wisdom in our walk with them.

When our second son was young, he used to have these incredibly grandiose ideas. At varying points in his life, he planned to build, as I recall, a snowmobile, a helicopter and an airplane all before the age of 12! It used to frustrate me to no end. He'd come to me for advice and help in building all these things. I would hardly know what to do. I didn't always want to discourage him. At the same time, I wanted him to have realistic expectations because I knew he kept setting himself up for failure each time. So I would just tell him each time, "Michael, I can't even build one of these things. Why don't we try building something that is a little more manageable?" That didn't usually dissuade him, mind you! He could be quite determined, even though history usually proved dad to be right. I might add, now that he has grown up, he's proven to be a remarkably handy lad!

Being There

Thirdly, it means *being there* when things go wrong. Not all kids have the ability, willingness or opportunity to talk things through, learn from others and thus solve their problems. Sometimes, they clam up. Nobody gets them talking. That's when things are likely to go wrong.

A recent newspaper article reported that Canada is the third highest nation in the world when it comes to teenage suicides. Teenage suicides in the country have doubled over the last twenty years. All over the country, there are young men and women who take their own life. Why is that?

As always, the reasons are many, but surely one reason is that the pain of living exceeds the pain of dying. They have become filled with hopelessness and despair. They see no way out of their present predicament and so choose to end it all. What is especially frightening about this is that so often it comes as an almost complete surprise to those closest to them. "I didn't know he had any problems," someone will say after the fact. "He was such a nice boy. He had everything going for him. What a shame." Shame indeed! But one of the greatest reasons for shame is that nobody picked up on the warning signals. Almost always, there are warning signals that imply a pending crisis. Here are some things to watch out for:[1]

- change in eating habits
- feeling helpless
- losing interest in doing things
- sleeplessness
- sudden outbursts of crying

- serious drop in grades
- extreme fatigue
- increased isolation from family and friends
- feeling of "nobody understands"
- expressing hostility

All of us feel like this some of the time, of course. But when it persists in a teenager, there is something seriously amiss. It is a cry for help. He or she is not fitting into life. Being there means we do what we can to help them through this very difficult time in life. If we cannot do it ourselves, at least we can avail ourselves of the resources. Writing it off as just part of the rebellious teenage years is dangerous.

The idea that all teenagers are destined to go through a sullen phase of rebelliousness is a bunch of nonsense, in my opinion. Yes, they need to be independent; yes, they will assert their authority; and yes, they will by times give their parents a hard time. But that doesn't mean they have to be disrespectful or rude or antisocial. Kids who manifest these characteristics over a period of time are going through a rough time and need help.

Love Them Unconditionally

The most important key to helping our kids form meaningful relationships is showing them unconditional love. Because this is such a major issue, we will discuss this more fully in the next chapter.

NOTES

1. Dr. Roger Allen and Ron Rose, *Common Sense Discipline: What to Say and Do When Kids Need Help* (Ft. Worth, TX: Worthy Publishing, 1986) pp. 203-204.

23 | Loving Your Kids Unconditionally

While he was still a long way off, his
father saw him and was filled with
compassion for him.
Luke 15:20

I was deeply impressed some time ago as I listened to the story of a father's unconditional love for his son. I was impressed because the father demonstrated unconditional love in the face of a glaring failure on the part of his son that cost the whole family considerable expense and misfortune. Here is the story as I remember it.

The father was a greenhouse grower who had many, many plants under glass. One spring when the nights were still cool but the days were increasingly hot, the man had to leave for the day and he delegated to his young teenage son the responsibility of opening the windows in the greenhouse. "When the sun rises and it becomes hot," he said, "all the plants will be scorched if the windows aren't opened." The son, of course, assured his father that he would take care of it. Father went away, but you know how it goes sometimes with kids. The young man was distracted. He got busy with other things and forgot all about his responsibilities.

367

Later that afternoon, his father came home and asked quite naturally, "You did open the windows in the greenhouse, did you not?" The colour drained first from the young man's face and then from his father's face when it became clear that this had not been done. In agonizing haste, the father drove over to the greenhouse with his son. All the way over there, the boy just kept apologizing, "I'm sorry, Dad, I'm sorry, Dad, I'm sorry." His father didn't say anything, but his face spoke volumes!

Sure enough, when they got to the greenhouse, their worst fears were realized. They walked into that place, and the temperature inside had risen to a phenomenal 146°F! Every last one of the more than 46,000 plants ready for market in that greenhouse were fried to a crisp! The economic consequences for the family would be devastating. Not only was the crop lost, but it was too late in the season to plant a new one.

I don't know about you, but if I were in that father's situation, I would be just a tad bit upset! And I'm sure the father was too. But the thing that impressed me so much about this story was that the father, faced with a colossal financial loss due to his son's negligence, turned to his son after surveying the damage, and said, "Son, you've made a mistake. I know you are sorry and I forgive you. I'll never mention it again."

And true to his word, he never mentioned it again. It was forgiven, it was forgotten, it was settled. That's unconditional love!

DEFINING UNCONDITIONAL LOVE

Unconditional love is love that has no conditions. It's not based on performance or accomplishments, but rather gives and keeps on giving of itself even when the object of love is unworthy and undeserving. Unconditional love is what God showed us when He gave His Son to die for our sins.

Unconditional love is what you see in Luke 15 in the story of the prodigal son. Here is a young man who squandered his inheritance in loose living, but eventually came to his senses and returned home. The Bible says, *...while he was still a long way off, his father saw him and was filled with compassion for him; he ran to his son, threw his arms around him and kissed him* (Luke 15:20). The story then goes on to tell us that the father threw a party because, he said, . ".*..this son of mine was dead and is alive again; he was lost and is found* (vs. 24). That's unconditional love and that is what our kids need if they are going to grow to emotional and spiritual maturity.

The reason for that is not hard to understand. Part of growing up, as we have noted previously, is learning to internalize the moral choices and values that we have been taught. It is not enough for our kids to choose to do the right thing because that's how they have been raised. They need to learn to make these choices for themselves. Rather than just having them imposed from the outside, they need to be written on their hearts. That means they need the space to learn by trial and error, in the confidence that the rug is not going to be pulled out from underneath them. They need to know that they are still loved and valued, even when their actions have caused us considerable pain.

For parents, that can be a costly business in more ways than one. When our oldest son, David, first started driving, I was in the car with him and said, "Son, if you continue taking corners this fast, the first time it snows, you are going to wipe out."

Well, wouldn't you know it! The first time it snowed after he got his licence, he was driving a car-load of kids home from high school in someone else's borrowed car, took a corner too fast, lost control and crashed into a telephone pole! The old car was a write-off. Our second son, Michael, had his foot caught between the front seat and the pillar of the car where the telephone pole hit, so he couldn't get out. This necessitated a call to the Fire Department for the "Jaws of Life." The result was a careless driving charge, which David challenged in court. Arguing as only he can, he won his case, partly because of the judge's sympathy and partly because road conditions that day had indeed deteriorated so fast with falling temperatures that there had been an excessive slate of accidents in town that afternoon. Of all the traffic cases in court that day, David's was the only one that was dismissed.

In retrospect, that was a dubious blessing. Roll the clock forward about a year. David is driving the family car on his way to a Sunday afternoon of skating. There goes the phone: "Dad, you are not going to believe this." Same problem again, on the same street, only a couple of blocks down. The car had fishtailed out of control and smashed tail-end first into another power pole, extensively damaging the rear end. There is nothing he can do but call the police. And wouldn't you believe it? The same policeman who had originally charged him with careless driving shows up to investigate this accident! He, of course, had been none too happy at having his earlier careless driving charge thrown out of court so he was more than delighted to lay a second charge. This time David didn't even bother trying to fight it, because he knew he didn't have a chance.

Many parents go through these things. Some have stories to tell which are far worse. How do you get through these painful and embarrassing moments, still loving your child unconditionally while at the same time making it clear that you do not approve or condone their actions? Here are some suggestions:

PRACTICING UNCONDITIONAL LOVE

See Each Child as Unique

There is a temptation for many parents to measure their kids against some ideal standard. For some parents, that standard is a selective memory of their own life and behaviour when they were children. You know the story: "When I was your age, I had to walk to school five miles uphill, against the wind, both ways!" The kids roll their eyes and make faces because they know what's coming next – comparisons with the "good old days."

Sometimes, that standard is a sibling. "Why can't you be smart like your brother or sister? They always have their homework done on time." Or else it's somebody down the street. "Why can't you behave like your friend does? She's always so pleasant and polite, not disrespectful like you are."

The intent behind this kind of comparison, more often than not I suspect, besides releasing parental frustration, is to try to shame the kid into better behaviour. Sometimes, I suppose, it actually works that way. In most cases, though, it doesn't because each of us hates to be compared with somebody else. We all want to be loved and accepted for who we are, warts, shortcomings, woundedness and all.

What we need to communicate to our kids, therefore, is that each of them is unique. Each is a unique expression of God's purpose, God's calling and God's destiny. I mean, God doesn't even make two snowflakes alike, let alone two people! For us to take some arbitrary standard, coloured as it is by our own prejudices and cultural background, and then apply that to our children does them a gross injustice. They aren't just a chip off the old block. They are their own persons in the sight of God and they need to be loved and respected for who God has made them to be.

I believe this is critically important, particularly today when so many people have lost any sense of being special. The downside of the theory of evolution is that we cease to be special. If we are here merely by blind chance, if there is no Creator God who has made us for His own transcendent purposes, then life gets reduced to living by animal instincts. "Eat, drink and be merry for tomorrow we die," becomes our creed.

I believe that is one reason why the suicide rate among young people is climbing so dramatically. The secularism of our culture produces kids who don't know what they are living for. They have no focus, no purpose, no goal beyond their own immediate needs. They experience never-ending pain as, one by one, their dreams are demolished and hope forsakes them. No wonder death is sometimes seen as an attractive alternative. If I don't matter to anybody, then nobody will miss me when I'm gone either.

That is why it is so important that we instill into our kids the belief that they do matter. They matter to God and they matter to us. We see them as unique individuals before the face of God. We value their thoughts, their feelings and their opinions. And even though we may not always approve of their behaviour, we value them as persons. We are proud of them. We believe that, in Christ, they have the potential to become everything that God has destined them to be. That's what creates a sense of security and belonging!

Wise parents recognize this and allow their kids the freedom to become the people God has designed them to be. Sometimes that means parents have to swallow their pride as their children turn out quite differently from what they as parents had hoped. Sometimes it means suffering embarrassment as your kids embark on an avenue of self-discovery that challenges acceptable patterns of behaviour.

John and Paula Sandford share a story about one of their kids. When he was in high school, he decided he was going to play in a rock band – a secular rock band. John Sandford, at that time, was pastoring the leading church in Wallace, Idaho, when rock-and-roll was even more disreputable than it is today, especially among evangelical church people. He had to make up his mind, first of all, whether he would allow his son to do that. As he prayed about it, it seemed that the Lord said that he should not only permit his son to play in the rock band, but that he, his father, was going to drive him around

from engagement to engagement! You can imagine how difficult a decision that was for John. Yet that is what he chose to
do. He knew that as a parent he had to give his son the freedom to make his own choices and that God would use that to
work out His own righteous purposes. God certainly honoured that decision. Today all of their children are actively
serving the Lord.[1]

Separate Who They Are From What They Do

Children can cause tremendous pain to their parents by
the choices they make and the things they do.

When I was in elementary school, I knew a young man
who years earlier had caused his parents considerable grief,
not to mention expense. As a child he had been playing in
the hayloft of his father's barn when he noticed some straw
from the previous year remaining on one of the beams. With
the logic of a child, he concluded the straw didn't belong
there and so he decided to get rid of it. He went to the
house, got some matches and proceeded to burn away the
straw! Well, he burned up the straw, all right. And the hay
and the barn! You can well imagine that his father was not a
happy camper.

When that sort of thing happens to us as parents, when
our kids make mistakes that are costly or result in social
embarrassment and humiliation, then it is easy to confuse
being and *doing*. That is to say, we fail to separate what our
kids *are* from what they *do*. Instead of being angry at their
behaviour and seeking to correct it, we personalize our anger
and our frustration and take it out on the child. We reject and
criticize the child instead of his or her behaviour. Name-call-
ing is a common example: "You no good, rotten, kid. I wish
I'd never had you. Get lost! I don't ever want to see you again.
A kid who behaves that way is not my son, or my daughter."
And so on. There are many variations of what amounts to calling down curses on our children.

It's very easy to fall into that pattern and all of us probably do it at one time or another, particularly if we are really angry or our child exhibits an especially annoying pattern of behaviour. For example, a child may be especially clumsy, or slow, or careless, or prone to making hasty decisions that haven't been thought through. It is so easy then to personalize our irritations: "You are so clumsy, so stupid, so slow, so forgetful. If your head wasn't attached, you'd forget that too." The intent, again, in addition to relieving us of our frustrations, is to try to shame the child into better behaviour. Sometimes that works. More often than not, however, the message that is communicated is, "You are a loser. You not only *do* things wrong, but you *are* wrong. There is something fundamentally defective about who you are."

That, of course, puts a child in a terrible predicament because it means he must change before he can be loved. If he doesn't change, then he won't be loved. The question is, how is he going to change? Character issues run deep. Unless we are loved unconditionally first, it will never be safe for us to make the changes that need to be made. God doesn't first require us to change before we receive His love. We first receive His love. Then we change.

Striving to Please

When we fail to make this distinction between "hating the sin and loving the sinner," we teach our kids one of the most profound, far-reaching lessons of life: If you want to be loved, you must live up to a certain standard of behaviour. If you fail to live up to this standard of behaviour, you will not be loved. This, of course has practical implications. Everybody needs and wants to be loved and so the natural response of a child in the face of love that is conditional is to try, at least for a while, to measure up. "Maybe if I clean up the house nice, or get better grades, or join the football team, Mom and Dad will be proud of me."

Kids desperately need and want their parents' love and approval and they will often work hard to try to get it. Should they succeed, because they know how to read their parents right, they will likely grow up equating love with performance. You are only worthy of love if you perform. Fail to perform, and you're not worthy of love.

That, of course, is what drives the elder brother in the story of the prodigal son. Here is a man who thinks his father loves him because he works so hard. By the same token, his father cannot possibly love his prodigal brother who has just gone and squandered his entire inheritance in loose living. And so when the father reaches out to the prodigal, throws a party as if nothing has ever happened, the elder brother is furious. It's just not fair. Here he is, working and slaving away from early morning to late at night. He doesn't get any party thrown in his honour. No sir. Nobody even takes note of him. Then along comes this good-for-nothing brother who deserves absolutely nothing, and everybody goes ecstatic over him. It offends his sense of fairness and he walks off in anger.

Why is he like that? Because he doesn't understand grace. He thinks the father should love him more because he worked for him so hard. He cannot understand that the Father's love is not conditioned by performance. It is based on relationship. The father loves the prodigal son every bit as much as he loves the elder brother because they are both his sons. That is the nature of grace. It is unmerited favour.

My experience is that, if the truth be known, a lot of Christians have trouble with that. Many of us, I suspect, have an easier time identifying with the sentiments of the elder brother than we do with either the father or the prodigal son. Who hasn't felt that his hard work and diligent labour was overlooked, while others much less worthy were heaped with attention and praise? Who hasn't been disappointed with God, at least a little bit, that He didn't seem to take more notice of the good things we have done for Him? That shows how deeply performance is written on our hearts. Love is something you earn. If you haven't earned it, then you are not worthy of it.

A person who grows up with that mentality will likely be a hard worker. He will strive to perform and will likely accomplish some pretty significant things. But it will not be motivated by true love, neither for God nor for other people. It will be motivated by a deep burning desire to be loved.

Bill and Lynne Hybels, in their book *Discovering Church: The Story and Vision of Willow Creek Community Church*, tell the very painful story of their own emotional burnout, which was occasioned, at least in part, by Bill's need to earn love. Raised in a family where the highest values included hard work, autonomy and self-sufficiency, Bill had learned early in life that hard work was a sure way to get approval and recognition. Subconsciously, he had carried that into the ministry with him, driving himself relentlessly, until neither he nor his wife could take it any longer.

> *"Many of us,"* [Bill] *says, "are crippled more than we realize by wounds and distortions we don't even know we're carrying, which cause us to behave destructively in relationships and in ministry. We may be harboring anger that leads us into harsh preaching or a controlling style of leadership. We may be filled with fear that makes us hesitant to walk out on limbs of faith. We may be shame-based and unable to stand up against criticism. We may be so hungry for love, as I was, that we will work ourselves nearly to death to try to get a poor substitute."*[2]

As Bill discovered the hard way, the sad fact of the matter is that nothing we accomplish can ever make us feel worthy of love. Love has to be written on our hearts, and it gets there through people who love us unconditionally for what we are, not merely for what we do.

Giving Up

That brings us to a second common response to conditional love: *we give up*.

Most kids will try to live up to their parents' expectations and standards at least for a little while. After all, they have a vested interest in receiving their love. However, when those expectations and standards are too high, or they keep changing as they are wont to do in dysfunctional families, there comes a point where the child just gives up. "There is no way that I am ever going to measure up to your expectations. I am sick and tired of trying to do the impossible. I just don't care any more!"

Our children share in original sin, just like we all do. Apart from God's grace, they cannot live up to all the expectations that we impose upon them. Things that may come easily for us as parents do not necessarily come easily for our children. Just because we were good in school does not mean they are going to be good in school. Just because we were good in sports does not mean they are going to be star athletes.

If, nevertheless, we insist that they live up to our expectations or those of others around us, there will come a time when they throw in the towel. Nobody can long live under that pressure and not give up. Then you get a kid who shuts himself off emotionally, stops trying to please his parents and starts hanging around with his own friends, where he can be himself.

That's why in the late '60s and '70s, the hippie movement arose out of middle-class America on the west coast of the United States. Many of these kids had been born into very successful middle-class families. Their fathers and mothers came through the war and the depression and wanted to give their children every material blessing they themselves had lacked. In the process of so doing, they gave them everything except their time and attention. They were so busy providing for their material needs, that they neglected their emotional and spiritual needs. Many of these kids when they grew up said, "We don't want that kind of lifestyle. We don't want bigger houses or better cars. We want meaningful relationships." And by the thousands, they opted out of society in favour of the promise of free love.

Interestingly enough, historically, the hippie movement gave way to the Jesus Revival. As many of the parents of these young people watched in horror as their children destroyed themselves with drugs and sexual promiscuity, they repented of their own sins and began earnestly praying for God to save their children. God graciously answered, and in a sovereign move of the Holy Spirit, brought many of these young men and women to faith. Many of them today are in leadership positions in the Body of Christ.

Keeping the Balance

How can we love our kids unconditionally and still encourage them to do their best? That is the fear of many parents. They say, "If I love my child unconditionally, does that mean that I have to approve of all of his or her actions and pretend that right and wrong don't matter any more?"

The answer is, "No!" The father in the story of the prodigal son did not lower the standard, nor, interestingly enough, did he go running after his son when he chose to go live in sin. At the same time, he was there with arms wide open for when his son came to his senses and returned home in repentance and faith.

What we need to be able to communicate to our children is that all of us struggle with the limitations of our sinful human nature. The struggles are as real for us as parents as they are for our kids. We cannot apply one standard to the kids and another standard to ourselves. What we want to do is help them to experience the grace of Jesus Christ.

Christ's standards never change and they never get lowered. At the same time, He doesn't just sit in heaven and say, "Now smarten up, or else I'm going to throw you out." No, as the song says,

You came from heaven to earth to show the way,
From the earth to the cross my debt to pay;
From the cross to the grave,
From the grave to the sky,
Lord, I lift Your name on high. [3]

When our son, Michael, was really little, he went through a period of time in his life when he just really had a hard time being good. He still has those occasionally, but not as often as he used to have! I remember distinctly one situation where we tried to discipline him several times in the course of one day. By the end of the day, we were both equally frustrated. He knew and I knew that he just didn't have what it took to be good. We also knew that more discipline wasn't going to impart that ability to him. He needed an infusion of grace. So I sat him down and said, "Michael, neither of us is very happy about what is happening here. I can't change you and you can't change you either, but I know Somebody who can. His name is Jesus. You need to ask Him to come into your life and change you." And he did. He was 5 years old when he did that and I can testify to this day that his life has not been the same since! What the law couldn't do, God did through the grace of Jesus Christ.

What a marvellous thing it is when God touches our lives with His grace, and how important it is that we teach our kids how to experience God's grace in the context of unconditional love!

Forgive Our Kids as God Has Forgiven Us

It's pretty easy to hold resentment for the pain, injury or failure caused by our children. It's pretty easy to want them to work it off, to demonstrate that they can really be trusted again. I am convinced that kids have no idea how much pain and grief they sometimes cause their parents. Not until I had kids of my own did I begin to appreciate what my parents had to put up with. For the first time, I could really understand why parents have this sense of responsibility towards their children.

In those moments, when we want to hold on to our frustration, anger or bitterness, that's the time to contemplate our own sins and shortcomings!

First of all, we are not perfect parents. Very often we are to blame, at least in part, for some of their mistakes and sins. Secondly, if God applied the letter of the law to our lives in the same way that we sometimes do to our children, then none of us would have a chance. Who of us haven't by times deliberately walked away from God and done some really stupid things? Yet God has always been there for us, gently wooing us back, disciplining us when we need it, but always in the context of unconditional love. That's what we need to do – forgive as we have been forgiven. That's not always easy to do, particularly if we have really been hurt and offended. But that is what the father does in the story of the prodigal son. Can you imagine how much pain this son caused his father? He squandered his inheritance and wasted his life. Yet when he returned in sorrow and repentance, the father was there to receive him and restore him. The more we have experienced that forgiving grace in our own lives, the easier it will be for us to do the same.

Please don't misunderstand me. I am not suggesting we justify sin or make excuses for it. Nor am I suggesting we save our children from experiencing the consequences of their sin. Love often needs to be tough. What I am suggesting is that when there is an awareness of failure, the onus is on us, the parents, to be there and extend forgiveness in any way that we can. The more mature and grace-filled we are, the more responsible we are to take whatever steps are needed to restore relationships. When I hear of relationships that are marred by alienation and a refusal to forgive and be reconciled, my heart just breaks. Scripture says, *If it is possible, as far as it depends on you, live at peace with everyone* (Rom. 12:18). That certainly includes our children!

Let me conclude this chapter with a word to those who have sinned against parents (which at some level includes all of us). Part of growing up and maturing, certainly as a Christian, is that you take responsibility for your behaviour and your actions towards your parents. That means going to them at the appropriate time and confessing things that you have done and said that were hurtful, apologizing for them and asking their forgiveness. I know that is not an easy thing to do! Most of us would prefer to let bygones be bygones and act as if nothing has happened. The Holy Spirit, however, will not usually allow us to get away with that.

One of the first things that happened in my own life after the Lord became significantly real to me was that He brought to mind a number of youthful pranks that I had been responsible for, including one or two that I had lied about when challenged. Tough as it was, I knew I had no choice but to deal with them. Since they involved my mother, I had to go to her, confess the nature of my misdeeds and ask her forgiveness. It being years after the fact, she of course didn't even remember them and gladly extended forgiveness.

It is easy to minimize the importance of this, particularly since parents are often embarrassed by our confessions. A typical response is: "Aw shucks, that was so long ago, I don't even remember it." And that may be true. Nevertheless, our sins do hurt other people, especially our parents, and many relationships maintain an undercurrent of pain unless and until these issues are resolved in a biblical fashion.

So, if you find yourself in a situation where you know you have hurt your parents, don't just assume that because you get along well today, it has been resolved satisfactorily. Go to them, confess it and ask them to extend forgiveness. It will do wonders, not only for your relationship, but also for your walk with the Lord.

NOTES

1. John and Paula Sandford, *Restoring the Christian Family* (Plainfield, NJ: Logos International, 1979) pp. 113-114.

2. Lynne and Bill Hybels, *Rediscovering Church: The Story and Vision of Willow Creek Community Church* (Grand Rapids, MI: Zondervan Publishing House, 1995) p. 118.

3. Rick Founds, "Lord, I Lift Your Name on High," © 1989, Maranatha! Music (Administered by The Copyright Company, Nashville, TN) All Rights Reserved. International Copyright Secured. Used By Permission.

24 | Effective Discipline

Discipline your children, and
they will give you rest.
Proverbs 29:17

Saturday Night magazine recently ran an article entitled, "Kids 'Я' Hell, and Parents are to Blame After
All." Here is how the author, Charles Foran, began
his article:

"In a recent one hour period, my 3-year-old daughter did
the following: threw yoghurt at her mother, slammed a
door in my face, screamed until she peed her pants, and
tried to throttle her baby sister for wrecking a Lego castle.

Her pre-school lends parents a guide to creative disci-
plining techniques. The book suggests that, during a con-
flict with the child, the adult simply go away for a while.
What a great idea! Maybe unwind in a café, fetch a film
downtown.... Instead, we call people with kids about the
same ages to commiserate. Turns out we aren't having such
a hard time. Turns out things could be a lot worse." [1]

He then goes on in the rest of the article to observe that
the present generation of parents is absolutely confused about

proper parenting techniques. This confusion, he says, is brought on in part by the rapid proliferation of self-help books, espousing a myriad of different child raising theories. He concludes his article by observing that, when all has been said and done, most people chuck all the manuals and go with what seems to work best for them.

I think he is right. It has been my observation that when it comes to raising children, everybody has his or her own pet theory. Usually these theories are based on what they have experienced in their own upbringing. If they have been disciplined too firmly as children, they will tend to be lax with their own children. If they have not been disciplined firmly enough, they will tend to be more severe in disciplining their own children and so on.

It has been my experience, furthermore, that relatively few, even Christian people, have ever sat down in any serious or systematic way to study what the Scriptures have to say about raising children. That is always a bit of a shocker to me because it seems so very self-evident that if God made the whole world, including the family, then He probably has some thoughts on how we should raise our children. With that in mind, we want to take a look in this chapter at what the Scriptures have to say about effective discipline.

Ephesians 6:4 says, *Fathers, do not provoke your children to anger, but bring them up in the discipline and instruction of the Lord* (RSV).

One of the key words in this verse is the word *discipline*. It means "to train or to correct." A second key word is *instruction* which means "to guide or teach."

Central to biblical thought is the notion that our children, like the rest of us, are conceived and born in sin. That is to say, they do not naturally want to love God, nor do they naturally want to put the interests of others ahead of their own. Instead, they are self-centered and selfish. My father used to say that anyone who does not believe that children are born inherently sinful has never raised a family of children. No one needs to teach them to bicker and argue and behave in self-serving ways. It comes quite naturally!

John and Paula Sandford have made the observation that our children might look like little angels with their big blue eyes and lovely radiant skin, but they are really just packages of sin, wrapped in skin! Somebody else has said that a child is just a long intestinal tract with a noise maker at one end and no sense of responsibility at the other!

The challenge, therefore, in raising children is to bring them up in such a way that by God's grace they can overcome their natural pull to sin, and choose to live righteously before God and other people, not because they have to, but because they want to!

How do we do that? *By applying effective biblical discipline.*

Affirmation

Discipline has two sides: positive and negative. The positive side of discipline is affirmation. We need to let them know that we love them and value them for what they are as well as for what they do.

Affirmation is a pretty common feature of our culture today. If anything, I suspect we go overboard. Few kids at school are ever criticized for the work they produce. They are all told they are budding geniuses, lest their fragile self-esteem be damaged! That is not a very healthy trend. Neither, of course, was an earlier trend where affirmation was to be avoided at all costs, lest the child become proud.

Older readers will perhaps remember those days. I've had people tell me that they were never told in their family that they were loved because they were just expected to take that for granted. And I know of people who were never complimented on the task they did because that was just a job that you were supposed to do. That's not biblical either! Even Jesus, at His baptism in the Jordan River, received affirmation from

His Father. The Bible says the heavens were opened and the Holy Spirit in the form of a dove descended upon His head. What did the Father say? *"You are my Son, whom I love; with You I am well pleased"* (Luke 3:22). That's affirmation!

Now, if Jesus needs affirmation, then certainly our kids need affirmation! We need to let them know we are proud of them and expect them to realize their God-given potential. That is what Paul does in his letters to his spiritual children. Time and again he says to them, "I am proud of you. I am proud of who you are in Christ and what you have accomplished in Him." In 2 Corinthians 7:4 he says, *"I have great confidence in you; I take great pride in you.* Again in verse 14, he says, *"For if I have expressed to him* [Titus] *some pride in you, I was not put to shame; but just as everything we said to you was true, so our boasting before Titus was true"* (RSV). That is not sinful pride. That is a healthy pride that lets us know we are on the right track and can, with confidence, throw ourselves into the task at hand.

Correction

There is, of course, another side to discipline. Our kids not only need affirmation, they also need correction.

Human nature being what it is, all the modelling and all the instruction in the world isn't going to guarantee they will live righteously. Their own sinful inclinations will get in the way. Peer pressure will try to drag them into places where they shouldn't go. They need help. They need adults in their lives who love them enough to help them stand firm both against their own inclinations and the temptations of the world around them.

I believe that is one reason our culture is in so much trouble. As Dr. Thomas Millar, a practicing child psychiatrist in Vancouver, points out in an article in the *Medical Post*, that many of today's parents were raised in the 1960s and are anti-authoritarian to the core.[2]

> [They] *have led their children to believe their lives should be constantly pleasurable, should never be boring or tedious. As a consequence the children develop no patience or persistence. They develop no tolerance for 'unpleasure' and when that unpleasure is anger, they let it all hang out with baseball bats and switch blades."*

What are the results?

> *Thirty percent of our children* [have] *behavioral or learning difficulties;* [there is] *an increasingly violent fringe group;* [and parents are] *turning away from parenthood and schools from instruction.*

He concludes his article with a plea for common sense discipline:

> *Children need a reasonable amount of one-to-one mothering in their pre-school years. And, when they turn 2, they need discipline to train them.*

Scripture puts it this way:

> *The rod and reproof give wisdom, but a mother is disgraced by a neglected child.... Discipline your children, and they will give you rest; they will give delight to your heart* (Prov. 29:15,17, NRSV).

How do we go about doing this?

Make Rules That Are Clear

I have found the book *Common Sense Discipline: What to Say and Do When Kids Need Help,* by Dr. Roger Allen and Ron Rose, particularly helpful on this score. One of their chapters gives some good practical help in establishing rules for kids.

For rules to be effective, say the authors, they must be:

- **Simple** — Kids must be able to repeat them and understand them.
- **Firm** — Rules are not bent by a flimsy excuse.

- **Fair** — They are applied equally to all children.
- **Flexible** — They can be adjusted to fit the circumstances.

They then give several lists of practical, everyday rules for a variety of different situations. For example, under the heading "Homework Rules" they suggest:

- After school, no T.V. until homework's done.
- I won't do homework for you, but I'll help you if you don't understand.
- If you miss an assignment, you can call a friend or a teacher to get the assignment.
- If you fall behind, you will have to study on weekends.

Under the heading "Rules for Meals" they suggest:

- Be polite about seconds.
- Come to breakfast after you have dressed.
- You may have dessert after you have eaten an appropriate portion of your meal.
- After a meal, everyone helps by clearing the table and putting away the food.

"Rules for Pets" are:

- You are responsible for feeding your pet.
- Your pet needs regular attention and play times.
- You will be expected to bathe your pet and clean its house/cage when I tell you it's appropriate.

And guess what, if you fail to take care of your pet, what am I going to do? I will sell it or give it to another kid who will provide better care for it. [3]

Enforce Rules Consistently

Dr. James Dobson, in his book *Dare to Discipline*, has a delightful little scenario about how not to apply discipline.

Eight-year-old Henry is sitting on the floor, playing with his games. Mom looks at her watch and says, "Henry, it's nearly nine o'clock [a thirty-minute exaggeration] so gather up your junk and go take your bath."

Now Henry knows, and Mom knows, that she doesn't mean for him to go take a bath. She merely meant for him to start thinking about going to take his bath. She would have fainted dead away if he had responded to her empty command.

Approximately ten minutes later, Mom speaks again, "Now, Henry [the pitch of voice is going up], it is getting later and you have to go to school tomorrow, and I want those toys picked up; then go get in that tub!" She still does not intend for Henry to obey, and he knows it. Her real message is, "We're getting closer, Hank."

Henry shuffles around and stacks a box or two to demonstrate that he heard her. Then he settles down for a few more minutes of play.

Six minutes pass, and Mom issues another command, this time with more passion and threat in her voice, "Now listen, young man, I told you to get a move on, and I meant it."

To Henry, this means that he must get his toys picked up and meander towards the bathroom door. If his Mom pursues him with a rapid step, then he must carry out the assignment posthaste. However, if Mom's mind wanders before she performs the last step of this ritual, Henry is free to enjoy a few more seconds reprieve.

Henry and his mom are involved in a one-act play; they both know the rules and the role being enacted by the opposite player. The entire scene is programmed, computerized, and scripted. Whenever Mom wants Henry to do something he dislikes, she progresses through graduated steps of phony anger, beginning with calm and ending with a red flush and a threat. Henry does not have to move until she reaches the peak anger point. [4]

This never happens at your house, I'm sure! I fear sometimes we simply train our children towards disobedience. We would do both them and ourselves a considerable favour if we would simply insist on appropriate and prompt obedience to the rules.

At our house when the kids were little, we used to count to three. "Please go and take your bath." Kids being what they are want to keep on playing, of course. "One, two..." (Every so often we would have to sneak in a two-and-a-half to make it work right!) "three." And they knew what was coming if they did not respond on the count of three. They would be sent to the bedroom for a little consultation with the "board of education."

The trouble with us as parents is that we are notoriously inconsistent in our discipline. Because we are often so undisciplined ourselves, we cannot discipline our children. When we are in a bad mood, kids can get away with nothing. When we are in a good mood, they can get away with murder. But all we are teaching them in the process is to keep their eye on our mood, so they will know which way the wind is blowing, and act accordingly.

The four to six p.m. time slot in many households is probably the most pressure-filled time for the mother. Mom is stirring the food in the kitchen, and the children are tugging on her clothes with, "Mommy this or Mommy that." A child begins to whine and Mommy says, "Not now, later." She starts off being very patient, but the pitch of her voice rises until it finally reaches a breaking point, and she either gives the child what he wants, or swats him one and sends him off flying. What has she done? All she has done is train the child, not in the way he should go, but that if he nags long enough he might just get what he wants; but he has to learn to keep his ear peeled to the pitch of her voice because if it reaches a certain point, he has to get out of there before he gets swatted one.

We need to be consistent in children's discipline, and that means we had better not make threats we cannot carry out. If children are fighting in the car, and you say, "If you don't quit fighting, I am going to put you out and make you walk home," who is going to believe you if you are 150 miles away from home? What parent in his right mind is going to make his kid walk home that distance?

Sometimes, though, strange things happen! I know a father whose children were in the back seat of the car, fighting like cats and dogs. He said to them, "If you don't behave, I am going to stop the car and put you in the trunk." Well, evidently, they didn't believe him because they kept right on fighting. So he stopped his car, took one of the kids by the scruff of the neck and locked him in the trunk of his car and drove off! Unfortunately for him, the driver of a car going the other way on this divided highway saw what was happening and called the police! And so, about 15 or 20 minutes down the road, a police car with its lights flashing pulled him over and the officer asked, "Sir, would you please open your trunk for me?" Fortunately, by this time he had pulled the child out of the trunk or else he would have been in major trouble. And quite properly so!

Use Discipline That Works

Scripture says:

The rod and reproof give wisdom, but a child left to himself brings shame to his mother (Prov. 29:15, RSV).

Do not withhold discipline from a child; if you beat him with a rod, he will not die. If you beat him with the rod, you will save his life from Sheol (Prov. 23:13,14, RSV).

Folly is bound up in the heart of a child, but the rod of discipline will drive it far from him (Prov. 22:15).

We live in a culture where we are almost embarrassed to read these verses, aren't we? While the Canadian criminal law still allows parents to use appropriate force in disciplining their children, increasingly the pressure is on to make spanking in any form an illegal method of discipline. Recently, David Peterson, of Warrensville, Illinois, was charged in a London,

Ontario courtroom for publicly spanking his 5-year-old daughter. Against the very explicit instructions of her father, this little girl had slammed the car door shut on her 2-year-old brother's finger. Father was not amused. He took the child, put her over the trunk of his car and swatted her bare bottom.

Well, he soon learned that there are some things that are not politically correct. A woman saw what he was doing and reported him to the police, who promptly charged him. The ensuing court case received widespread publicity. Eventually, the father was found not guilty as there was no evidence that inappropriate force had been used.

Nevertheless, the case illustrates the changing social climate of our culture. More recently yet, a father in British Columbia went to court for a very similar situation. He was found guilty. [5]

The fear, of course, is that violence begets violence. Few people, it seems, can distinguish between spanking that is done in love and for the child's good and spanking that is motivated by parental anger and lack of self control. The irony is that the more our culture has rejected biblical norms for discipline, the more we have created a generation of kids that cannot be controlled. Hence, the rise of child abuse. The devil has us coming and going. First, he persuades us that kids need no discipline. Then, when we no longer know what to do with them, he encourages us to lose our cool and vent our frustrations on them. Then, he persuades us to pass laws barring any form of physical punishment, thus ensuring that there is another whole generation that is unmanageable. And so the cycle repeats itself over and over again.

I would be the first to agree that child abuse in any form should have no place in any of our homes. I would also be one of the first to agree that when a child refuses to listen to any other form of correction, a good spanking is one of the most effective ways of helping him to reconsider his chosen course. At our house, we had four very simple rules:

1. Kids are expected to obey their parents.
2. Kids who knowingly and deliberately disobey will get spanked.
3. Parents may never spank in anger.
4. Parents and kids shall make up and forget what has happened.

We have found that to have been marvellously blessed of God. We have been able to avoid the turmoil that is so characteristic of many households today. Three of our four kids are grown up and neither they, nor we, have any regrets about our chosen course of action.

But someone says, what about other forms of discipline? What about reasoning things out with your children or sending them to their rooms? Isn't that much better than spanking them? Undoubtedly, there is room for a variety of different discipline methods. We have never resorted to sending our kids to their rooms because there is an element of lingering rejection in that which, I believe, is worse than a spanking. What we found with spanking is that it cleared the air and the relationship was restored without any lingering undercurrent of, "You don't love me anymore."

As for reasoning a child into obedience, many parents think their children are miniature adults and need to understand everything. As a child gets older, of course, he should understand more and more the reasons behind our decisions. Even so, there will always be times when a child is either not ready or doesn't want to understand the logic behind your position. To seek to persuade them logically can be a tremendous exercise in frustration. Sometimes they just have to do things because the parent says so! That's why parents are parents. Far from resenting that, kids are often looking for some firm structure in their lives.

The bottom line is this: The pain of disobedience must outweigh the pleasure of disobedience! Fair and consistent discipline is the key if our kids are going to learn the difference between right and wrong. *Discipline your children, and they will give you rest; they will give delight to your heart* (Prov. 29:17, NRSV). My wife and I have certainly found that to be true!

NOTES

1. Charles Foran, "Kids 'Я' Hell, and Parents Are to Blame After All," *Saturday Night*, December, 1994, p. 123.

2. Dr. Thomas Millar, "Unreared Children are Leading to the Destruction of Society," *The Medical Post*, 27 April 1993, p. 8.

3. Dr. Roger Allen and Ron Rose, *Common Sense Discipline: What to Say and Do When Kids Need Help* (Ft. Worth, TX: Worthy Publishing, 1986) pp. 227-229.

4. Adapted from *The New Dare to Discipline* by Dr. James Dobson. ©1970, 1992. (Used by permission of Tyndale House Publishers, Inc., Wheaton, IL. All Rights Reserved. International Copyright Secured) pp. 37-40.

5. "Al Riopel of Esquimalt, BC, was recently fined $300 and placed on six months' probation after pleading guilty to assaulting his 9-year-old daughter. He admitted to strapping her twice on her backside because she had lied to him. The girl complained the next day to her school counsellor. But Riopel says he had only pleaded guilty so that his four children would not have to testify in court. 'My kids knew I wouldn't touch them – except for lying,' he says." From: Frank Stirk, "Family Issues Alert/Pastor's Briefing," *Focus on the Family (Canada)*, 6 February 1996.

25 | Living With Regret

Against You, You only, have I sinned
and done what is evil in Your sight.
Psalm 51:4

Some time ago in one of our worship services, I spoke on the story of Esau, how he was immoral and irreligious and sold his birthright for a single meal (see Gen. 25). I pointed out that while God is anxious and willing to forgive our failures and sins, these sometimes have lasting consequences. Scripture says concerning Esau, *For you know that afterward, when he desired to inherit the blessing, he was rejected, for he found no chance to repent, though he sought it with tears* (Heb. 12:17, RSV). Much as he wanted to undo the past, it was no longer possible. He had to live with the sad consequences of his earlier decisions.

After the service, one of the women in our church was deeply troubled and in tears. And understandably so. She and her husband had raised a fine family of children. Unfortunately, in their adulthood, each child rejected the faith of the parents. One of the reasons for that was that during their growing up years, their father had held a grudge against the church. Someone had wronged him and that wrong was not easily overlooked. As a result, the kids grew up wanting nothing to do with the church.

After their last child had moved out and they were left with an empty nest, the parents eventually moved into our area. Looking for a new church home, they were drawn to our worship services where they met the Lord in a powerful way and renewed their commitment to Him.

Needless to say, they longed for their children to share their new-found faith. Here lay the source of their grief. No matter how much they loved their now-grown children, how gently they sought to witness to them of their saving faith in Jesus Christ, all efforts were rejected. Having been raised without a living faith, the children to this day continue to live as if there is no God.

This, of course, produces considerable guilt for the parents. "What if we hadn't been so stubborn? What if we had raised them in the fear and the nurture of God?" Most of the time, they have peace with it and are able to leave it in the hands of the Lord. Every so often, though, it comes back with a vengeance. "What if we had done things differently? What if...?"

All of us, I think, know what it is to live with regrets. All of us wish sometimes we could turn the clock back and do things over and do them right. Probably nowhere is that more obviously true than when it comes to raising children. To see our children suffer on account of the mistakes we have made is difficult indeed.

The question is, what do we do with our regrets? What do we do with the shameful mistakes we have made?

DAVID AND BATHSHEBA

The story of David's adulterous affair with Bathsheba in 2 Samuel 11-12 gives us some keen insights on how to live with regret. First, some background information.

David, you may recall, was one of the biblical kings in Israel. He was a man after God's own heart in the sense that he truly loved God and was committed to His purposes. That did not mean, however, that he was without sin. One day, while wandering on the flat roof of his palace, he happened to see a beautiful woman by the name of Bathsheba taking a bath on the roof of her house. Overcome with desire, he sent for her, went to bed with her, only to discover some time later that she was pregnant with his child.

What to do now? The woman was married and her husband, Uriah, was one of the soldiers in David's army. In a flash of inspiration, he ordered the husband to come home for furlough, in the hope that he would sleep with his wife and thus cover up David's sin. No dice! The man came home alright, but refused to sleep with Bathsheba while the rest of his fellow soldiers were out fighting for their lives. In desperation now, David sent word to Joab, his friend and commander-in-chief of the army, to make sure that Uriah would be killed in battle. Joab, who was no angel either, obliged. Uriah died. After an appropriate period of mourning, David married Bathsheba and thought he had gotten away with it.

Enter Nathan, a prophet of the Lord. He holds David accountable. *"You are the man!"* he says after David indignantly judges the wrongdoer in Nathan's parable of the rich man who steals his poor neighbour's sheep. *"This is what the Lord, the God of Israel, says... 'You struck down Uriah the Hittite with the sword and took his wife to be your own. You killed him with the sword of the Ammonites. Now, therefore, the sword will never depart from your house, because you have despised me and took the wife of Uriah the Hittite to be your own'"* (2 Sam. 12:7, 9-10). Nathan also told David, *"...because by this deed you have scorned the Lord, the child that is born to you shall die"* (2 Sam. 12:14, RSV). Talk about having to live with consequences! David's life was never the same again. What can we learn from this story? Several things:

Face Our Failures Squarely

Note how David responds to Nathan's accusation (vs. 13): *"I have sinned against the Lord."* In Psalm 51, which is one of the great psalms that he wrote after his sin with Bathsheba, he says, *For I know my transgressions, and my sin is always before me. Against You, You only, have I sinned and done what is evil in Your sight* (Ps. 51:3-4).

The natural temptation, of course, is to minimize or deny our failures. "I did the best I could. It is not really that bad. Everybody does it. We are, after all, only human and so what can we be expected to do?" When that doesn't work, our next stage is to try to blame somebody else. "If my kids were more co-operative and weren't so sassy, I would have a much easier time being a good parent." "If that woman hadn't been so thoughtless and taken her bath outdoors on the roof where I could see her, I wouldn't be in this mess today. Where is her sense of decency, anyway?" "If my spouse weren't so cold and distant, I wouldn't have to look around for someone else to pay me a little attention."

David, who has been living with a pretty heavy dose of guilt for a good many months by the time Nathan confronts him, doesn't resort to any of these tactics. He faces his sin head on. He says, *"I have sinned against the Lord."* I suspect that he probably found it a relief to be finally found out. *"When I kept silent,"* he says in Psalm 32:3-5, *"my bones wasted away through my groaning all day long. For day and night Your hand was heavy upon me; my strength was sapped as in the heat of the summer. Then I acknowledged my sin to You, and did not cover up my iniquity. I said, 'I will confess my transgressions to the Lord' – and You forgave the guilt of my sin."*

We need to do the same. We need to embrace our sin squarely and face it honestly. Sometimes I am afraid that we confess our sins too glibly and claim forgiveness too easily. We need to look at them in depth, try to understand what happened and why. We need to cry out with David, *Cleanse me with hyssop, and I will be clean; wash me, and I will be whiter than snow* (Ps. 51:7). If we don't do that, we will not likely get to the root of our problems and are thus likely to repeat them. Furthermore, we will probably spend the rest of our life trying to prove to ourselves and everybody else that we are not really as bad as we or others may think we are.

Let me give some examples.

Jeff and Natalie

Natalie is a young woman who married Jeff against her parents' forceful objections. The reasons her parents were opposed to the marriage were two-fold: 1) Jeff is not a believer and shows no interest in becoming one; and 2) his character is such they are not at all confident he will be able to keep a job and provide for his family.

Natalie, with all the wisdom of a 17-year-old, thinks her parents are over-reacting. She is in love with Jeff and believes her love will change him. So she marries him.

As time goes on, her parents' predictions prove uncannily accurate. Once married, Jeff drops all pretense of church going. At first he allows her to keep going by herself, but soon actively starts discouraging her. What is more, his lack of character starts to show. He shows no interest in work. Instead, he hangs around with the old crowd. He drinks too much. When Natalie says something about it, he gets defensive, even angry, and gradually the relationship begins to deteriorate.

What is Natalie going to do? If she acknowledges that she has a problem, she will have to admit that her parents were right and she was wrong when she married Jeff. That's pretty hard to do. If she tells her mother that she and Jeff are having problems, she is likely to be confronted with an "I told you so." That she doesn't want either.

So the chances are she will stay in denial as long as possible. "It's just a little disagreement," she'll tell herself when they've had one of their many blowups. When her parents or friends question her about her bruises or black eye, "Oh, I bumped into the door of my cupboard. How silly of me!" For as long as possible, she needs to prove to herself and everyone else that the marriage is really working. Only when it becomes obvious that things are out of control will she finally admit to it. By then, of course, the damage has been done and it is most likely too late to do anything about it.

Robert and Melissa

Robert and Melissa were both sexually promiscuous in their teenage years. Robert used to pride himself on his many female "conquests." Melissa was a real party girl. When she found herself pregnant at age 16, it didn't take her long to figure out this was one baby she didn't want. All alone, she drove herself to the clinic that day to terminate the pregnancy. Not even her boyfriend, let alone her parents, knew about it. For a while she changed her way of life. Eventually, she drifted back into more promiscuity, except this time she was wiser and much more "careful." Then she met Robert and after a brief but passionate courtship, they got married.

Some years later, she had the first of several miscarriages. Eventually, their son was born. Tragically, he was severely allergic to peanut oil, and one day when nobody was watching, he ingested a chocolate bar containing peanuts, had a reaction and died. Understandably, the parents were grief-stricken. But more than that, they felt guilty. Melissa, particularly, wondered secretly if maybe God was punishing her for her promiscuous life-style. Robert tried not to think about it too deeply and threw himself into work with a vengeance. Neither of them dared put their secret thoughts and fears into words. Both lived in the misery of their own private pain. Gradually, they drifted apart, until their collective misery made them cry out for help. Only narrowly were they able to salvage their relationship.

We need to face our sin squarely and work through the issues that are involved. If we don't, they're bound to hound us for years to come.

Do What We Can to Make it Right

For David in this story, that means at least two things. 1) He cries out for God to spare the child's life: *The Lord struck the child that Uriah's wife had borne to David, and he became ill. David pleaded with God for the child* (2 Sam. 12:15-16). 2) He comforts and restores Bathsheba: *Then David comforted his wife Bathsheba, and he went to her and lay with her. She gave birth to a son, and they named him Solomon* (vs. 24).

David could have easily turned his back on his wife and child and pretended there was never a problem. But he didn't. He took full responsibility for his actions and did what he could to make it better. For us as parents, this means going to our children if we have failed them, asking them for forgiveness and doing what we can to make it right. At the same time, we need to give them as much space as they need in order to be fully reconciled to us.

My experience has been that when it comes to reconciliation in the Christian community, we are often too glib and fail to give people space to work out their anger and frustration in a truly healthy way. We muster a quick, "I'm sorry," and hope that will solve the problem. We forget that true reconciliation is a very complex process. It involves giving the injured party enough space to work through the anger and pain that are often a very real part of having been wronged.

Let me illustrate. Some years ago, I was asked to mediate a reconciliation process between a father and his adult daughter. When she was between the ages of 12 and 16, he had sexually molested her in a most tragic fashion. As she got older, she found a boyfriend and soon she was sleeping with him. When her father found this out, he was absolutely livid and without any further ado, kicked her out of the house.

She was heart-broken and absolutely furious because as she said, "Everything I have learned about sex, I have learned from you. Why punish me for something you have taught me is normal?"

This led her on a twenty year journey of alcoholism, drugs, prostitution and crime. She even did time in jail. God, however, was merciful. He reached down into her brokenness and brought her to conversion and faith in Jesus Christ. She sobered up, got her life back on track and then wanted to work things out with her father.

Understandably, she was afraid, and didn't know what kind of reaction she would receive from her father. Other members in the family also professed to have been abused by him and he had denied it all, so she was quite apprehensive about confronting him. Therefore, she asked me to mediate.

On the appointed day, the three of us met together. She shared with her dad some of her hurt and what that had all led to in her life. To the father's credit, he didn't deny any of her allegations. He faced his failures and he faced them squarely. He even asked her for forgiveness.

I thought the meeting was really quite successful. After it was over, I asked her how she thought it had gone and was surprised at how negatively she felt about it. When I pressed her on it, it became immediately evident that she was disappointed in his reaction. Though she was glad he didn't try to deny it, she was disappointed at what she perceived was an attempt on his part to gloss over the past. As she was trying to verbalize the deep pain and anguish that she had experienced as a result of the abuse, he kept saying, "There is nothing I can do about that anymore. I have already apologized for it. You have to forgive me." And that was true, but she wasn't ready to forgive yet. She first needed to work out her pain and anger, and she felt he wasn't giving her the proper space to do so.

What he didn't realize is that true forgiveness is far more than saying, "I am sorry," important as that is. It means giving the other person enough space to work out the hurt and the anger they harbour so that when forgiveness is extended, it is both real and lasting.

THE PROCESS OF FORGIVENESS

Please refer to *Figure 25.1*. This is a chart outlining the process of forgiveness.[1] Note the sequence of events. An offensive event will cause both hurt and anger. Suppose, for example, that a parent abandons his or her child. The child in all likelihood will experience hurt. If that hurt is severe enough, it will turn into anger. How deep that hurt and anger go is determined by two sets of conditions, one on the part of the offender and one on the part of the offended person.

Offender Factors

Note the following under this heading:

• *Severity.* Not everything we do to one another hurts or angers us equally. A child who receives a well-deserved slap on the wrist isn't going to be half as hurt and offended as the child who gets wrongfully accused and punished.

• *Acknowledgement of wrong.* This makes a big difference. When somebody hurts us and says, "I was wrong in hurting you, please forgive me," that takes a lot of the sting out of the hurt. But if somebody says, "It wasn't my fault, it was your fault," then you live with that unresolved conflict of having an injustice done to you and no place to go with it.

• *Intentionality.* Whether people hurt you accidentally or on purpose makes a big difference. Somebody who hurts you accidentally isn't likely to leave you as hurt and angry as a person who takes dead aim at you and deliberately tries to do you in. Intentional hurt produces personal overtones that are lacking in accidental hurt.

• *Frequency.* How many times the injury happens makes a big difference also. If your spouse succumbs to temptation and

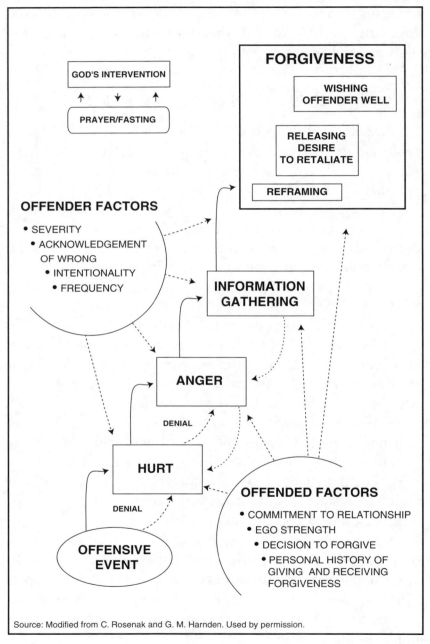

Figure 25.1
The Process of Forgiveness

commits a one-time act of marital unfaithfulness, that is bad enough and may take a long time to work through. If, however, it keeps happening again and again, even after repeated assurances that it won't happen again, then the damage is much more severe and the chances of restoration and forgiveness much more difficult.

Similarly, a parent who occasionally loses his or her cool with a child is one thing. A parent who verbally or physically abuses a child regularly is quite another. Frequency makes quite a difference.

Offended Factors

Under *Offended Factors* note the following:

• ***Commitment to the relationship.*** Somebody who is close to you can hurt you much more than somebody who is not close. What my mailman does, says or thinks leaves me relatively cold (as long as he gets my mail to me on time!). What my wife says, thinks or does has a much greater capacity to wound me to the core of my heart. That, of course, is why so many people fear intimacy. The closer you are to each other, the greater the possibility of betrayal.

• ***Ego strength.*** Some people take offense much easier than others. Some people have thick skin. You can say or do almost anything and it doesn't bother them. It runs off their backs like water off the back of the proverbial duck. They are strong in their own right. Most of us have times like that. We feel strong. We can take quite a lot. Other days, we are not as strong, we feel vulnerable and things that wouldn't bother us otherwise, set us off. We are then easily offended and hurt.

That is one of the reasons different kids in the same family respond so differently to a similar environment. When parents are confronted by one black sheep in the family, they will sometimes say, "I don't know what happened to him. I raised all my kids the same way. The rest all turned out fine. Only this one went the wrong way." What often happens, of course, is that one child is much more sensitive than another. Things that don't bother someone else may make a deep impact on that child's life. Ego strength makes the difference.

• *Decision to forgive.* A person who decides early on that he or she is going to walk and live in forgiveness has a much easier time letting go of hurt and anger than a person who nurses that hurt and anger and decides to hold on to it.

• *A personal history of forgiving and receiving forgiveness.* A person who has faced his own sin and experienced God's forgiveness has a much easier time extending forgiveness to somebody else. Once you recognize that you, too, are a sinner saved by grace, you become much more tolerant of other people's failures.

· · · · · · · ·

All of these, then, are factors that determine how much hurt and anger results from the original offensive event.

What happens when you start trying to work it out? The hurt and the anger come back. Unless you are in denial, the more you talk and think about what happened, the more you feel the original pain. The more pain you feel, the angrier you become. The angrier you become, the more you need to gather information. "How could you do this to me? Why did you and Mom split up when I was just 3 years old? Didn't you love me anymore? Why weren't you there for me?"

Children particularly, tend not to know the full facts and, therefore, tend to assume that they are probably the cause. "If Dad abused me, there must have been something I did wrong to make him come on to me." "If Dad and Mom split up, it is probably my fault since I was such a rotten kid."

Even as adults, we often feel this way. Someone treats us badly, is angry with us or gives us a hard time, and the first thing we say is, "What did I do to deserve this?" And we start asking questions: "Why were you unfaithful to me? Why did you hurt me like that? What else did you do behind my back that I don't know about?"

Note in the diagram the broken arrows that point back from *Information Gathering* to *Anger* and then to *Hurt*. What that means is that the more we dialogue about what happened and the more answers, straight or evasive, I get, the angrier I become and the more hurt I feel.

That is what was happening in the meeting between the adult woman and her father that I was trying to mediate. The more she talked about the abuse, the more hurt and anger she felt. She wasn't ready by any standard of measurement to forgive him until she had full opportunity to get it out of her system and she felt that he fully understood the pain he had caused her. His attempts at letting bygones be bygones only served to fuel her anger more. She needed time to work it out.

Bill Hybels tells the story of learning the hard way how painful reconciliation can be. Willow Creek Church, which today is world-renowned for its Seeker Services, started in the mid-'70s in a theatre. Almost immediately, the church grew by leaps and bounds as many people came to know Christ.

Then came what the Willow Creek people call, "The Great Train Wreck" of the early '80s. In the midst of an extensive building program, half their staff quit and about a third of their members left. The reason for this was a perception on the part of many that Hybels was trying to consolidate his power in the church. What in fact was happening was that he and the elders of the church were trying to protect the reputation of a leading staff member who had fallen into sexual sin.

Understandably, all these misunderstandings and defections were hard to take. Hardest of all was when Nancy Beach and her husband left. Nancy had been a teenager when she had first joined Bill and others in what would later become Willow Creek. A gifted dramatist, she had pioneered the drama ministry at Willow Creek. Her loss was a terrific and painful blow to Hybels.

For five years, she and her husband were gone from the church. Eventually, they felt led to come back, but the past needed to be resolved. So she and Bill decided to meet to try to work out the issues of hurt and anger. The way Bill tells the story, it took a dozen meetings or more for the two of them to come to grips with their hurt and anger! The first few were so bad that, but for the grace of God, both of them would have given up hope of ever working out their difficulties with each other. But they persevered and eventually they came out of what Bill likes to call "the tunnel of chaos." Today, Nancy Beach remains an integral part of the Willow Creek ministry.[2]

Once the *hurt-anger-information gathering cycle* has sufficiently run its course, we are then ready to enter the forgiveness stage.

The Forgiveness Stage

Note from the diagram that this stage also has three components: reframing, releasing our desire to retaliate and wishing the offender well.

Reframing means developing a new understanding of what happened and why. Much anger and bitterness is the result of faulty or incomplete understanding of what happened and why. With those misunderstandings cleared out of the way, the injured party is now ready to form a new understanding of what really transpired and why. Let's return for a moment to that father-daughter relationship I was asked to mediate.

Though the daughter was far from satisfied after the first meeting, it did accomplish some very significant purpose in her life. As they talked and her father acknowledged his failures, he tried, without shifting blame from himself, to explain to her a little bit concerning his own history. He told her how he had been raised in a family of girls where, for some strange reason, it was common for him to be put into the same bed as his sisters, even when they were teenagers! Not only that, but as a teenager he was seduced by a much older woman. And on and on his story went.

None of that, of course, excused his actions, but it sure helped his daughter to understand where he was coming from. Instead of always wondering, "What did I do to bring this on?" she saw much more clearly the baggage her father had carried in his own life. For her, this was tremendously relieving because she had always assumed that there had to be something wrong with her. Why would he pick her and not somebody else? So as she got new information and began to put together the pieces that didn't fit together before, she was able to reframe reality. She was able to understand the whole situation in a new light.

Once we have reframed the issue, we are now ready to *release the desire to retaliate*. Getting even runs deep in the human heart. Until the hurt and anger are all processed, everything inside us says, "I want to hurt you back for what you have done to me." Fortunately, most of us never get to carry out all the nifty little ways we have planned to get even, but it sure feels good thinking about it! In the end, of course, it just keeps the bitterness and the anger going. Once we understand more clearly what has happened and we have processed the hurt and the anger, we are now in a position to say, "Alright, I choose to let go of my anger and my desire to retaliate. I will choose to forgive."

How do we know forgiveness has truly been accomplished? When you finally get to the point where you not only no longer desire to get even, but you can *wish the offender well*, you know you have forgiven. When you can truly and honestly say, "Lord bless this person who has hurt me," then you know that you have come to a point where your anger has run its course and you have done what you needed to do for reconciliation to be accomplished.

Before we leave this topic, notice yet the place of prayer and fasting in *Figure 25.1*. This whole process is very much dependent on God's gracious intervention. As we and others pray, sometimes with fasting, asking God to step in, amazing things can happen as the Lord softens both our own heart and that of the others who are involved. Few things give God more glory than long-seated resentments that are finally processed and truly forgiven from the heart. It ought to be one of the hallmarks of the believers.

Leave the Results in God's Hands

Notice what happens in 2 Samuel 12 as David cries out to God for the life of his child: All his servants are getting worried because they think he is going crazy with grief, and when the child dies, they are afraid to tell him because of what he may do to himself. However, he hears them whispering, catches on to what is going on and, much to their surprise, gets up off the ground, changes his clothes, eats and goes into the house of God to worship.

When the servants ask him about the reason for his sudden turnabout in view of the child's death, he responds as follows:

> *"While the child was still alive, I fasted and wept. I thought, 'Who knows? The Lord may be gracious to me and let the child live.' But now that he is dead, why should I fast? Can I bring him back again? I will go to him, but he will not return to me"* (2 Sam. 12:22-23).

David understood that he had done what he could. Having accepted blame and having cried out to God in desperation asking Him to change His mind, the verdict had been given and David humbled himself under the mighty hand of God. He said, "Lord, not my will but Yours be done."

He let it go. That is a lesson we all need to learn sooner or later. There are times in life when no matter what we do, how much we repent or cry out to God, things are just not going to change. We need to leave them in the hands of God.

That is particularly true with our children. I know a great many parents who struggle with children who have been alienated, either from God, the church, their parents or all three. They've done their level best to restore the relationship. They have accepted blame where due. They have tried to make it right. But their children refuse to be reconciled. When that happens, we need to be able to say, "They are adults in their own right. They are responsible for the choices and decisions they make. They will have to live with the consequences."

When all of us stand before the judgment seat of God, nobody in that day is going to be able to say, "Well, it's what my Mom and Dad did to me that caused me to be the way that I am today." It's not whatever has been done to us that determines our destiny. It is how we respond to that which we have experienced. Sooner or later, all of us have to acknowledge that we all live in a sinful world, and we all fail. There isn't a perfect parent around and ultimately each one of us, as children, need to take responsibility for our own lives. We can do what we can to try to resolve all of it, but when all has been said and done, we are responsible to forgive as God has forgiven us.

When we do, there are some amazing things that can happen. Notice, how this story ends:

> *Then David comforted his wife, Bathsheba, and he went to her and lay with her. She gave birth to a son, and they named him Solomon. The Lord loved him* (2 Sam. 12:24).

Think this through, for a moment. Here is a child born out of a marriage that had its origins in adultery, that was built on the foundation of murder and that set loose a whole cycle of violence in David's house from which he never quite got away. You would think God would say, "That marriage is illegitimate; that child has no right to live either." But instead the Bible says, *the Lord loved him.*

Solomon, as Scripture tells us, goes on to build the temple of God and to become one of the forebears of Jesus Christ. Talk about redeeming human sin and misery! This has to be about the ultimate!

Does God condone David's sin? Of course not! Does God condone the immorality, the murder or the unfaithfulness? No, God does not. Did David have to pay a price for his sin?

Yes, he did. But does it stop there? No! God can make good things come out of even the worst. That's called grace. And that is the word with which I want to end this book.

No matter how big our sins, how colossal our failures, how deep-rooted our dysfunctions, God is bigger than all of them. When in repentance and faith we turn to Him, throwing ourselves on His mercy, we find that He is able to redeem even the worst of our failures and weave them into the tapestry of His new creation.

NOTES

1. Adapted from Charlotte M. Rosenak and G. Mack Harnden, "Forgiveness in the Psychotherapeutic Process: Clinical Applications" (Overland Park, KS: Christian Psychological Services. Used by permission).

2. Lynne and Bill Hybels, *Rediscovering Church: The Story and Vision of Willow Creek Community Church* (Grand Rapids, MI: Zondervan, 1995).

26 | Epilogue: A Tale of Two Families

The generation of the upright will be blessed... [but] the longings of the wicked will come to nothing.
Psalm 112:2,10

Throughout this book, we have been looking at the importance of the family. We have seen that the individual choices we make have an impact, not only on our own lives, but also on those of our children to the third and fourth generation. The choices we make, therefore, are very important and far-reaching in their consequences.

A classic example of that is a comparative study of the Jukes and Edwards families.[1]

Max Jukes and Jonathan Edwards were contemporaries who both lived in New York State during the late 1700s. Max Jukes was a self-professed atheist. He refused to take his children to church, even when they asked to go. He has 1,026 known descendants. Of that number, 300 were sent to prison for an average term of 13 years; 190 were public prostitutes; and 680 were admitted alcoholics. His family is estimated to have cost the state of New York hundreds of thousands of dollars, with little or no contribution made in return.

Jonathan Edwards, on the other hand, was a devout Christian who played an active role in the Great Awakening, a religious revival that swept the American colonies during the first half of the 18th century.

He has some 929 known descendants. Of these, 430 were ministers, 86 were university professors, 13 became university presidents, 75 authoured good books, 5 were elected to the United States Congress and 2 to the Senate, and one became Vice President of the United States. Far from costing the state of New York one penny, his family contributed immeasurably to the well-being of society.

Of course, not all families are so clearly black and white. Most of them are a curious mixture of good and bad, success and failure. Yet the fact remains, the choices we make matter, and the consequences of those choices can often be clearly traced for generations.

How important it is, therefore, for us to make the right choices. God, in Christ, through His infinite compassion, has made it possible for us to break out of old destructive patterns and to start new and healthy ways of living. As we avail ourselves of His compassion for ourselves and pass it along to our children, He will certainly bless us and help us to overcome barriers to wholeness. That, in turn, will start a cycle of healing and blessing that will benefit our children and their descendants for generations to come.

We can then not only get excited about the possibility of change for ourselves, but we can pass on a wonderful new legacy to our children – the possibility of becoming highly functional and highly successful people, no matter how dysfunctional the world may have been, or may become.

To God be the glory!

NOTES

1. From: *Family Happiness is Homemade*, September 1986.

Bibliography

Allen, Roger and Ron Rose. *Common Sense Discipline: What to Say and Do When Kids Need Help.* Ft. Worth, TX: Worthy Publishing, 1986.

Anderson, Neil T. *Setting Your Church Free.* Ventura, CA: Regal Books, 1994.

Carder, Dave, Earl Henslin, John Townsend, Henry Cloud, Alice Brawand. *Secrets of Your Family Tree: Healing for Adult Children of Dysfunctional Families.* Chicago: Moody Press, 1991.

Cavanaugh, Michael. *God's Call to the Single Adult.* (Available from Mobilized to Serve, 7245 College St., Lima, NY, 14485)

Chambers, Oswald. *My Utmost for His Highest.* New York: Dodd, Mead and Co., 1935.

Cloud, Henry and John Townsend. *Boundaries: When to Say YES; When to Say NO; To Take Control of Your Life.* Grand Rapids, MI: Zondervan Publishing House, 1992.

_____. *Safe People.* Grand Rapids, MI: Zondervan, 1995.

Covey, Stephen R. *The Seven Habits of Highly Effective People: Restoring the Character Ethic.* New York: Simon and Schuster, Fireside ed., 1989.

Dawson, John. *Healing America's Wounds*. Ventura, CA: Regal Books, 1994.

Dobson, James. *Dare to Discipline*. Wheaton, IL: Tyndale House Publishers, 1988.

_____. *Love Must be Tough: New Hope for Families in Crisis*. Waco, TX: Word Books, 1983.

_____. *Preparing for Adolescence*. Ventura, CA: Gospel Light Publications, 1978.

Downing, Fred. *The Family System's Workshop* video.

Fried, John and Linda. *Adult Children: The Secrets of Dysfunctional Families*. Deerfield Beach, FL: Health Communications, 1988.

Friesen, James G. *Uncovering the Mystery of MPD*. San Bernardino, CA: Here's Life Publishers, Inc., 1991.

Fulghum, Robert. *All I Really Need to Know I Learned in Kindergarten: Uncommon Thoughts on Common Things*. New York: Villard Books, 1986, 1988.

Horton, Martha. *Growing Up In Adulthood*. Tarrytown, NY: Triumph Books, 1992.

Hurnard, Hannah. *Hearing Heart*. Wheaton, IL: Tyndale House Publishers, Inc., 1978.

Hybels, Lynne and Bill. *Rediscovering Church: The Story and Vision of Willow Creek Community Church*. Grand Rapids, MI: Zondervan, 1995.

James, John W. and Frank Cheny. *The Grief Recovery Handbook*. New York: Harper & Row Publications, 1988.

McDonald, Arlys Norcross. *Repressed Memories: Can You Trust Them?* Grand Rapids, MI: Fleming H. Revell, 1995.

Medved, Michael. *Hollywood vs. America: Popular Culture and the War on Traditional Values*. New York: HarperCollins Publishers, Inc., 1992.

Payne, Leanne. *Listening Prayer*. Grand Rapids, MI: Hamewith Books, 1994.

_____. *Restoring the Christian Soul Through Healing Prayer: Overcoming the Three Great Barriers to Personal and Spiritual Completion in Christ*. Wheaton, IL: Crossway Books, 1991.

_____. *The Broken Image: Restoring Personal Wholeness Through Healing Prayer*. Westchester, IL: Crossway Books, 1981.

_____. *The Healing Presence*. Wheaton, IL: Crossway Books, 1989.

Piper, John, and Wayne Grudem, eds. *Recovering Biblical Manhood and Womanhood: A Response to Evangelical Feminism.* Wheaton, IL: Crossway Books, 1991.

Ross, Colin A. *Multiple Personality Disorder: Diagnosis, Clinical Features, and Treatment.* New York: John Wiley & Sons, 1989.

_____. *The Osiris Complex: Case-Studies in Multiple Personality Disorder.* Toronto: University of Toronto Press, 1994.

Sandford, John and Paula. *Restoring the Christian Family.* Plainfield, NJ: Logos International, 1979.

Satinover, Jeffrey. *Homosexuality and the Politics of Truth.* Grand Rapids, MI: Hamewith Books, 1996.

Schrader, Christopher M. *Righteous Anger: Christ's Expression as a Model.* Belleville, ON: Essence Publishing, 1996.

Seamands, David A. *Healing of Memories.* Wheaton, IL: Victor Books, 1985.

_____. *Putting Away Childish Things.* Wheaton, IL: Victor Books, 1982.

Verny, Thomas and John Kelly. *The Secret Life of the Unborn Child.* Don Mills, ON: Collins Publishers, 1981.

Visser, John. *To Have and to Hold: Biblical Reflections on Marriage.* Belleville, ON: Maranatha Publications, 1993.

Weatherby, W.J. *Chariots of Fire.* New York: Quicksilver Books/Dell Publishing Co., 1982.

Whitfield, Charles L. *Healing the Child Within: Discovery and Recovery for Adult Children of Dysfunctional Families.* Deerfield Beach, FL: Health Communications, Inc., 1987.

Wilson, Sandra D. *Released From Shame: Recovery for Adult Children of Dysfunctional Families.* Downer's Grove, IL: InterVarsity Press, 1990.

_____. "Evangelical Christian Adult Children of Alcoholics: A Preliminary Study." *Journal of Psychology and Theology,* 17, 1989. 263-273.

Woititz, Janet Beringer. *Adult Children of Alcoholics.* Deerfield Beach, FL: Health Communications, 1983.

INDEX

Scripture Index

For more information or to place an order,
please contact your local Christian Bookstore
or:

PUBLISHING

20 Hanna Court
Belleville, ON K8P 5J2
Phone (613) 962-2360; Fax (613) 962-3055
1-800-238-6376
E-mail: publishing@essencegroup.com
Internet: http://www.essencegroup.com

Setting the Captives Free provides practical and biblical help in learning how God's people can be effectively used of God to make a difference in a hurting world. Beginning with the ministry of Christ, author John Visser discusses how God, in Christ, sets people free and then shares that ministry with His people through the power of the Holy Spirit. A must read for those who long to see God's Kingdom come!

Includes study Guide. Excellent for group study.

ISBN 1-896400-01-9, Softcover

104 pages .... $**12** *95* CDN $**9** *95* US

Everyone longs for the most out of life. We all want wholeness—physical health, emotional happiness, deep loving relationships, and peace and meaning in life. But can it be found?

In this book you will find answers to how you can. You will see that it begins in harmonious living that balances the four basic human needs: physical, social, mental and spiritual. By choosing the best that science can offer through modern medicine, safe and proven alternatives, and spiritual healing that leads to true peace, *you can start a personal journey toward wholeness.*

Author: Hendrik Visser, M.D.

ISBN 1-55306-233-7, Softcover

320 pages .... $**18** *95* CDN $**14** *95* US

Both blessings and curses are biblical realities! While we prefer to dwell on blessings, honesty compels us to admit that curses are every bit as much a part of biblical reality. Accordingly, this book aims to answer three questions: What are blessings and curses? What do they look like and where do they come from? How are they passed on from one generation to the next? What are the provisions God has made in Christ to break the power of the curse and replace it with the blessing?

Blessings & Curses illustrates how much Jesus delivers us from the power of the curse and restores us to the promised blessings of God.

ISBN 1-55306-889-0, Softcover

320 pages .... $**22** **95**

- Why do some marriages flourish, while so many others fail?
- Why do so many couples have difficulty establishing true intimacy?
- What is appropriate sexual behaviour inside and outside of marriage?
- How can I help my children to successfully resist temptation in a sex-crazed culture?

These and many other questions are discussed by veteran pastor and counsellor John Visser in this book. Beginning with the creation story of Adam and Eve, the author looks at God's original plan for marriage, how sin has affected it, and how God in Christ seeks to reconcile us to Himself and to each other.

ISBN 1-896400-94-9, Softcover

200 pages................................... $**14** **95** CDN $**10** **95** US

Order Form

Ordered By: (please print)

Name: _____

Address: _____

City: _____ Prov./State: _____

Postal/Zip Code: _____ Telephone: _____

Please send me the following book(s): (All Prices in Cdn. Dollars.)

Qty.	Title	Unit Price	Total
_____	*Blessings & Curses*	$22.95	$_____
_____	*Olive Shoots Around Your Table*	$22.95	$_____
_____	*Healing for Your Hurts*	$18.95	$_____
_____	*Setting the Captives Free*	$12.95	$_____
_____	*To Have and To Hold*	$14.95	$_____

Shipping ($4.00 first book - $1.00 each add. book): $_____

G.S.T. @ 7%: $_____

Total: $_____

Payable by Cheque, Money Order or **VISA**

VISA #:_____ Expiry:_____

Signature:_____

Send to: *Essence Publishing*
20 Hanna Court
Belleville, ON K8P 5J2

Or call our toll-free number, 1-800-238-6376, ext. 7575
or visit our on-line bookstore at
www.essencebookstore.com

Quantity Discounts of
Olive Shoots Around Your Table
are available for group study.

Call 1-800-238-6376 for details.